Taste of Home
Low-Fat
Country
Cooking

Editor: Julie Schnittka
Food Editor: Coleen Martin
Associate Food Editor: Sue A. Jurack
Senior Home Economist: Mary Fullmer
Art Director: Ellen Lloyd
Design Director: Jim Sibilski
Assistant Editor: Kristine Krueger
Test Kitchen Assistant: Suzi Hampton
Food Photography Artist: Stephanie Marchese
Photography: Scott Anderson, Glenn Thiesenhusen,
Mike Huibregtse, Judy Anderson
Photo Studio Coordinator: Anne Schimmel
Illustrations: Thomas Hunt

© 1997, Reiman Publications, L.P.
5400 S. 60th St., Greendale WI 53129
International Standard Book Number: 0-89821-210-3
Library of Congress Catalog Card Number: 97-65129
All rights reserved.
Printed in U.S.A.

PICTURED ABOVE. Porcupine Meatballs (page 177).

PICTURED ON THE COVER. Clockwise from upper right: Extra-Quick Yeast Rolls
(page 87), Mom's Roast Beef (page 176) with Oven-Roasted Potatoes (page 224),
Cherry Cobbler (page 266) and Citrus Broccoli Toss (page 224).

Filling, Flavorful <u>and</u> Low-Fat? The Proof's in These Pages!

IF you're like most of us, favorite foods—creamy rich Chicken 'n' Dumplings, for instance, or sumptuously sweet Grandma's Chocolate Pudding—provide fond memories. Unfortunately, if you've cut back on fat in your daily diet, that's all they may be—memories.

Not anymore, though…*starting today!*

With this unique cookbook, you can once more enjoy both of those classic country treats—plus over 450 other delicious down-home dishes —week after week, while still shrinking the amount of fat you and your family consume.

In fact, if you don't tell your family they're eating low-fat meals, they'll likely never know. And you won't notice either. We've made sure of that!

Perhaps you've discovered the same dismaying dilemma we have. Finding a "light" recipe is easy these days…but finding a low-fat recipe that you and your family want to eat again and again—a hearty, stick-to-your-ribs country one—is all but impossible.

That's what makes *this* cookbook truly different. It's been put together by the editors of *Taste of Home*, the most popular food publication in the country. Only "real food for real people" is included in that recipe-packed magazine. And the exact same applies to *Low-Fat Country Cooking*.

You can be confident any of the hundreds of recipes in this book will quickly become a new family favorite at your house—because each is already the family favorite of the country cook who contributed it. Plus, each has been thoroughly tested for taste appeal in the *Taste of Home* kitchen.

At the same time, all 455 recipes have been analyzed and certified as being low-fat by a Registered Dietitian, who's also tallied up a quick-reference chart of nutritional information for each recipe.

A few additional notes:

Many of the recipes in this book are naturally low in fat. In other cases, Home Economists in the *Taste of Home* kitchen simply substituted a lighter ingredient or two or made minor adjustments in the preparation to further reduce fat and calories.

Occasionally, you'll see we've included a recipe with higher nutritional numbers. Don't worry if you're counting—you can still make it part of your menus! Just serve it a little less often and combine it with other foods that will provide a balance of nutrients over time.

Finally, to give yourself even more options, keep an eye out while grocery shopping. New light food products are regularly being introduced, expanding the range of low-fat recipes. Feel free to substitute them for similar higher-fat ingredients where appropriate.

With that, dig in and enjoy *Low-Fat* (and *Filling* and *Flavorful*) *Country Cooking!*

FOR ADDITIONAL COPIES of *Low-Fat Country Cooking* or information on other books, write: *Taste of Home* Books, P.O. Box 990, Greendale WI 53129. **Credit card orders call toll-free 1-800/558-1013.**

Putting It Together

The recipes in this book all work fine by themselves. But, if you like, you can also "mix and match" them to create complete low-fat menus that combine foods with complementary tastes and colors! Here are a few suggestions to get you started...

Mom's Roast Beef (p. 176)
Oven-Roasted Potatoes (p. 224)
Extra-Quick Yeast Rolls (p. 87)
Citrus Broccoli Toss (p. 224)
Cherry Cobbler (p. 266)

Calories per Serving: 526
Total Fat per Serving: Less than 13 gm
Calories from Fat: 21%

Three-Green Salad (p. 56)
Oven-Barbecued Pork Chops (p. 213)
Ginger-Orange Squash (p. 232)
Cranberry Orange Bread (p. 91)

Calories per Serving: 450
Total Fat per Serving: 12 gm
Calories from Fat: 24%

Asparagus-Stuffed Potatoes (p. 223)
Grilled Citrus Chicken (p. 161)
Creamy Sliced Tomatoes (p. 59)

Calories per Serving: 460
Total Fat per Serving: Less than 12 gm
Calories from Fat: 22%

Buttermilk Biscuits (p. 95)
Chicken and Barley
  Boiled Dinner (p. 163)
Raspberry Peach Jam (p. 252)

Calories per Serving: 487
Total Fat per Serving: Less than 14 gm
Calories from Fat: 24%

Shepherd's Pie (p. 193)
Lemon-Basil Carrots (p. 237)
Spinach Apple Salad (p. 60)

Calories per Serving: 493
Total Fat per Serving: 14 gm
Calories from Fat: 26%

Additional Ideas for Low-Fat Menus...

Pasta Meatball Stew (p. 132)
Lettuce with Sour Cream Dressing (p. 64)
Sesame French Bread (p. 83)
Raspberry Baked Apples (p. 276)
Calories per Serving: 494
Total Fat per Serving: Less than 5 gm
Calories from Fat: 7%

Cranberry-Orange Molded Salad (p. 54)
Turkey Tetrazzini (p. 167)
Pumpkin Spice Muffins (p. 91)
Calories per Serving: 495
Total Fat per Serving: Less than 9 gm
Calories from Fat: 15%

Barbecued Pork Sandwiches (p. 127)
Stuffed Cherry Tomatoes (p. 33)
Stuffed Celery Snacks (p. 25)
Carrot Spice Cake (p. 272)
Calories per Serving: 501
Total Fat per Serving: Less than 8 gm
Calories from Fat: 13%

Here's How You Can Make Your Own Family-Favorite Recipes Lower in Fat

THE 455 RECIPES in *Low-Fat Country Cooking* supply an abundance of new ideas for your cooking day in and day out. Likely, though, you also have some favorite standby recipes—dishes you and your family have enjoyed for years—that you would love to make more often...if only they were lower in fat.

With that in mind, here are some general suggestions on how you can adapt recipes from your own file to reduce fat whenever you like right in your own kitchen:

Use Lower-Fat Alternatives

● Make *chili*, *meatballs*, *meat loaf* or *cabbage rolls*—but substitute ground turkey breast for part or all of the ground beef or pork.

● Use reduced-fat cheese in *cheddar cheese soup* or *macaroni and cheese*—but, because it melts differently, shred it finely and stir it in at the last minute.

● On your favorite *wheat* or *English muffin bread* or *toast*, use jelly, fruit spread, fat-free margarine or honey as the spread.

● Substitute egg whites or egg substitute for fresh whole eggs in *cheesecake*, *cornmeal muffins* or *pumpkin pie*.

● In place of cream, use evaporated skim milk in *chowder*, *brownies* or *caramel apple cake*.

● Top *gingerbread*, *banana cream pie* or *creamy fruit desserts* with light or fat-free whipped topping instead of whipped cream.

Adjust Ingredients

● Try a small amount of a sharp highly flavored cheese—Swiss, sharp cheddar or Parmesan, for example—in place of mild cheddar cheese in your *au gratin potatoes*, *beefy taco dip* or *brunch egg casserole*.

● Combine fat-free mayonnaise with nonfat yogurt in *creamy potato salad*, *coleslaw* or *onion dip*.

● Use half the amount of buttered crumbs or shredded cheese the recipe calls for to make a topping for *tuna noodle casserole* or *shepherd's pie*.

● Cook rice and noodles without added butter or margarine to serve with *Swiss steak* or in making *stir-fries*, *stuffed peppers* or *rice pudding*.

Change Techniques

● Trim visible fat from meat before making *steak and onion pie*, *breaded pork chops* or *beef roll-ups*.

● Remove poultry skin when you prepare *Brunswick stew* or *chicken cacciatore*.

● Consider broiling, grilling, microwaving or roasting on a rack *London broil*, *kabobs*, *pork roast* or *roast turkey*.

● When baking *nut breads* or *muffins*, toast nuts and coconut, then chop finely and distribute throughout for the same flavor from half the amount.

● Thicken gravies and sauces for your *pot roast*, *chicken dumplings* or *stews* with pureed vegetables.

● Drizzle *baked lemon chicken* or *roasted chicken and potatoes* with a small amount of olive oil or vegetable oil instead of basting with butter.

● Use margarine for baking *cakes* or *apple crumb bars* ...and reduced-fat margarine for topping *vegetables* or *noodles* or tossing *bread crumbs*.

● Mist your *potato skins*, *parsley potatoes* or *oven-roasted potatoes* with nonstick cooking spray instead of brushing with butter.

● Rely on only a small amount of fat for sauteing or stir-frying *pepper steak* or *vegetables*.

● Use nonstick pans or coat pans with nonstick cooking spray if your recipe calls for greased pans to make *cakes*, *pancakes* or *casseroles*.

● Skim fat while cooking *chicken noodle soup*, *beef stew* or *barbecue sauces*.

About the "Nutritional Information" Boxes...

THIS is how the recipes in this book are analyzed in the "Nutrition Information" box to the side of each one:

● All information is listed for one serving.

● Garnishes and optional ingredients are not included.

● Only the amount of marinade absorbed into the food is calculated.

● Margarine is calculated at 80% vegetable oil; reduced-fat margarine is calculated at 53% vegetable oil.

Keep in mind that, since certain foods can have a wide range of values, these numbers are considered estimates.

* * *

For your reference, these are the daily recommendations for a moderately active adult:

Calories	2,000
Total Fat	65 gm
Calories from fat	30%
Saturated Fat	20 gm
Cholesterol	300 mg
Sodium	2,400 mg
Carbohydrate	300 gm
Protein	50 gm

Note: If you have specific dietary needs or have questions about how the recipes in *Low-Fat Country Cooking* fit into your diet, consult a qualified health professional.

Fast Fat Figuring

● To quickly estimate your daily allotment of fat in grams, divide your ideal weight by 2.

● Calorie needs are based on a variety of factors—age, size, gender, overall health and activity level. But for a quick estimate of your daily allotment, multiply your current weight by 10 if you are inactive...by 12 if you are moderately active...and by 15 if you are very active.

● Experts recommend that no more than 30% of daily calorie intake come from fat. Here's a fast way to calculate the percent of calories from fat: Multiply the grams of fat by 9...divide that number by the total number of calories...then multiply that number by 100.

WAKE UP TO FLAVOR. *Top to bottom: Vegetable Frittata and Oatmeal Waffles (both recipes on page 11).*

Breakfast & Brunch

Vegetable Frittata

Janet Eckhoff, Woodland, California

(Pictured at left)

Egg dishes are a quick and inexpensive way to offer your family a tasty meal. With such great flavor and convenience, this is one recipe you'll likely prepare often.

2 tablespoons vegetable oil, *divided*	1 garlic clove, minced
1/2 cup chopped onion	2 medium red potatoes, cooked and cubed
1/2 cup chopped green pepper	1 small zucchini, cubed
1/2 cup chopped sweet red pepper	Egg substitute equivalent to 6 eggs
	Dash pepper

Heat 1 tablespoon oil in a 10-in. cast-iron or ovenproof skillet; saute onion, peppers and garlic until tender. Remove vegetables with a slotted spoon; set aside. In the same skillet over medium heat, lightly brown potatoes in remaining oil. Add vegetable mixture and zucchini; cook for 4 minutes. In a bowl, combine egg substitute and pepper; pour over vegetables. Cover and cook for 8-10 minutes or until eggs are nearly set. Broil 6 in. from the heat for 2 minutes or until eggs are completely set. Cut into wedges. **Yield:** 6 servings.

Oatmeal Waffles

Mrs. Francis Stoops, Stoneboro, Pennsylvania

(Pictured at left)

This recipe can be used to make pancakes as well as waffles. Both are delicious because of their hearty whole-grain flavor. For a special treat, serve them topped with fruit or a flavored syrup!

Egg substitute equivalent to 2 eggs	1 cup whole wheat flour
2 cups buttermilk	1/2 teaspoon salt
1 cup quick-cooking oats	1 teaspoon baking soda
1 tablespoon molasses	1 teaspoon baking powder
1 tablespoon vegetable oil	Confectioners' sugar and fresh strawberries, optional

In a large bowl, combine egg substitute and buttermilk. Add oats and mix well. Stir in molasses and oil. Combine flour, salt, baking soda and baking powder; stir into the egg mixture. Pour batter onto a preheated waffle maker coated with nonstick cooking spray. Bake according to manufacturer's directions. If desired, dust with confectioners' sugar and top with strawberries. **To make pancakes:** Drop batter by about 1/4 cupfuls onto a hot griddle coated with nonstick cooking spray. Turn when bubbles begin to form on top of pancake. **Yield:** 8 waffles (4 inches) or 16 pancakes.

Grandma's Breakfast Fruit

Ethelyn Aanrud, Amherst Junction, Wisconsin

(Pictured above)

This versatile recipe is similar to the "Sweet Soup" that is served at our family's traditional Scandinavian holiday suppers. I've found this fruit mixture to be delicious for breakfast spooned over dry cereal.

NUTRITIONAL
INFORMATION

Serving Size: 1/8 recipe

Calories: 174
Total Fat: trace
Calories from Fat: 0%
Saturated Fat: trace
Cholesterol: 0 mg
Sodium: 2 mg
Carbohydrate: 45 gm
Protein: 1 gm

3 large cooking apples, peeled and thickly sliced
1/2 cup pitted prunes
3/4 cup raisins
1 orange, peeled and sectioned
3 cups plus 3 tablespoons water, *divided*
1/2 cup sugar
1/2 teaspoon ground cinnamon
2 tablespoons cornstarch

In a saucepan, combine apples, prunes, raisins, orange and 3 cups water. Bring to a boil; reduce heat and simmer 10 minutes. Stir in sugar and cinnamon. Combine cornstarch and remaining water; stir into saucepan. Bring to a boil, stirring constantly. Cook 2 minutes. Chill. **Yield:** 8 servings.

Hearty Ham Scramble

Marsha Ransom, South Haven, Michigan

Ham and potatoes are comforting additions to ordinary scrambled eggs. My family enjoys this dish so much I sometimes make it for dinner.

NUTRITIONAL
INFORMATION

Serving Size: 1/6 recipe

Calories: 141
Total Fat: 4 gm
Calories from Fat: 25%
Saturated Fat: 1 gm
Cholesterol: 17 mg
Sodium: 614 mg
Carbohydrate: 11 gm
Protein: 15 gm

1/3 cup chopped onion
1/4 cup chopped green pepper
2 medium potatoes, peeled, cooked and cubed
1-1/2 cups julienned fully cooked low-fat ham
Egg substitute equivalent to 6 eggs
2 tablespoons water
Dash pepper

In a large skillet coated with nonstick cooking spray, cook onion and green pepper until crisp-tender. Add potatoes and ham; cook and stir for 5 minutes. In a bowl, combine egg substitute, water and pepper; pour over ham mixture. Cook over low heat, stirring occasionally, until eggs are completely set. **Yield:** 6 servings.

Open-Faced Chicken Benedict

Cathy Tyrrell, Colorado Springs, Colorado

My husband enjoyed this recipe when he was growing up, so my mother-in-law passed it on to me when I wanted to surprise him with a special Valentine's Day breakfast.

6 boneless skinless
  chicken breast halves
1/2 cup all-purpose flour
1 teaspoon paprika
1/4 teaspoon pepper, *divided*
6 slices Canadian bacon,
  trimmed

1/2 cup light sour cream
1/2 cup light mayonnaise
1 tablespoon lemon juice
1 teaspoon prepared
  mustard
3 English muffins, split
  and toasted

Pound chicken to 1/4-in. thickness. In a large resealable plastic bag, combine flour, paprika and 1/8 teaspoon pepper. Add chicken, one piece at a time, and shake to coat. In a large skillet coated with non-stick cooking spray, cook chicken until browned and juices run clear. Transfer to a platter and keep warm. Brown bacon in the same skillet, turning once; remove and keep warm. For sauce, combine sour cream, mayonnaise, lemon juice, mustard and remaining pepper in a small saucepan. Cook, stirring constantly, until heated through; keep warm over low heat (do not boil). Place English muffin halves on a baking sheet. Top each with a slice of bacon, one chicken breast half and 2 tablespoons sauce. Broil until bubbly. **Yield:** 6 servings.

NUTRITIONAL INFORMATION

Serving Size: 1/6 recipe

Calories: 372
Total Fat: 14 gm
Calories from Fat: 34%
Saturated Fat: 4 gm
Cholesterol: 103 mg
Sodium: 699 mg
Carbohydrate: 23 gm
Protein: 36 gm

Raspberry Pancakes

Karen Edland, McHenry, North Dakota

Most people have eaten blueberry pancakes before but are pleasantly surprised by this version calling for raspberries. It's my favorite.

2/3 cup all-purpose flour
1 tablespoon sugar
1 teaspoon baking powder
3/4 teaspoon baking soda
1/3 cup nonfat plain yogurt
1 egg

1 tablespoon margarine,
  melted and cooled
1/2 cup skim milk
1 cup fresh raspberries
Confectioners' sugar and
  raspberry jam, optional

Whisk together flour, sugar, baking powder and baking soda; set aside. In large bowl, whisk together yogurt, egg, margarine and milk. Stir flour mixture into liquid mixture until just combined. Fold in raspberries. Heat a griddle coated with nonstick cooking spray over medium-high heat. Drop batter by 1/4 cupfuls onto griddle; cook for 1 minute or until bubbles form on top of pancakes. Turn and cook 1 minute more. If desired, dust with confectioners' sugar and serve with jam. **Yield:** 4 servings.

NUTRITIONAL INFORMATION

Serving Size: 1/4 recipe
(calculated without confectioners' sugar and jam)

Calories: 181
Total Fat: 5 gm
Calories from Fat: 23%
Saturated Fat: 1 gm
Cholesterol: 55 mg
Sodium: 445 mg
Carbohydrate: 28 gm
Protein: 7 gm

Sausage Strata

Gayle Grigg, Phoenix, Arizona

(Pictured above)

For the perfect combination of eggs, sausage, bread and cheese, this is the dish to try. I like it because it bakes up tender and golden, slices beautifully and goes over well whenever I serve it.

1 pound bulk turkey sausage	6 slices white bread, cut into 1/2-inch cubes
Egg substitute equivalent to 6 eggs	1 cup (4 ounces) shredded reduced-fat cheddar cheese
2 cups skim milk	
1 teaspoon ground mustard	

In a skillet, brown and crumble sausage; drain and set aside. In a large bowl, combine egg substitute, milk and mustard. Stir in bread cubes, cheese and sausage. Pour into an 11-in. x 7-in. x 2-in. baking dish coated with nonstick cooking spray. Cover and refrigerate for 8 hours or overnight. Remove from the refrigerator 30 minutes before baking. Bake, uncovered, at 350° for 40 minutes or until a knife inserted near the center comes out clean. **Yield:** 10 servings.

Broiled Grapefruit

Terry Bray, Haines City, Florida

I was never a fan of grapefruit until I had it broiled at a restaurant—it was so tangy and delicious! I finally got the recipe and now make it often.

1 large grapefruit, halved	2 tablespoons sugar
2 teaspoons margarine, softened	1/2 teaspoon ground cinnamon

Cut membrane out of the center of each grapefruit half. Cut around each section so it will be easy to spoon out when eating. Place 1 teaspoon margarine in the center of each half. Combine sugar and cinnamon; sprinkle over each. Broil until butter is melted and sugar is bubbly. Serve immediately. **Yield:** 2 servings.

Potatoes O'Brien

Nila Towler, Baird, Texas

I usually serve these colorful potatoes for breakfast. But they're great as a tasty potato side dish for just about any meal.

1 tablespoon cooking oil
1/2 cup chopped onion
1/2 cup chopped green pepper
1/2 cup chopped sweet red pepper

4 medium red potatoes, cubed
1/4 cup low-sodium beef broth
1/2 teaspoon Worcestershire sauce

Heat oil in a skillet; saute the onion, peppers and potatoes over medium heat for 4 minutes. Combine broth and Worcestershire sauce; pour over vegetables. Cover and cook for 10 minutes or until potatoes are tender, stirring occasionally. Uncover and cook until liquid is absorbed, about 3 minutes. **Yield:** 4 servings.

NUTRITIONAL INFORMATION

Serving Size: 1/4 recipe

Calories: 134
Total Fat: 4 gm
Calories from Fat: 27%
Saturated Fat: trace
Cholesterol: 0
Sodium: 50 mg
Carbohydrate: 23 gm
Protein: 3 gm

Baked Applesauce

Mary Mootz, Cincinnati, Ohio

(Pictured below)

Once you taste this applesauce, you won't want the store-bought variety anymore. Baking the apples locks in their delicious flavor!

2 large tart apples, peeled and sliced
3 tablespoons sugar

1/4 teaspoon ground cinnamon
1/4 teaspoon vanilla extract

Place apples in a 1-qt. baking dish coated with nonstick cooking spray. In a small bowl, combine sugar, cinnamon and vanilla; mix well. Sprinkle over apples. Cover and bake at 350° for 40-45 minutes or until apples are tender. Uncover and mash with a fork. Serve warm. **Yield:** 2 servings.

NUTRITIONAL INFORMATION

Serving Size: 1/2 recipe

Calories: 194
Total Fat: 1 gm
Calories from Fat: 5%
Saturated Fat: trace
Cholesterol: 0
Sodium: trace
Carbohydrate: 50 gm
Protein: trace

Pine Nut Pancakes

Ed Horkey, Ahwatukee, Arizona

Back when I was a youngster, pine nuts helped me earn my Boy Scout Cooking Merit Badge. I decided on these pancakes for my project.

1-1/2 cups reduced-fat biscuit/baking mix	1/4 cup raisins
1 cup puffed rice cereal	2 tablespoons pine nuts, toasted
1/3 cup finely chopped banana	1 egg
1/3 cup shredded peeled apple	3/4 cup milk
	1/2 teaspoon vanilla extract

In a bowl, combine baking mix, cereal, banana, apple, raisins and pine nuts. In another bowl, beat egg, milk and vanilla; stir into the dry ingredients just until moistened. Pour batter by 1/4 cupfuls onto a lightly greased hot griddle; turn when bubbles form on top of pancakes. Cook until second side is golden brown. Serve immediately. **Yield:** 10 pancakes.

Breakfast Burritos

Mary Smith, Huntington, Indiana

(Pictured below)

One morning, I decided to try the leftover taco filling from the night before in my eggs. They were really delicious served in tortillas.

Egg substitute equivalent to 8 eggs	1/2 cup shredded reduced-fat cheddar cheese
2 tablespoons finely chopped onion	1/2 cup cooked taco-seasoned ground round
2 tablespoons finely chopped green pepper	4 fat-free flour tortillas (6 inches), warmed
1 drop hot pepper sauce	Salsa, optional

In a bowl, combine egg substitute, onion, green pepper, hot pepper sauce and cheese. Cook and stir in a nonstick skillet until eggs begin to set. Add taco meat; cook until eggs are completely set. Spoon onto a warmed tortilla and roll up; top with salsa if desired. **Yield:** 4 servings.

Blueberry French Toast

Patricia Walls, Aurora, Minnesota

(Pictured above)

With luscious blueberries inside and in a sauce that drizzles over each slice, this is the best breakfast dish I've ever tasted.

12 slices day-old white bread, crusts removed
2 packages (8 ounces *each*) light cream cheese
1 cup fresh *or* frozen blueberries
Egg substitute equivalent to 12 eggs
2 cups skim milk
1/3 cup maple syrup

SAUCE:
1 cup sugar
2 tablespoons cornstarch
1 cup water
1 cup fresh *or* frozen blueberries

Cut bread into 1-in. cubes; place half in a 13-in. x 9-in. x 2-in. baking dish coated with nonstick cooking spray. Cut cream cheese into 1-in. cubes; place over bread. Top with blueberries and remaining bread. In a large bowl, combine egg substitute, milk and syrup; mix well. Pour over bread mixture. Cover and chill 8 hours or overnight. Remove from refrigerator 30 minutes before baking. Cover and bake at 350° for 30 minutes. Uncover; bake 25-30 minutes longer or until golden brown and the center is set. In a saucepan, combine sugar and cornstarch; add water. Bring to a boil over medium heat; boil for 3 minutes, stirring constantly. Stir in blueberries; reduce heat. Simmer for 8-10 minutes or until berries have burst. Serve over French toast. **Yield:** 8 servings (1-3/4 cups sauce).

NUTRITIONAL INFORMATION

Serving Size: 1/8 recipe

Calories: 449
Total Fat: 11 gm
Calories from Fat: 22%
Saturated Fat: 6 gm
Cholesterol: 35 mg
Sodium: 681 mg
Carbohydrate: 67 gm
Protein: 20 gm

Polish Apple Pancakes

Jane Zielinski, Rotterdam Junction, New York

(Pictured above)

My mom used to make these wonderful pancakes for me as an after-school snack. Now I serve them as a main course or as a side dish with a variety of breakfast entrees.

NUTRITIONAL
INFORMATION

Serving Size: 2 pancakes
(calculated without sugars)

Calories: 143
Total Fat: 3 gm
Calories from Fat: 19%
Saturated Fat: 1 gm
Cholesterol: 27 mg
Sodium: 171 mg
Carbohydrate: 27 gm
Protein: 4 gm

1 cup all-purpose flour
1 tablespoon sugar, optional
1/2 teaspoon salt
1 egg
1 cup skim milk

1 tablespoon vegetable oil
5 medium apples, peeled and
thinly sliced
Confectioners' sugar, optional

In a bowl, combine flour, sugar if desired and salt. In another bowl, lightly beat egg; add milk and oil. Add to dry ingredients and stir until smooth. Fold in apples. Heat a griddle coated with nonstick cooking spray; pour batter by 1/2 cupfuls onto hot griddle and spread to form a 5-in. circle. Turn when bubbles begin to form on top. Cook until the second side is golden brown and apples are tender. Dust with confectioners' sugar if desired. **Yield:** 8 servings (16 pancakes).

Zucchini Scramble

Betty Claycomb, Alverton, Pennsylvania

These scrambled eggs have garden-fresh taste that's sure to please anyone. I like this recipe because I can use other fresh vegetables when they are available. It also makes a tasty light lunch or dinner.

NUTRITIONAL
INFORMATION

Serving Size: 1/6 recipe

Calories: 100
Total Fat: 4 gm
Calories from Fat: 37%
Saturated Fat: 2 gm
Cholesterol: 7 mg
Sodium: 114 mg
Carbohydrate: 4 gm
Protein: 12 gm

3 small zucchini
(about 1 pound), sliced
1 medium onion, chopped
2 tablespoons margarine

Egg substitute equivalent
to 6 eggs
1/2 cup reduced-fat shredded
cheddar cheese

In a skillet coated with nonstick cooking spray, saute zucchini and onion until tender. Add the egg substitute; cook and stir until completely set. Sprinkle with cheese. Remove from the heat; cover until cheese melts. **Yield:** 6 servings.

Breakfast Pizzas

Olive Ranck, Williamsburg, Indiana

I taught high school economics classes for years. I always included a session on eggs, and this is a recipe my students enjoyed.

Egg substitute equivalent
  to 4 eggs
   3 tablespoons finely
    chopped green pepper
   3 tablespoons skim milk
  1/2 teaspoon dried oregano

4 English muffins
4 tablespoons pizza sauce
1/2 cup bulk turkey sausage,
  cooked and drained
2 tablespoons grated
  Parmesan cheese

In a bowl, combine egg substitute, green pepper, milk and oregano. In a skillet coated with nonstick cooking spray, cook and stir egg mixture over medium heat until eggs are completely set. Remove from the heat. Split and toast English muffins; spread with pizza sauce. Spoon the egg mixture onto muffins. Sprinkle with sausage and cheese. Place under broiler for a few minutes to heat through. **Yield:** 4 servings.

NUTRITIONAL INFORMATION

Serving Size: 1/4 recipe

Calories: 278
Total Fat: 10 gm
Calories from Fat: 31%
Saturated Fat: 2 gm
Cholesterol: 13 mg
Sodium: 588 mg
Carbohydrate: 32 gm
Protein: 15 gm

Ambrosia Fruit

Marsha Ransom, South Haven, Michigan

This recipe is a perfect way to capture the taste of fresh fruit anytime of year.

1 can (20 ounces)
  unsweetened pineapple
  tidbits
1/4 cup packed brown sugar
1/2 teaspoon grated orange
  peel

2 medium oranges
2 medium unpeeled apples,
  diced
1 tablespoon shredded
  coconut

Drain pineapple, reserving 1/4 cup juice in a saucepan; set pineapple aside. Add brown sugar and orange peel to the juice; heat until sugar dissolves. Peel and section oranges into a large bowl; add the apples and pineapple. Add pineapple juice mixture and stir gently. Chill. Just before serving, sprinkle with coconut. **Yield:** 6 servings.

NUTRITIONAL INFORMATION

Serving Size: 1/6 recipe

Calories: 132
Total Fat: 1 gm
Calories from Fat: 4%
Saturated Fat: trace
Cholesterol: 0
Sodium: 6 mg
Carbohydrate: 33 gm
Protein: 1 gm

Easy Cherry Fruit Soup

Virginia Shellum, Nicollet, Minnesota

My husband's family is from Scandinavia, where fruit soups are common.

1 can (21 ounces) cherry
  pie filling
1 can (8 ounces)
  unsweetened pineapple
  chunks, undrained
2 cups water
1 cup pitted prunes

2/3 cup chopped dried
  apricots
1 tablespoon margarine
2 lemon slices
1 teaspoon quick-cooking
  tapioca

In a 3-qt. casserole, combine all ingredients. Cover and bake at 325° for 1 hour. Serve warm. **Yield:** 8 servings.

NUTRITIONAL INFORMATION

Serving Size: 1/8 recipe

Calories: 175
Total Fat: 1 gm
Calories from Fat: 5%
Saturated Fat: trace
Cholesterol: 0
Sodium: 42 mg
Carbohydrate: 42 gm
Protein: 1 gm

Popeye Special

Marcy Cella, L'Anse, Michigan

(Pictured above)

A combination of vegetables and ground round make this a hearty breakfast.

1 pound ground round
1/2 pound fresh mushrooms, sliced
1/2 pound fresh spinach, torn
6 green onions, sliced
1/4 cup chopped celery
1/4 cup chopped sweet red pepper
1/4 teaspoon garlic powder
1/2 teaspoon pepper
Egg substitute equivalent to 6 eggs

In a large skillet, brown beef and mushrooms; drain. Add spinach, onions, celery, red pepper, garlic powder and pepper. Cook and stir for 1 minute. Add egg substitute; cook and stir until the eggs are completely set. Serve immediately. **Yield:** 6 servings.

NUTRITIONAL INFORMATION

Serving Size: 1/6 recipe

Calories: 139
Total Fat: 5 gm
Calories from Fat: 32%
Saturated Fat: 2 gm
Cholesterol: 48 mg
Sodium: 157 mg
Carbohydrate: 4 gm
Protein: 21 gm

Triple Berry Wake-Up Breakfast

Leandra Holland, Westlake, California

This recipe earned "most outstanding" honors in our state's "Berry-Off" cooking contest. Strawberries make this stuffed French toast scrumptious.

1/4 cup fat-free cream cheese, softened
2 tablespoons strawberry spreadable fruit
4 slices white bread, crusts removed
1/2 pint fresh strawberries, sliced
1 egg
2 tablespoons skim milk
Strawberry syrup *or* confectioners' sugar, optional

Combine cream cheese and spreadable fruit; spread on two slices of bread. Top with sliced berries, making a complete blanket over the cheese. Top each with the remaining bread. In a bowl, beat egg and milk. Heat a frying pan or griddle coated with nonstick cooking spray over medium-high heat. Dip sandwiches in egg mixture and fry until golden brown on both sides. If desired, serve with syrup or dust with confectioners' sugar. **Yield:** 2 servings.

NUTRITIONAL INFORMATION

Serving Size: 1/2 recipe
(calculated without syrup and confectioners' sugar)

Calories: 262
Total Fat: 5 gm
Calories from Fat: 18%
Saturated Fat: 2 gm
Cholesterol: 109 mg
Sodium: 466 mg
Carbohydrate: 40 gm
Protein: 14 gm

Apple-Topped Oatcakes

Lois Hofmeyer, Aurora, Illinois

(Pictured below)

These oatcakes with apple topping are a tasty, wholesome combination.

1-1/2 cups hot skim milk
3/4 cup old-fashioned oats
1 egg
1 tablespoon vegetable oil
2 tablespoons molasses
1 cup all-purpose flour
1-1/2 teaspoons baking powder
3/4 teaspoon ground
   cinnamon
1/4 teaspoon ground ginger
1/4 teaspoon baking soda
1/4 teaspoon salt

3 egg whites
LEMON APPLES:
1 tablespoon margarine
5 medium tart apples,
   peeled and sliced
1 tablespoon lemon juice
1 teaspoon grated lemon
   peel
1/2 cup sugar
1 tablespoon cornstarch
1/8 teaspoon ground nutmeg

NUTRITIONAL INFORMATION

Serving Size: 1/8 recipe

Calories: 264
Total Fat: 5 gm
Calories from Fat: 17%
Saturated Fat: 1 gm
Cholesterol: 28 mg
Sodium: 261 mg
Carbohydrate: 50 gm
Protein: 7 gm

In a large bowl, combine milk and oats; let stand for 5 minutes. Stir in egg, oil and molasses. Combine dry ingredients; stir into oat mixture just until moistened. Beat egg whites until soft peaks form; fold gently into batter. Set aside. Heat margarine in a skillet until foamy. Add apples, lemon juice and peel; cook, uncovered, for 8-10 minutes, stirring occasionally. Meanwhile, cook oatcakes. Pour batter by 1/4 cupfuls onto a hot griddle coated with nonstick cooking spray. Cook until bubbles form; turn and cook until browned on other side. For apples, combine sugar, cornstarch and nutmeg; add to apple mixture and cook 2 minutes longer or until tender. Serve warm over oatcakes. **Yield:** 8 servings.

SATISFYING SNACKS. Clockwise from top right: Appetizer Meatballs, Creamy Taco Dip (both recipes on page 23), Pineapple Cheese Dip and Cinnamon Popcorn (both recipes on page 24).

Appetizers & Snacks

Appetizer Meatballs

Pat Waymire, Yellow Springs, Ohio

(Pictured at left)

These tasty meatballs are a perennial favorite at our Christmas parties. But with such wonderful flavor, you'll get requests year-round.

1 pound ground round	SAUCE:
Egg substitute equivalent to 1 egg	1/2 cup ketchup
1/2 cup soft bread crumbs	1/2 cup chopped onion
1/4 cup skim milk	1/3 cup sugar
1/3 cup finely chopped onion	1/3 cup vinegar
1/2 teaspoon Worcestershire sauce	1 tablespoon Worcestershire sauce
	1/8 teaspoon pepper

Combine the first six ingredients; mix well. Shape into 1-in. balls. In a skillet over medium heat, brown meatballs; drain. Place in a 2-1/2-qt. baking dish. Combine sauce ingredients. Pour over meatballs. Bake, uncovered, at 350° for 50-60 minutes or until meatballs are done. **Yield:** 4 dozen.

NUTRITIONAL INFORMATION

Serving Size: 3 meatballs

Calories: 85
Total Fat: 3 gm
Calories from Fat: 26%
Saturated Fat: 1 gm
Cholesterol: 24 mg
Sodium: 199 mg
Carbohydrate: 9 gm
Protein: 8 gm

Creamy Taco Dip

Denise Smith, Lusk, Wyoming

(Pictured at left)

You'll know this snack is a hit at your next gathering when you come home with an empty pan!

1 package (8 ounces) fat-free cream cheese, softened	1 cup shredded lettuce
1/2 cup (4 ounces) nonfat sour cream	1 cup (4 ounces) fat-free shredded cheddar cheese
1/2 cup taco sauce	1 medium tomato, diced
1 teaspoon ground cumin	1/4 cup chopped ripe olives
1 can (15 ounces) fat-free refried beans	1/4 cup canned chopped green chilies
	Baked tortilla chips

In a mixing bowl, beat cream cheese and sour cream until smooth. Stir in taco sauce and cumin; set aside. Spread the refried beans over the bottom of a serving platter or 13-in. x 9-in. x 2-in. dish. Spread cream cheese mixture over the beans, leaving about 1 in. uncovered around the edges. Top with layers of lettuce, cheese, tomato, olives and chilies. Serve with tortilla chips. **Yield:** 20 servings.

NUTRITIONAL INFORMATION

Serving Size: 1/4 cup
(calculated without tortilla chips)

Calories: 45
Total Fat: 1 gm
Calories from Fat: 10%
Saturated Fat: trace
Cholesterol: 0
Sodium: 270 mg
Carbohydrate: 5 gm
Protein: 5 gm

Cinnamon Popcorn

Caroline Roberts, Findlay, Ohio

(Pictured on page 22)

This crisp, lightly sweet snack is great for traveling since it's not sticky.

2 quarts plain popped
 popcorn
1 egg white, lightly beaten
1/2 cup sugar

1 teaspoon ground
 cinnamon
1/4 teaspoon salt, optional

Place popcorn in a 15-in. x 10-in. x 1-in. baking pan. In a small bowl, mix egg white, sugar, cinnamon and salt if desired. Pour over popcorn and mix thoroughly. Bake at 300° for 20 minutes. Cool. Store in an airtight container. **Yield:** 2 quarts.

Pineapple Cheese Dip

Deborah Hill, Coffeyville, Kansas

(Pictured on page 22)

The combination of flavors makes this dip very interesting as well as delicious. It's a challenge to not eat a lot while you're making it.

1 can (8 ounces)
 pineapple tidbits
2 packages (8 ounces
 each) light cream cheese,
 softened
1 can (8 ounces) water
 chestnuts, drained and
 chopped

3 tablespoons chopped
 fresh chives
1/2 teaspoon salt-free
 seasoning blend
1/4 teaspoon pepper
3/4 cup chopped pecans
Assorted reduced-fat crackers

Drain the pineapple, reserving 1 tablespoon juice. In a small bowl, combine pineapple, cream cheese, water chestnuts, chives, seasoning blend, pepper and pecans. Stir in reserved juice; mix well. Cover and chill. Serve with crackers. **Yield:** 4 cups.

Creamy Chicken Spread

Lynn Scheiderer, Bishop, California

This tasty chicken spread came from a member of the Texas church where my husband served as pastor. It's great on bread or crackers.

1-1/2 cups chopped cooked
 chicken
1 package (8 ounces)
 fat-free cream cheese,
 softened

1/2 cup chopped celery
1/2 cup fat-free mayonnaise
2 tablespoons chopped
 onion
1 teaspoon onion powder

Place all ingredients in a food processor; process until coarsely chopped. **Yield:** 2-1/2 cups.

Salmon Spread

Carolyn Stewart, Anchorage, Alaska

(Pictured above)

This quick spread splendidly showcases one of Alaska's greatest resources—salmon! I know it'll be a hit where you live, too.

2 cans (15 ounces *each*) salmon, drained, boned and flaked
1 package (8 ounces) fat-free cream cheese, softened
1 tablespoon finely chopped onion
1 tablespoon prepared horseradish
1 tablespoon lemon juice
2 tablespoons fat-free mayonnaise
1-1/2 teaspoons dill weed
1 cup (8 ounces) nonfat sour cream
Fresh dill *or* parsley, optional
Toasted bread rounds *or* reduced-fat crackers

In a mixing bowl, combine the first seven ingredients; mix well. Spread on a serving platter and shape into a loaf or ball. Top with sour cream. Garnish with dill or parsley if desired. Serve with bread rounds or crackers. **Yield:** 10 appetizer servings.

Stuffed Celery Snacks

Patsy Faye Steenbock, Shoshoni, Wyoming

The creamy filling with each bite of celery makes for a satisfying snack.

1 package (8 ounces) fat-free cream cheese, softened
1/3 cup shredded carrot
1-1/2 teaspoons dried parsley flakes
1/4 teaspoon dried thyme
Dash onion powder
24 celery pieces (3 inches)

In a small bowl, combine cream cheese, carrot and seasonings. Stuff into celery. Cover and chill for at least 1 hour. **Yield:** 2 dozen.

Creamy Caramel Dip

Karen Laubman, Spruce Grove, Alberta

(Pictured above)

Because I feed three hungry "men" (my husband and our two little boys), I love satisfying snacks like this dip that are easy to make. We appreciate this cool treat, especially in summer.

1 package (8 ounces) light cream cheese, softened	2 teaspoons lemon juice
3/4 cup packed brown sugar	1 cup cold skim milk
1 cup (8 ounces) nonfat sour cream	1 package (3.4 ounces) instant vanilla pudding mix
2 teaspoons vanilla extract	Assorted fresh fruit

In a mixing bowl, beat cream cheese and brown sugar until smooth. Add the sour cream, vanilla, lemon juice, milk and pudding mix, beating well after each addition. Cover and chill for at least 1 hour. Serve with fruit. **Yield:** 3-1/2 cups.

Savory Potato Skins

Andrea Holcomb, Torrington, Connecticut

For a simple hot snack that really hits the spot on a cool fall evening, put together a plate of these crisp potato skins.

4 large baking potatoes, baked	1 teaspoon paprika
1 teaspoon salt, optional	Nonfat sour cream and chives, optional
1 teaspoon garlic powder	

Cut potatoes in half lengthwise; scoop out pulp, leaving a 1/4-in.-thick shell. (Save pulp for another use.) Cut shells lengthwise into quarters and place on a baking sheet coated with nonstick cooking spray. Mist shells with nonstick cooking spray. Combine salt if desired, garlic powder and paprika; sprinkle over the skins. Broil until golden brown, 5-8 minutes. If desired, combine sour cream and chives and serve with potato skins. **Yield:** 32 shells.

NUTRITIONAL
INFORMATION

Serving Size: 2 tablespoons
(calculated without fruit)

Calories: 61
Total Fat: 1 gm
Calories from Fat: 20%
Saturated Fat: 1 gm
Cholesterol: 3 mg
Sodium: 106 mg
Carbohydrate: 11 gm
Protein: 2 gm

NUTRITIONAL
INFORMATION

Serving Size: 4 shells
(calculated without salt,
sour cream and chives)

Calories: 40
Total Fat: trace
Calories from Fat: 1%
Saturated Fat: trace
Cholesterol: 0
Sodium: 5 mg
Carbohydrate: 9 gm
Protein: 1 gm

Honey-Mustard Turkey Meatballs

Bonnie Durkin, Nescopeck, Pennsylvania

(Pictured below)

I serve these often during the holidays. It's nice to have a turkey meatball that doesn't taste like you should have used beef. These meatballs can be prepared ahead and frozen, so you can treat even drop-in guests to a hot snack.

1 pound ground turkey breast
1 egg, lightly beaten
3/4 cup crushed reduced-fat butter-flavored crackers
1/2 cup shredded part-skim mozzarella cheese
1/4 cup chopped onion
1/2 teaspoon ground ginger
6 tablespoons Dijon mustard, *divided*
1-1/4 cups unsweetened pineapple juice
1/4 cup chopped green pepper
2 tablespoons honey
1 tablespoon cornstarch
1/4 teaspoon onion powder

NUTRITIONAL INFORMATION

Serving Size: 3 meatballs

Calories: 176
Total Fat: 8 gm
Calories from Fat: 40%
Saturated Fat: 2 gm
Cholesterol: 48 mg
Sodium: 337 mg
Carbohydrate: 14 gm
Protein: 11 gm

In a bowl, combine turkey, egg, cracker crumbs, cheese, onion, ginger and 3 tablespoons mustard. Form into 30 balls, 1 in. each. Place in a greased 13-in. x 9-in. x 2-in. baking dish. Bake, uncovered, at 350° for 20-25 minutes or until juices run clear. In a saucepan, combine pineapple juice, green pepper, honey, cornstarch and onion powder; bring to a boil, stirring constantly. Cook and stir 2 minutes more; reduce heat. Stir in remaining mustard until smooth. Brush meatballs with about 1/4 cup sauce and return to the oven for 10 minutes. Serve remaining sauce as a dip for meatballs. **Yield:** 2-1/2 dozen.

Mini Hamburgers

Judy Lewis, Sterling Heights, Michigan

I guarantee these will be the first snack cleared from your table. They may be small, but they're packed with lots of flavor.

1/2 cup chopped onion	40 mini rolls, split
1 pound lean ground round	8 ounces light process
1 egg, beaten	American cheese slices,
1/4 teaspoon ground sage	cut into 1-1/2-inch
1/8 teaspoon pepper	squares, optional

In a skillet coated with nonstick cooking spray, saute onion. Transfer to a bowl; add meat, egg and seasonings. Spread over bottom halves of the rolls; replace tops. Place on baking sheets; cover with foil. Bake at 350° for 20 minutes. If desired, place a cheese square on each hamburger; replace tops and foil and return to the oven for 5 minutes. **Yield:** 40 appetizers.

Parmesan-Garlic Popcorn

Sharon Skildum, Maple Grove, Minnesota

This recipe proves that popcorn doesn't have to be topped with butter in order to be tasty. Here seasonings and a little Parmesan cheese give great flavor.

2-1/2 quarts plain popped popcorn	1 teaspoon garlic powder
1/4 cup grated Parmesan cheese	1 teaspoon dried parsley flakes
	1/2 teaspoon dill weed

Place popcorn in a large bowl and mist with nonstick cooking spray. In a small bowl, combine Parmesan cheese, garlic powder, parsley and dill; sprinkle over popcorn and toss lightly. Serve immediately. **Yield:** 2-1/2 quarts.

Soft Pretzels

Lori Hoogland, Catawba, Wisconsin

Our three kids enjoy every step of making these soft homemade pretzels. Each one has a chance to add ingredients, knead the dough and brush on the egg.

1 package (1/4 ounce) active dry yeast	1 teaspoon salt
1-1/2 cups warm water (110° to 115°)	4 cups all-purpose flour
1 tablespoon sugar	1 egg, beaten
	Coarse salt, optional

NUTRITIONAL INFORMATION

Serving Size: 1 sandwich
(calculated without cheese)

Calories: 110
Total Fat: 4 gm
Calories from Fat: 30%
Saturated Fat: 1 gm
Cholesterol: 12 mg
Sodium: 163 mg
Carbohydrate: 15 gm
Protein: 4 gm

NUTRITIONAL INFORMATION

Serving Size: 1-1/4 cups

Calories: 67
Total Fat: 2 gm
Calories from Fat: 23%
Saturated Fat: 1 gm
Cholesterol: 2 mg
Sodium: 59 mg
Carbohydrate: 10 gm
Protein: 3 gm

NUTRITIONAL INFORMATION

Serving Size: 1 pretzel
(calculated without coarse salt)

Calories: 98
Total Fat: trace
Calories from Fat: 4%
Saturated Fat: trace
Cholesterol: 11 mg
Sodium: 111 mg
Carbohydrate: 20 gm
Protein: 3 gm

In a large bowl, dissolve yeast in water. Add sugar, salt and enough flour to make a soft dough. Turn onto a floured board; knead until smooth and elastic, about 6-8 minutes. Pinch off about 2 tablespoons of dough for each pretzel. Shape into traditional pretzel twists or letters or animals as desired. Place on greased baking sheets. Brush with egg; sprinkle with salt if desired. Bake at 425° for 15 minutes or until golden brown. Cool on a wire rack. **Yield:** 20 servings.

Hot and Spicy Cranberry Dip

Dorothy Pritchett, Wills Point, Texas

This festive dip featuring cranberries makes appearances at all of our holiday gatherings. The spices really lend a delicious difference.

1 can (16 ounces) jellied cranberry sauce	1 garlic clove, minced
2 tablespoons prepared horseradish	1/4 teaspoon cayenne pepper
2 tablespoons honey	Pineapple chunks and orange sections, optional
1 tablespoon Worcestershire sauce	Light pork sausage breakfast links, cooked and halved, optional
1 tablespoon lemon juice	

In a medium saucepan, combine the first seven ingredients; bring to a boil. Reduce heat; cover and simmer for 5 minutes. Serve warm with pineapple, oranges and sausages if desired. **Yield:** 2 cups.

Fireside Clam Logs

Mrs. Chester Forwood, Merced, California

Sandwich bread makes an instant "coating" that bakes up nice and brown. Family and friends love these one-of-a-kind appetizers.

3 cans (6-1/2 ounces *each*) minced clams, rinsed and drained	1 teaspoon Worcestershire sauce
1/2 cup light mayonnaise	3/4 teaspoon garlic powder
1/3 cup sliced green onions	1/2 teaspoon hot pepper sauce
1/3 cup grated Parmesan cheese	24 thin slices sandwich bread, crusts removed

In a medium bowl, combine the first seven ingredients; mix well. Chill until ready to use. Flatten each slice of bread with a rolling pin; spread with 1 tablespoon of clam mixture. Roll up jelly roll style and cut in half. Place 1 in. apart on a baking sheet coated with nonstick cooking spray. Mist rolls with nonstick cooking spray. Bake at 425° for 10-12 minutes or until lightly browned. Serve immediately. **Yield:** 4 dozen.

Easy Entertaining

When planning a menu for a party, look for foods you can prepare in advance. Hot and Spicy Cranberry Dip can be made ahead, chilled and quickly reheated before serving. Or assemble, shape and chill the Fireside Clam Logs until ready to bake. You'll appreciate the extra time you have to visit.

NUTRITIONAL INFORMATION

Serving Size: 2 tablespoons
(calculated without fruit and sausages)

Calories: 53
Total Fat: trace
Calories from Fat: 1%
Saturated Fat: trace
Cholesterol: 0
Sodium: 38 mg
Carbohydrate: 14 gm
Protein: trace

NUTRITIONAL INFORMATION

Serving Size: 2 pieces

Calories: 88
Total Fat: 3 gm
Calories from Fat: 27%
Saturated Fat: 1 gm
Cholesterol: 3 mg
Sodium: 218 mg
Carbohydrate: 13 gm
Protein: 3 gm

Summertime Melon Soup

Valerie Black, Fairfield Bay, Arkansas

My summertime soup always elicits a sweet response. Guests never fail to request the recipe. To make it look even better, I often serve it in cantaloupe "bowls".

5 cups seeded cubed
  watermelon
1 pint fresh strawberries
1/4 cup light sour cream
2 tablespoons skim milk

2 tablespoons sugar
4 cantaloupes, optional
Additional fresh strawberries,
  optional

Combine watermelon and strawberries. Puree in batches in a blender, adding sour cream, milk and sugar to the last batch. Pour into a 2-qt. container; mix well. Cover and chill at least 3 hours. To serve soup in cantaloupe bowls, cut cantaloupes in half; hollow out melon and seeds, leaving about a 1/2-in. shell. Cut a decorative edge if desired. Reserve melon for another use. Add soup to shell; garnish with a strawberry if desired. **Yield:** 8 servings.

NUTRITIONAL INFORMATION

Serving Size: 1/8 recipe
(calculated without cantaloupe and strawberries)

Calories: 65
Total Fat: 1 gm
Calories from Fat: 14%
Saturated Fat: trace
Cholesterol: 2 mg
Sodium: 9 mg
Carbohydrate: 13 gm
Protein: 1 gm

Dairy Delicious Dip

Karen Kenny, Harvard, Illinois

(Pictured below)

Munching on fruit becomes so much more fun when there's a sweet, creamy dip to dunk your slices in. I especially enjoy its ease of preparation.

1 package (8 ounces) light
  cream cheese, softened
1/2 cup nonfat sour cream
1/4 cup sugar

1/4 cup packed brown sugar
2 tablespoons maple syrup
Assorted fresh fruit

In a small mixing bowl, combine cream cheese, sour cream, sugars and syrup; beat until smooth. Chill. Serve with fruit. **Yield:** 2 cups.

NUTRITIONAL INFORMATION

Serving Size: 2 tablespoons
(calculated without fruit)

Calories: 65
Total Fat: 2 gm
Calories from Fat: 32%
Saturated Fat: 1 gm
Cholesterol: 5 mg
Sodium: 86 mg
Carbohydrate: 10 gm
Protein: 2 gm

Chutney Cracker Spread

Carolyn Eastham, South Bend, Washington

Store-bought chutney makes this savory spread a delicious alternative to the usual cheese spread. Plus, it can be whipped up in no time.

1 package (8 ounces)
   fat-free cream cheese,
   softened
2 tablespoons nonfat sour
   cream
1 teaspoon curry powder

1/2 cup sliced green onions
   with tops
1/2 cup chopped unsalted
   dry-roasted peanuts
1 bottle (9 ounces) chutney
Assorted reduced-fat crackers

In a small mixing bowl, beat the cream cheese, sour cream and curry powder until smooth. Fold in the onions and peanuts. Spread about 1/2 in. thick on a serving plate. Chill. Just before serving, pour chutney over all. Serve with crackers. **Yield:** 1-1/2 cups.

NUTRITIONAL INFORMATION

Serving Size: 2 tablespoons
(calculated without crackers)

Calories: 108
Total Fat: 3 gm
Calories from Fat: 25%
Saturated Fat: trace
Cholesterol: 0
Sodium: 120 mg
Carbohydrate: 16 gm
Protein: 4 gm

Curried Chicken Balls

Judy Sloter, Alpharetta, Georgia

These flavorful chicken balls are so hearty that no one will suspect they're lighter fare. Most folks who try these prefer them to hot beef meatballs.

6 ounces fat-free cream
   cheese, softened
2 tablespoons orange
   marmalade
2 teaspoons curry powder
1/4 teaspoon salt
1/4 teaspoon pepper

3 cups finely minced
   cooked chicken
3 tablespoons minced
   green onions
3 tablespoons minced
   celery
1 cup finely chopped
   fresh parsley

In a mixing bowl, combine the first five ingredients. Beat until smooth. Stir in chicken, onions and celery. Shape into 1-in. balls; roll in parsley. Cover and chill until firm. **Yield:** 5 dozen.

NUTRITIONAL INFORMATION

Serving Size: 3 pieces

Calories: 55
Total Fat: 2 gm
Calories from Fat: 28%
Saturated Fat: trace
Cholesterol: 19 mg
Sodium: 99 mg
Carbohydrate: 2 gm
Protein: 7 gm

Sweet and Spicy Popcorn

Flo Burtnett, Gage, Oklahoma

This crisp snack has a fun and different flavor. I took some to my neighbor's one evening when we were visiting and it didn't last long!

1 tablespoon sugar
1 teaspoon chili powder
1/2 teaspoon ground
   cinnamon

1/4 teaspoon salt, optional
Dash cayenne pepper
6 cups plain popped
   popcorn

Place sugar, chili powder, cinnamon, salt if desired and cayenne pepper in a resealable plastic bag or other 2-qt. airtight container. Mix. Add popcorn. Mist popcorn with nonstick cooking spray. Close bag and shake. Repeat one or two times until popcorn is coated. **Yield:** 6 cups.

NUTRITIONAL INFORMATION

Serving Size: 1-1/2 cups
(calculated without salt)

Calories: 78
Total Fat: 1 gm
Calories from Fat: 14%
Saturated Fat: trace
Cholesterol: 0
Sodium: 7 mg
Carbohydrate: 16 gm
Protein: 2 gm

Asparagus Appetizer Spread

Linda Stotts, Lowell, Ohio

(Pictured above)

The first time I made this spread was for a potluck get-together. It received such great comments that I've been making it ever since. The asparagus and ham pair nicely with smooth sour cream and cream cheese.

NUTRITIONAL INFORMATION

Serving Size: 1/8 recipe
(calculated without garnish
and crackers)

Calories: 153
Total Fat: 9 gm
Calories from Fat: 55%
Saturated Fat: 3 gm
Cholesterol: 34 mg
Sodium: 429 mg
Carbohydrate: 6 gm
Protein: 11 gm

1 pound fresh asparagus, trimmed
1-1/2 cups (12 ounces) light sour cream, *divided*
1 package (8 ounces) light cream cheese, softened
1 envelope unflavored gelatin
1 cup finely chopped fully cooked low-fat ham
1 tablespoon chopped chives
1/8 teaspoon pepper
Additional ham and asparagus, optional
Assorted reduced-fat crackers

Cook asparagus in a small amount of water until tender. Drain, reserving 1/4 cup liquid. Cool. Puree asparagus until smooth. Add 1 cup sour cream and the cream cheese; blend well. In a saucepan, combine gelatin and reserved liquid; heat slowly until the gelatin is dissolved. Remove from the heat; stir in the asparagus mixture, ham, chives and pepper. Pour into a 1-qt. round-bottom bowl coated with nonstick cooking spray. Cover and chill until set, about 6 hours. Unmold onto a plate and spread with reserved sour cream. Garnish with additional ham and asparagus if desired. Serve with crackers. **Yield:** 8 servings.

Hot Beef Dip

Sonya Hanks, Snyder, Texas

As a busy science teacher, I appreciate fast, flavorful foods that fit into my schedule. My family likes this dip so much I often serve it as a meal.

1 pound ground round
2/3 cup chopped onion
1/2 cup chopped green pepper
4 garlic cloves, minced
1 can (8 ounces) tomato sauce
1/4 cup ketchup
1 teaspoon sugar
3/4 teaspoon dried oregano
1/4 teaspoon pepper
1 package (8 ounces) light cream cheese, softened
1/4 cup grated Parmesan cheese
Baked tortilla chips *or* reduced-fat crackers

In a large skillet, cook beef, onion, green pepper and garlic until meat is browned. Drain. Add the tomato sauce, ketchup, sugar, oregano and pepper; simmer for 10 minutes. Remove from the heat and stir in cheeses until melted. Transfer to a fondue pot or chafing dish; serve warm with tortilla chips or crackers. **Yield:** 20 servings.

NUTRITIONAL INFORMATION

Serving Size: 3 tablespoons
(calculated without tortilla chips or crackers)

Calories: 85
Total Fat: 6 gm
Calories from Fat: 57%
Saturated Fat: 3 gm
Cholesterol: 19 mg
Sodium: 204 mg
Carbohydrate: 4 gm
Protein: 6 gm

Stuffed Cherry Tomatoes

Rita Reifenstein, Evans City, Pennsylvania

(Pictured below)

Try this simple recipe for a crowd-pleasing appetizer. They may be small, but these tasty tomatoes have big garden-fresh flavor enhanced by the cool, zesty filling.

11 ounces fat-free cream cheese, softened
2 tablespoons fat-free mayonnaise
1 package (.4 ounce) ranch salad dressing mix
3 dozen cherry tomatoes
Alfalfa sprouts, optional

In a mixing bowl, blend cream cheese, mayonnaise and salad dressing mix until smooth. Cut a thin slice off tops of tomatoes and carefully remove insides; invert on paper towel to drain. Fill with cream cheese mixture. Serve on a bed of alfalfa sprouts if desired. **Yield:** 3 dozen.

NUTRITIONAL INFORMATION

Serving Size: 3 tomatoes

Calories: 40
Total Fat: trace
Calories from Fat: 4%
Saturated Fat: trace
Cholesterol: 0
Sodium: 285 mg
Carbohydrate: 5 gm
Protein: 4 gm

Continental Cheese Spread

Mrs. Thomas Wigglesworth, Absecon, New Jersey

Around the holidays, I like to keep the ingredients for this spread on hand for drop-in guests. It makes last-minute entertaining extra easy.

1 package (8 ounces) fat-free cream cheese, softened
1 tablespoon skim milk
1 garlic clove, minced
3 tablespoons grated Parmesan cheese
1 tablespoon minced fresh parsley
1 tablespoon minced green onion
1/2 teaspoon dried thyme
1/8 teaspoon pepper
Assorted reduced-fat crackers

In a bowl, beat cream cheese and milk until fluffy. Add garlic, Parmesan cheese, parsley, onion, thyme and pepper. Mix until well blended. Spoon into a small container. Cover and refrigerate at least 1 hour. Serve with crackers. **Yield:** 1 cup.

Salmon Appetizers

Evelyn Gebhardt, Kasilof, Alaska

(Pictured below)

I've found this recipe to be a terrific addition to a festive Mexican meal or as a delicate prelude to a steak dinner.

1 can (15 ounces) salmon or 2 cups cooked salmon, drained, boned and flaked
1 package (8 ounces) fat-free cream cheese, softened
4 tablespoons salsa
2 tablespoons chopped fresh parsley or cilantro
1/4 teaspoon ground cumin
8 flour tortillas (8 inches)

In a small bowl, combine salmon, cream cheese, salsa, parsley and cumin. Spread about 2 tablespoons over each tortilla. Roll up tightly and wrap individually with plastic wrap. Refrigerate for 2-3 hours. Slice into bite-size pieces. **Yield:** 4 dozen.

Clam Dip

Sherri Gentry, Dallas, Oregon

This seafood delight is perfect for a bridal buffet, but I also make this appetizer when company's coming. It's a hit at family get-togethers, too!

1 package (8 ounces)
  fat-free cream cheese,
  softened
2 tablespoons fat-free
  mayonnaise
1 teaspoon lemon juice

Dash garlic powder
1 can (6-1/2 ounces)
  minced clams, drained
1/4 cup sliced green onions
Fresh vegetables

In a mixing bowl, beat cream cheese, mayonnaise, lemon juice and garlic powder until smooth. Fold in clams and onions. Chill. Serve with vegetables. **Yield:** 1-1/4 cups.

NUTRITIONAL
INFORMATION

Serving Size: 2 tablespoons
(calculated without vegetables)

Calories: 51
Total Fat: trace
Calories from Fat: 7%
Saturated Fat: trace
Cholesterol: 12 mg
Sodium: 195 mg
Carbohydrate: 3 gm
Protein: 8 gm

Chilled Rhubarb Soup

Laurel Anderson, Pinole, California

I like to start a variety of my summer meals with this refreshing soup.

3 cups sliced fresh *or*
  frozen rhubarb (1/2-inch
  pieces)
1-1/4 cups orange juice

1 pint fresh strawberries,
  sliced
3/4 cup sugar

In a 3-qt. saucepan, bring rhubarb, orange juice and strawberries to a boil. Reduce heat; cover and simmer for 10 minutes. Remove from heat; stir in sugar. In a blender or food processor, blend half the fruit mixture at a time until smooth. Chill. **Yield:** 4 servings.

NUTRITIONAL
INFORMATION

Serving Size: 1 cup

Calories: 22
Total Fat: 1 gm
Calories from Fat: 2%
Saturated Fat: trace
Cholesterol: 0
Sodium: 6 mg
Carbohydrate: 55 gm
Protein: 2 gm

Carrot Dip

Raegan Dexter, Union Grove, Wisconsin

This creamy appetizer features nothing but great flavor. You don't have to be a carrot fan to enjoy it. I like it even more because it's so easy to fix!

1 package (8 ounces)
  fat-free cream cheese,
  softened
1/2 cup fat-free mayonnaise
2 medium carrots, finely
  shredded
3 green onions, thinly sliced

1/2 teaspoon Worcestershire
  sauce
Dash garlic powder
1 small firm head iceberg
  lettuce
Fresh vegetables *or* reduced-fat
  crackers

In a small bowl, mix cream cheese and mayonnaise until smooth. Stir in carrots, onions, Worcestershire sauce and garlic powder. Chill for at least 1 hour. To make a lettuce serving bowl, hollow out the head of lettuce, keeping the core at the bottom intact and removing enough interior leaves so that a 1-in. shell remains. Add dip; serve with vegetables or crackers. **Yield:** 1-3/4 cups.

NUTRITIONAL
INFORMATION

Serving Size: 2 tablespoons
(calculated without
vegetables and crackers)

Calories: 26
Total Fat: trace
Calories from Fat: 1%
Saturated Fat: trace
Cholesterol: 0
Sodium: 211 mg
Carbohydrate: 3 gm
Protein: 2 gm

Vegetable Dip

Denise Goedeken, Platte Center, Nebraska

This cool and creamy dip, paired with fresh garden vegetables, is a real family favorite for snacking.

1-1/2 cups (12 ounces) nonfat
   sour cream
3/4 cup fat-free mayonnaise
1 tablespoon dried minced
   onion
1 teaspoon dill weed

1 teaspoon dried parsley
   flakes
1 teaspoon garlic powder
Dash Worcestershire sauce
Fresh vegetables

In a small bowl, combine sour cream, mayonnaise, onion, dill, parsley, garlic powder and Worcestershire sauce. Chill for at least 1 hour. Serve with fresh vegetables. **Yield:** 2 cups.

Snappy Asparagus Dip

Debra Johnson, Bonney Lake, Washington

At the first sign of spring, I reach for this recipe that calls for fresh asparagus.

1 pound fresh asparagus,
   trimmed
1 cup (8 ounces) nonfat
   sour cream
1/2 cup salsa

Dash lime juice
Dash cayenne pepper
Fresh vegetables *or* baked
   tortilla chips

Cook asparagus in a small amount of water until tender. Drain and cool. In a blender or food processor, puree asparagus until smooth. Stir in sour cream, salsa, lime juice and cayenne. Chill. Serve with fresh vegetables or tortilla chips. **Yield:** 2 cups.

Cranberry Meatballs

Deborah Hill, Coffeyville, Kansas

Typically, my husband doesn't care for cranberries. So I was thrilled when he raved about these meatballs.

Egg substitute equivalent
  to 2 eggs
1 cup cornflake crumbs
1/3 cup ketchup
2 tablespoons light soy
  sauce
1 tablespoon dried parsley
  flakes
2 tablespoons dehydrated
  onion

1/4 teaspoon pepper
2 pounds ground turkey
  breast
SAUCE:
1 can (16 ounces) jellied
  cranberry sauce
1 cup ketchup
3 tablespoons brown sugar
1 tablespoon lemon juice

In a mixing bowl, combine the first eight ingredients. Shape into 72 meatballs, 1 in. each. Place in a 15-in. x 10-in. x 1-in. baking pan coated with nonstick cooking spray. Bake at 350° for 20-25 minutes or until done. In a large saucepan, combine sauce ingredients. Cook, stirring frequently, until the cranberry sauce is melted. Add the meatballs and heat through. **Yield:** 6 dozen.

Fresh Fruit Soup

Jenny Sampson, Layton, Utah

(Pictured below)

This soup is a great start to a Mexican meal, but I've also served it with butter cookies at a baby shower.

1 can (12 ounces) frozen
  orange juice concentrate,
  thawed
1-1/2 cups sugar
  1 cinnamon stick (2 inches)
  6 whole cloves

1/4 cup cornstarch
  2 tablespoons lemon juice
  2 cups sliced fresh
    strawberries
  2 bananas, sliced
  2 cups halved green grapes

In a large saucepan, mix orange juice with water according to package directions. Remove 1/2 cup of juice; set aside. Add sugar, cinnamon stick and cloves to saucepan; bring to a boil. Reduce heat and simmer for 5 minutes. Blend cornstarch and reserved orange juice to form a smooth paste; stir into pan. Bring to a boil; cook and stir until thickened, about 2 minutes more. Remove from the heat and stir in lemon juice. Pour into a large bowl; cover and chill. Just before serving, remove the spices and stir in fruit. **Yield:** 10 servings (2-1/2 quarts).

NUTRITIONAL INFORMATION

Serving Size: 1 cup

Calories: 237
Total Fat: 1 gm
Calories from Fat: 2%
Saturated Fat: trace
Cholesterol: 0
Sodium: 4 mg
Carbohydrate: 59 gm
Protein: 1 gm

THIRST-QUENCHERS. *Clockwise from bottom: Sparkling Punch, Frosty Pineapple Nog (both recipes on page 39) and Hot Apple Cider (recipe on page 40).*

Refreshing Beverages

Sparkling Punch

Karen Ann Bland, Gove, Kansas

(Pictured at left)

As a table brightener, I fix a bowl of this festive fruit punch—it's a refreshing beverage you can mix together in moments.

3 cups water
2 cups cranberry juice
1 can (6 ounces) frozen
   orange juice concentrate,
   thawed

1 can (6 ounces) frozen
   lemonade concentrate,
   thawed
1/2 cup sugar
1-1/2 liters lemon-lime soda,
   chilled

In a large bowl, combine the first five ingredients; mix until sugar is dissolved. Chill for 1-2 hours. Just before serving, stir in soda. **Yield:** 24 servings (3 quarts).

NUTRITIONAL INFORMATION

Serving Size: 1/2 cup

Calories: 87
Total Fat: trace
Calories from Fat: 0%
Saturated Fat: 0
Cholesterol: 0
Sodium: 13 mg
Carbohydrate: 23 gm
Protein: 0

Frosty Pineapple Nog

DeAnn Alleva, Columbus, Ohio

(Pictured at left)

This frothy, cool beverage is perfect for sipping under a big shade tree. Rich buttermilk makes it satisfying, and the pineapple adds a tropical flair.

3 cups buttermilk
1 can (8 ounces) crushed
   pineapple with juice,
   chilled

1/4 cup sugar
1 teaspoon vanilla extract
5 ice cubes
Fresh mint sprigs, optional

In a blender container, combine buttermilk, pineapple, sugar and vanilla. Cover and blend for 30 seconds or until combined. With blender running, add ice cubes, one at a time, through opening in lid. Blend until mixture is frothy and nearly smooth. Pour into chilled glasses. If desired, garnish with a sprig of mint. **Yield:** 6 servings.

NUTRITIONAL INFORMATION

Serving Size: 3/4 cup

Calories: 134
Total Fat: trace
Calories from Fat: 0%
Saturated Fat: trace
Cholesterol: 7 mg
Sodium: 203 mg
Carbohydrate: 28 gm
Protein: 4 gm

Iced Strawberry Tea

Laurie Andrews, Milton, Ontario

When strawberry season begins, my family looks forward to this colorful and refreshing thirst-quencher.

1 pint fresh strawberries
4 cups cold tea
1/3 cup sugar

1/4 cup lemon juice
Ice cubes

Set aside five whole strawberries. Puree the rest in a blender; strain into a pitcher. Stir in tea, sugar and lemon juice until sugar dissolves. Chill. Serve over ice; garnish with the whole berries. **Yield:** 5 servings.

NUTRITIONAL INFORMATION

Serving Size: 1 cup

Calories: 78
Total Fat: trace
Calories from Fat: 3%
Saturated Fat: trace
Cholesterol: 0
Sodium: 7 mg
Carbohydrate: 20 gm
Protein: trace

NUTRITIONAL INFORMATION

Serving Size: 1 cup

Calories: 154
Total Fat: trace
Calories from Fat: 0%
Saturated Fat: trace
Cholesterol: 0
Sodium: 28 mg
Carbohydrate: 39 gm
Protein: trace

Hot Apple Cider

Marlys Benning, Wellsburg, Iowa

(Pictured on page 38)

When I was planning a bridal shower, I reached for this recipe because of its no-fuss convenience. It was nice to greet guests with this cider's wonderful aroma.

2/3 cup packed brown sugar	3 cinnamon sticks (3
1 teaspoon whole cloves	inches), broken
1 teaspoon ground allspice	1 gallon apple cider

Fill the filter-lined basket of a large automatic *percolator* with the brown sugar, cloves, allspice and cinnamon sticks. Prepare as you would coffee according to manufacturer's directions, but substitute cider for water. **Yield:** 16 servings. **Editor's Note:** Do not use a drip-style coffeemaker for this recipe.

NUTRITIONAL INFORMATION

Serving Size: 1/2 cup

Calories: 142
Total Fat: trace
Calories from Fat: 2%
Saturated Fat: trace
Cholesterol: 1 mg
Sodium: 10 mg
Carbohydrate: 35 gm
Protein: trace

Leprechaun Lime Punch

Gloria Warczak, Cedarburg, Wisconsin

Friends and family have come to look forward to our annual St. Patrick's Day party. After our guests arrive, we toast the occasion with this punch.

1 can (46 ounces) lime citrus drink	1/4 cup lime juice
2 cans (12 ounces *each*) frozen limeade concentrate, thawed	1 carton (1 quart) lime sherbet, softened
1/4 cup sugar	1 bottle (2 liters) lemon-lime soda, chilled
	Lime slices, optional

In a punch bowl, combine citrus drink, limeade, sugar, lime juice and sherbet; stir until smooth and sugar is dissolved. Add soda; stir to mix. Float lime slices on top of punch if desired. Serve immediately. **Yield:** 32 servings (1 gallon).

NUTRITIONAL INFORMATION

Serving Size: 3/4 cup

Calories: 106
Total Fat: trace
Calories from Fat: 4%
Saturated Fat: trace
Cholesterol: 0
Sodium: 28 mg
Carbohydrate: 25 gm
Protein: 1 gm

Cappuccino Mix

Lois Britton, Selma, Alabama

This homemade cappuccino mix is better than any store-bought brands I've tried. I like to make several batches of the mix to share with friends around the holidays. It's a special gift from the kitchen.

1 cup powdered fat-free nondairy creamer	2/3 cup instant coffee granules
1 cup instant chocolate drink mix	1/2 teaspoon ground cinnamon
1/2 cup sugar	1/4 teaspoon ground nutmeg

Combine all ingredients; mix well. Store in an airtight container. To serve, add 3 tablespoons mix to 3/4 cup boiling water; stir. **Yield:** 16 servings (3 cups mix).

Rhubarb Slush

Theresa Pearson, Ogilvie, Minnesota

(Pictured above)

This thirst-quenching slush is a fun way to use rhubarb. I love to serve it for special get-togethers like a ladies' brunch or holiday meal. The rosy color and tangy flavor of this springtime crop come through in every sip.

3 cups chopped fresh *or*
  frozen rhubarb
1 cup water
1/3 cup sugar
1 cup apple juice

1 can (6 ounces) frozen
  pink lemonade
  concentrate, thawed
1 bottle (2 liters) lemon-
  lime soda, chilled

In a saucepan, combine rhubarb, water and sugar; bring to a boil. Reduce heat; cover and simmer for 5 minutes or until rhubarb is tender. Cool for about 30 minutes. In a food processor or blender, puree mixture, half at a time. Stir in apple juice and lemonade. Pour into a freezer container; cover and freeze until firm. Let stand at room temperature for 45 minutes before serving. For individual servings, scoop 1/3 cup into a glass and fill with soda. To serve a group, place all of the mixture in a large pitcher or punch bowl; add soda and stir. Serve immediately. **Yield:** 10 servings.

NUTRITIONAL INFORMATION

Serving Size: 1 cup

Calories: 159
Total Fat: trace
Calories from Fat: 1%
Saturated Fat: trace
Cholesterol: 0
Sodium: 26 mg
Carbohydrate: 41 gm
Protein: trace

Serving Size: 1 cup
(calculated without
whipped topping)

Calories: 5
Total Fat: trace
Calories from Fat: 1%
Saturated Fat: 0 gm
Cholesterol: 0
Sodium: 5 mg
Carbohydrate: 1 gm
Protein: trace

Hot Ginger Coffee

Audrey Thibodeau, Lancaster, New Hampshire

(Pictured below)

I like to sit by the fire and sip this coffee on a cold winter day. It's a great warm-up after shoveling snow, skiing, skating or snowmobiling.

6 tablespoons ground coffee (not instant)
1 tablespoon grated orange peel
1 tablespoon chopped crystallized *or* candied ginger*

1/2 teaspoon ground cinnamon
6 cups cold water
Light whipped topping, optional

Combine the coffee, orange peel, ginger and cinnamon; pour into a coffee filter. Add water to coffeemaker and brew according to manufacturer's directions. Pour into mugs; garnish with whipped topping if desired. **Yield:** 6 servings. ***Editor's Note:** Look for crystallized or candied ginger in the spice or baking section of your grocery store.

Spiced Lemonade

Kim Van Rheenen, Mendota, Illinois

Serve this drink over ice in summer or warmed in winter—it's always refreshing. If you have a cold, a warm mug of spiced lemonade will make you feel much better. It'll quench a big thirst, too!

6 cups water, *divided*
3/4 cup sugar
2 cinnamon sticks (3 to 4 inches)
6 whole cloves
1 large lime, thinly sliced
1 lemon, thinly sliced
3/4 cup fresh lemon juice

In a large saucepan, bring 4 cups water, sugar, cinnamon and cloves to a boil. Reduce heat; simmer for 10 minutes. Remove from the heat; discard cinnamon and cloves. Cool. Pour into a large pitcher. Stir in lime, lemon, lemon juice and remaining water. Chill at least 1 hour. Can also be served warm. **Yield:** 8 servings (2 quarts).

NUTRITIONAL INFORMATION

Serving Size: 1 cup

Calories: 78
Total Fat: trace
Calories from Fat: 0%
Saturated Fat: trace
Cholesterol: 0
Sodium: trace
Carbohydrate: 21 gm
Protein: trace

Orange Julius

Rita Swanson, Three Hills, Alberta

This is a refreshing drink year-round, but it's also nice to serve around the holidays. It's a good alternative to sugared soft drinks, too.

1 can (6 ounces) frozen orange juice concentrate, thawed
1 cup skim milk
1 cup water
1/4 cup sugar
1 teaspoon vanilla extract
10 to 12 ice cubes

In a blender, combine orange juice concentrate, milk, water, sugar and vanilla. Cover and blend until smooth. With blender running, add ice cubes, one at a time, through the opening in lid. Blend until smooth. Serve immediately. **Yield:** 5 servings.

NUTRITIONAL INFORMATION

Serving Size: 3/4 cup

Calories: 112
Total Fat: trace
Calories from Fat: 1%
Saturated Fat: trace
Cholesterol: 1 mg
Sodium: 26 mg
Carbohydrate: 25 gm
Protein: 2 gm

Wassail Punch

Dorothy Anderson, Ottawa, Kansas

On Christmas Eve, we traditionally begin our dinner with this punch and assorted appetizers. The wonderful cinnamon, spice and fruit aroma fills the house and adds to the festive atmosphere.

2 quarts apple cider
2 cups orange juice
2 cups pineapple juice
1/2 cup lemon juice
1/2 cup sugar
12 whole cloves
4 cinnamon sticks (3 to 4 inches)
Orange slices and additional cloves, optional

In a large kettle, bring the first seven ingredients to a boil. Reduce heat; simmer for 10-15 minutes. Remove cinnamon and cloves. Serve warm. If desired, stud orange slices with cloves and float in punch bowl. **Yield:** 18 servings (3-1/2 quarts). **Editor's Note:** Be sure bowl is safe for hot liquid.

NUTRITIONAL INFORMATION

Serving Size: 3/4 cup

Calories: 104
Total Fat: trace
Calories from Fat: 1%
Saturated Fat: trace
Cholesterol: 0
Sodium: 12 mg
Carbohydrate: 26 gm
Protein: trace

Lemony Iced Tea

Sharon Emery, New Burnside, Illinois

This beverage is one of our favorites to serve during the hot humid summer months. We keep a jug in the refrigerator ready to serve for family and guests.

2 quarts water
3/4 cup sugar
1/2 cup lemon juice
1/2 cup white grape juice
1/4 cup unsweetened lemon-flavored instant tea mix
Ice cubes
Lemon slices, optional

In a large pitcher, combine water, sugar, lemon juice, grape juice and tea mix. Stir well to dissolve the sugar. Serve over ice with lemon slices if desired. **Yield:** 9 servings.

Strawberry Watermelon Slush

Patty Howse, Great Falls, Montana

Ripe for a refreshing treat? Try this—it'll quench everyone's thirst sweetly. After a long, hot summer day, we like to relax on the back porch with a glass of this slush.

2 cups cubed seeded watermelon
1 pint fresh strawberries, halved
1/3 cup sugar
1/3 cup lemon juice
2 cups ice cubes

Combine the first four ingredients in a blender; process until smooth. Gradually add ice, blending until slushy. Serve immediately. **Yield:** 5 servings.

Hot Chocolate Mix

Debbie Klejeski, Sturgeon Lake, Minnesota

Why settle for pre-packaged hot chocolate powders when this homemade mix is so easy to make and much more delicious?

1 package (8 quarts) nonfat dry milk
1 jar (6 ounces) fat-free nondairy coffee creamer
1 container (16 ounces) instant chocolate drink mix
1/2 cup confectioners' sugar

Place all ingredients in a very large bowl or kettle. Stir until well blended. Store in airtight containers or pack into small gift containers. To serve, add 1/4 cup chocolate mix to 2/3 cup hot water. **Yield:** 48 servings (3 quarts dry mix).

Blackberry Fizz

Andrea Eberly, Sarasota, Florida

(Pictured above)

For a festive beverage with a distinctive berry flavor and a hint of spice, try this recipe. We save it for holidays and special times with family and friends. It's a delightful drink people will remember.

3 quarts fresh *or* frozen
　blackberries
4 cups water
3 cups sugar
1 tablespoon whole cloves

1 tablespoon whole allspice
2 cinnamon sticks
　(4 inches), broken
2 bottles (2 liters) diet
　lemon-lime soda

Crush blackberries in a large kettle. Add water and bring to a boil. Reduce heat to medium and cook for 10 minutes. Strain through a jelly bag, reserving juice and discarding pulp. Add water to juice if necessary to equal 2 qts.; pour into a large kettle. Slowly stir in sugar until dissolved. Place spices in a cheesecloth bag; add to juice. Simmer, uncovered, for 30 minutes. Bring to a boil; remove the spice bag and discard. Pour hot into hot jars, leaving 1/4-in. headspace. Adjust caps. Process for 15 minutes in a boiling-water bath. To serve, mix two parts soda to one part concentrate. **Yield:** 48 servings (4 pints concentrate).

NUTRITIONAL INFORMATION

Serving Size: 1/2 cup

Calories: 75
Total Fat: trace
Calories from Fat: 2%
Saturated Fat: trace
Cholesterol: 0
Sodium: 13 mg
Carbohydrate: 19 gm
Protein: trace

Banana Brunch Punch

Mary Anne McWhirter, Pearland, Texas

(Pictured above)

A cold glass of refreshing punch really brightens a brunch. It's nice to serve a crisp beverage like this that's more spectacular than plain juice. With bananas, lemonade and pineapple juice, it can add tropical flair to any day.

NUTRITIONAL INFORMATION

Serving Size: 1/2 cup

Calories: 79
Total Fat: trace
Calories from Fat: 1%
Saturated Fat: trace
Cholesterol: 0
Sodium: 9 mg
Carbohydrate: 20 gm
Protein: trace

6 medium ripe bananas
1 can (12 ounces) frozen orange juice concentrate, thawed
1 can (6 ounces) frozen lemonade concentrate, thawed
3 cups warm water, *divided*
2 cups sugar, *divided*
1 can (46 ounces) pineapple juice
3 bottles (2 liters *each*) lemon-lime soda
Orange slices, optional

In a blender or food processor, blend bananas and concentrates until smooth. Remove half of the mixture and set aside. Add 1-1/2 cups of warm water and 1 cup sugar to mixture in blender; blend until smooth. Place in a large freezer container. Repeat with remaining banana mixture, water and sugar; add to container. Cover and freeze until solid. One hour before serving, take punch base out of freezer. Just before serving, place in a large punch bowl. Add pineapple juice and soda; stir until well blended. Garnish with orange slices if desired. **Yield:** 80 servings (10 quarts).

Orange Sherbet Party Punch

Lannis Blunk, Mascoutah, Illinois

This punch is always a big hit. It's especially good for weddings and special parties where you have guests of all ages.

4 cups water, *divided*
2 packages (3 ounces *each*) strawberry gelatin
1-1/2 cups sugar
1 cup lemon juice
1 can (46 ounces) pineapple juice

1 can (46 ounces) orange juice
1/2 gallon orange sherbet, softened
1 bottle (1 liter) ginger ale, chilled

Heat 2 cups water to boiling; add gelatin and sugar, stirring until dissolved. Add lemon, pineapple and orange juices and remaining water; chill until ready to serve. Just before serving, stir in sherbet and ginger ale. **Yield:** 52 servings (6-1/2 quarts).

NUTRITIONAL INFORMATION

Serving Size: 1/2 cup

Calories: 111
Total Fat: 1 gm
Calories from Fat: 5%
Saturated Fat: trace
Cholesterol: 1 mg
Sodium: 24 mg
Carbohydrate: 26 gm
Protein: 1 gm

Citrus Mint Cooler

Kathy Burkholder, Bakersfield, California

In California, where lemons, oranges and mint are so abundant, my family has found great enjoyment sitting in the shade and drinking a tall glass of this thirst-quenching cooler.

1 cup fresh lemon juice (about 6 lemons)
1 cup fresh orange juice (about 3 oranges)
2 cups sugar

2-1/2 cups water
10 mint sprigs
1 bottle (1 liter) ginger ale
Additional water
Ice cubes

Place the first five ingredients in a saucepan; bring to a boil, stirring until sugar dissolves. Cover; remove from the heat and let steep until cool. Strain. Cover and refrigerate. To serve, fill glasses or a pitcher with equal amounts of fruit juice, ginger ale and water. Add ice and serve immediately. **Yield:** 15 servings.

NUTRITIONAL INFORMATION

Serving Size: 1 cup

Calories: 137
Total Fat: trace
Calories from Fat: 0%
Saturated Fat: trace
Cholesterol: 0
Sodium: 5 mg
Carbohydrate: 35 gm
Protein: trace

Aunt Frances' Lemonade

Debbie Blackburn, Camp Hill, Pennsylvania

My sister and I spent a week each summer with Aunt Frances, who always had this delicious lemonade in a stoneware crock in the refrigerator. It tastes so much like fresh citrus.

5 lemons
5 limes
5 oranges

3 quarts water
1-1/2 cups sugar
Ice cubes

Squeeze the juice from four of the lemons, limes and oranges; pour into a gallon container. Thinly slice the remaining fruit and set aside for garnish. Add water and sugar to juices; mix well. Store in the refrigerator. Serve on ice with fruit slices. **Yield:** 16 servings (1 gallon).

NUTRITIONAL INFORMATION

Serving Size: 1 cup

Calories: 87
Total Fat: trace
Calories from Fat: 1%
Saturated Fat: trace
Cholesterol: 0
Sodium: 1 mg
Carbohydrate: 23 gm
Protein: trace

TOSSED TOGETHER. *Top to bottom: Celebration Salad (recipe on page 49), Basil Tomato Salad (recipe on page 50) and Apple Chicken Salad (recipe on page 49).*

Satisfying Salads

Celebration Salad

Barbara Berger, Breckenridge, Colorado

(Pictured at left)

No matter what size your celebration is, this salad will fit right in. It's been a standby at family gatherings, as well as church functions, for some 30 years. We never tire of it around here.

16 cups torn salad greens
1 package (16 ounces) frozen peas, thawed
1 large red onion, thinly sliced into rings
4 celery ribs, thinly sliced
1 block (12 ounces) reduced-fat cheddar cheese, julienned

12 turkey bacon strips, cooked and crumbled
1/2 cup fat-free sour cream
1/2 cup fat-free mayonnaise
1 tablespoon Dijon mustard
2 teaspoons sugar
1/2 teaspoon ground nutmeg
1/4 teaspoon pepper

In a large salad bowl, toss the greens, peas, onion, celery, cheese and bacon. In a small bowl, combine remaining ingredients; pour over salad and toss to coat. Serve immediately. **Yield:** 16 servings.

NUTRITIONAL INFORMATION

Serving Size: 1 cup

Calories: 111
Total Fat: 2 gm
Calories from Fat: 19%
Saturated Fat: 1 gm
Cholesterol: 12 mg
Sodium: 436 mg
Carbohydrate: 11 gm
Protein: 13 gm

Apple Chicken Salad

Anne Stevens, Lake Charles, Louisiana

(Pictured at left)

This tasty salad recipe is a favorite of mine because it's colorful, a little different and also contains healthy ingredients. I rely on it whenever I want to prepare a special meal just for myself.

1 medium apple, cored and chopped
1 cup diced cooked chicken breast
2 tablespoons fat-free mayonnaise

2 tablespoons diced green pepper
1 teaspoon diced pimiento
Pinch crushed rosemary
Pinch lemon-pepper seasoning
Lettuce leaf

In a small bowl, combine the first seven ingredients. Chill until ready to serve. Place lettuce leaf on a serving plate and top with salad. **Yield:** 1 serving.

NUTRITIONAL INFORMATION

Serving Size: 1 recipe

Calories: 238
Total Fat: 5 gm
Calories from Fat: 17%
Saturated Fat: 1 gm
Cholesterol: 85 mg
Sodium: 228 mg
Carbohydrate: 27 gm
Protein: 23 gm

Basil Tomato Salad

Barb Gumieny, Wauwatosa, Wisconsin

(Pictured on page 48)

A light basil-based dressing gives great flavor to tomatoes in this salad.

2 tablespoons olive oil
2 tablespoons cider vinegar
2 teaspoons chopped fresh
  basil *or* 1 teaspoon dried
  basil
1/4 teaspoon pepper

3 cups cooked rice, cooled
2 medium tomatoes,
  chopped
1 medium cucumber,
  seeded and chopped
1 small red onion, chopped

In a small bowl, whisk together oil, vinegar, basil and pepper. Add rice, tomatoes, cucumber and onion; toss. Chill. **Yield:** 8 servings.

NUTRITIONAL INFORMATION

Serving Size: 3/4 cup

Calories: 118
Total Fat: 4 gm
Calories from Fat: 28%
Saturated Fat: 1 gm
Cholesterol: 0
Sodium: 5 mg
Carbohydrate: 19 gm
Protein: 2 gm

Orange Buttermilk Salad

Carol Van Sickle, Versailles, Kentucky

This make-ahead salad is refreshing with just the right amount of sweetness.

1 can (20 ounces) crushed
  unsweetened pineapple,
  undrained
1 package (6 ounces)
  orange gelatin

2 cups buttermilk
1 carton (8 ounces) frozen
  light whipped topping,
  thawed

In a saucepan, bring pineapple with juice to a boil. Remove from the heat; add gelatin and stir to dissolve. Add buttermilk and mix well. Cool to room temperature. Fold in whipped topping. Pour into an 11-in. x 7-in. x 2-in. dish. Refrigerate several hours or overnight. Cut into squares. **Yield:** 12 servings.

NUTRITIONAL INFORMATION

Serving Size: 1/12 recipe

Calories: 145
Total Fat: 3 gm
Calories from Fat: 19%
Saturated Fat: 3 gm
Cholesterol: 3
Sodium: 107 mg
Carbohydrate: 26 gm
Protein: 3 gm

Fresh Fruit Bowl

Marion Kirst, Troy, Michigan

The glorious colors used here make this a great summer salad. Slightly sweet and chilled, it makes a nice accompaniment to a grilled entree.

4 cups cantaloupe cubes
4 cups honeydew cubes
1 tablespoon light corn
  syrup

1 pint fresh strawberries
2 cups fresh pineapple
  chunks
2 oranges, sectioned

In a large bowl, combine melon cubes and corn syrup. Cover and refrigerate overnight. Just before serving, stir in remaining fruit. **Yield:** 16 servings (4 quarts).

NUTRITIONAL INFORMATION

Serving Size: 1 cup

Calories: 55
Total Fat: trace
Calories from Fat: 5%
Saturated Fat: trace
Cholesterol: 0
Sodium: 8 mg
Carbohydrate: 14 gm
Protein: 1 gm

Strawberry-Glazed Fruit Salad

Jeri Dobrowski, Beach, North Dakota

(Pictured above)

I first tasted this delightful salad at a friend's house when she served it with dinner. After sampling it, no one would ever believe how incredibly easy it is to prepare.

1 quart fresh strawberries, halved
1 can (20 ounces) unsweetened pineapple chunks, drained
4 firm bananas, sliced
1 jar *or* pouch (16 ounces) strawberry glaze

In a large bowl, gently toss strawberries, pineapple and bananas; fold in the glaze. Chill for 1 hour. **Yield:** 8 servings. **Editor's Note:** Strawberry glaze can often be found in the produce section of your grocery store.

NUTRITIONAL INFORMATION

Serving Size: 1/8 recipe

Calories: 185
Total Fat: 1 gm
Calories from Fat: 3%
Saturated Fat: trace
Cholesterol: 0
Sodium: 64 mg
Carbohydrate: 44 gm
Protein: 1 gm

Marinated Mushroom Salad

Sandra Johnson, Tioga, Pennsylvania

(Pictured below)

Packed with mushrooms and loads of crunchy colorful ingredients, this salad is perfect at picnics and parties. It's also convenient since you make it ahead of time.

2-1/2 quarts water
3 tablespoons lemon juice
3 pounds small fresh mushrooms
2 carrots, sliced
2 celery ribs, sliced
1/2 medium green pepper, chopped
1 small onion, chopped
1 tablespoon minced fresh parsley
1/2 cup sliced stuffed olives
1 can (2-1/4 ounces) sliced ripe olives, drained

DRESSING:
1/2 cup fat-free Italian salad dressing
1/2 cup red *or* white wine vinegar
1 garlic clove, minced
1/2 teaspoon dried oregano

In a large saucepan, bring water and lemon juice to a boil. Add mushrooms and cook for 3 minutes, stirring occasionally. Drain; cool. Place mushrooms in a large bowl with carrots, celery, green pepper, onion, parsley and olives. Combine all dressing ingredients in a small bowl or a jar with tight-fitting lid; shake or mix well. Pour over salad. Cover and refrigerate overnight. **Yield:** 8 servings.

Cucumber-Dill Pasta Salad

Kelly Azzopardi, Harrow, Ontario

I came up with this recipe when I was asked to bring a dish to a last-minute get-together. It was a quick, tasty creation.

3 cups cooked pasta
1/2 cup thinly sliced carrot
1/2 cup thinly sliced celery
1 cup parboiled broccoli
   florets
1 green onion, thinly sliced

1/4 cup chopped onion
1/2 cup reduced-fat cucumber
   salad dressing
1 teaspoon dill weed
Pepper to taste

Combine all ingredients in a large salad bowl. Chill until serving time. **Yield:** 6 servings.

NUTRITIONAL INFORMATION

Serving Size: 1/6 recipe

Calories: 150
Total Fat: 3 gm
Calories from Fat: 20%
Saturated Fat: 1 gm
Cholesterol: 0
Sodium: 227 mg
Carbohydrate: 25 gm
Protein: 5 gm

Cool Lime Salad

Elnora Johnson, Union City, Tennessee

I've been making this recipe for years. Since my husband has special dietary needs, one-portion recipes work out very well for us.

1/2 cup undrained
   unsweetened crushed
   pineapple
2 tablespoons lime gelatin

1/4 cup low-fat cottage cheese
1/4 cup light whipped
   topping

In a small saucepan, bring pineapple to a boil. Remove from the heat and stir in gelatin until dissolved. Cool to room temperature. Stir in cottage cheese and whipped topping. Chill until set. **Yield:** 1 serving.

NUTRITIONAL INFORMATION

Serving Size: 1 recipe

Calories: 258
Total Fat: 3 gm
Calories from Fat: 9%
Saturated Fat: 2 gm
Cholesterol: 2 mg
Sodium: 311 mg
Carbohydrate: 48 gm
Protein: 10 gm

Festive Pineapple Boat

Susan Phelan, Tallahassee, Florida

My fondest childhood memories are centered in the kitchen with my mother making recipes like this.

1 large fresh ripe pineapple
2 medium firm bananas,
   sliced
2 kiwifruit, peeled and
   sliced
1/4 cup packed brown sugar

2 tablespoons coarsely
   chopped pecans
Dash ground cinnamon
Dash ground nutmeg
2 tablespoons flaked
   coconut

Stand pineapple up and cut about a third off of one side, leaving the top attached. Remove fruit from the cutoff section; discard outer peel. Remove fruit from the remaining pineapple, leaving a 1/2-in. shell intact. Cut pineapple into bite-size pieces; toss with bananas and kiwi. Spoon into "boat". Combine brown sugar, pecans, cinnamon and nutmeg; sprinkle over fruit. Sprinkle with coconut. Serve immediately. **Yield:** 8 servings.

NUTRITIONAL INFORMATION

Serving Size: 1/8 recipe

Calories: 102
Total Fat: 2 gm
Calories from Fat: 17%
Saturated Fat: 1 gm
Cholesterol: 0
Sodium: 4 mg
Carbohydrate: 22 gm
Protein: 19 gm

Fresh and Fruity

Citrus fruit will keep at room temperature for 1 to 2 weeks. For longer storage, refrigerate in a plastic bag or crisper.

Sweet-and-Sour Salad

Sheryl Christian, Watertown, Wisconsin

The magic words for me when it comes to cooking are "quick" and "easy". This recipe fills the bill!

8 ounces elbow macaroni *or* mostaccioli
1 medium green *or* sweet red pepper, coarsely chopped
1/2 medium cucumber, sliced
1 small onion, coarsely chopped

1 cup cider vinegar
3/4 cup sugar
1 tablespoon dried parsley flakes
1 teaspoon garlic powder
1/4 teaspoon pepper

Cook pasta according to package directions; drain and rinse with cold water. Place in a bowl; add pepper, cucumber and onion. In a jar with tight-fitting lid, combine remaining ingredients; shake until sugar is dissolved. Pour over salad; toss. Chill. **Yield:** 6 servings.

Cranberry-Orange Molded Salad

Judy Kimball, Haverhill, Massachusetts

(Pictured below)

This colorful side dish will complement virtually any meal. Cinnamon and cloves combined with the cranberry sauce and orange sections give this salad an interesting, zesty taste.

1 package (6 ounces) raspberry gelatin
2 cups boiling water
1 can (16 ounces) whole-berry cranberry sauce

1/4 teaspoon ground cinnamon
Dash ground cloves
2 cups diced orange sections
Lettuce leaves

In a large bowl, dissolve gelatin in boiling water. Stir in cranberry sauce, cinnamon and cloves. Chill until partially set. Add the orange sections. Pour into a 6-cup mold coated with nonstick cooking spray. Chill until set, about 3 hours. Unmold onto a lettuce-lined platter. **Yield:** 10 servings.

Red Potato Salad

Shirley Helfenbein, Lapeer, Michigan

(Pictured above)

I remember digging up small red potatoes in our garden and bringing them home for Mom to use in this salad.

3/4 cup nonfat sour cream
1/2 cup fat-free mayonnaise
  or salad dressing
2 tablespoons vinegar
1 teaspoon celery seed
3/4 cup sliced green onions

6 medium red potatoes
  (2 pounds), peeled,
  cooked and cubed
1/3 cup sliced radishes
1/4 cup chopped celery
2 hard-cooked eggs, chopped

In a small bowl, combine sour cream, mayonnaise, vinegar and celery seed; set aside. In a large bowl, combine onions, potatoes, radishes, celery and eggs. Add dressing and toss lightly. Cover and chill. **Yield:** 8 servings.

NUTRITIONAL INFORMATION

Serving Size: 1/8 recipe

Calories: 148
Total Fat: 2 gm
Calories from Fat: 9%
Saturated Fat: trace
Cholesterol: 53 mg
Sodium: 230 mg
Carbohydrate: 29 gm
Protein: 5 gm

Strawberries and Romaine with Poppy Seed Dressing

Laurie Andrews, Milton, Ontario

My family runs a strawberry farm, so it's no surprise that I've collected countless recipes featuring that flavorful fruit. This is a recipe I use often.

1 bunch romaine, torn
1 quart fresh strawberries,
  sliced
1 small sweet onion, sliced
1/2 cup fat-free mayonnaise
  or salad dressing

1/3 cup sugar
2 tablespoons vinegar
1/4 cup skim milk
1 tablespoon poppy seeds

Combine romaine, berries and onion in a large bowl. In a jar with tight-fitting lid, combine remaining ingredients; shake well. Pour over salad; toss lightly. Serve immediately. **Yield:** 8 servings.

NUTRITIONAL INFORMATION

Serving Size: 1/8 recipe

Calories: 99
Total Fat: 1 gm
Calories from Fat: 8%
Saturated Fat: trace
Cholesterol: trace
Sodium: 118 mg
Carbohydrate: 22 gm
Protein: 2 gm

Three-Green Salad

Gina Squires, Salem, Oregon

(Pictured above)

For a crisp, refreshing side dish, this tasty salad can't be beat. The bold flavor and crunch really wake up your taste buds. It's the perfect salad to go with an Italian meal.

4 cups torn iceberg lettuce
4 cups torn leaf lettuce
4 cups torn fresh spinach
1 medium cucumber, sliced
2 carrots, sliced
2 celery ribs, sliced
6 broccoli florets, sliced
3 cauliflowerets, sliced

6 radishes, sliced
4 green onions, sliced
5 fresh mushrooms, sliced
1 bottle (8 ounces)
  fat-free Italian dressing
2 tablespoons grated
  Parmesan cheese

In a large salad bowl, toss the greens and vegetables. Cover and chill. Just before serving, add dressing and Parmesan cheese; toss. **Yield:** 12 servings.

Tossed Salad with Creamy Garlic Dressing

Phyllis Hickey, Bedford, New Hampshire

I often mix some escarole and spinach with leaf lettuce for this salad. I always receive compliments on the pleasant dressing. My family agrees it's better than any store-bought variety we've ever tasted.

1/4 cup red wine vinegar	1-1/2 cups (12 ounces) nonfat
1/4 cup water	sour cream
2 tablespoons minced onion	1/4 teaspoon pepper
1 to 2 garlic cloves, minced	8 cups torn salad greens
1/3 cup sugar	1 large carrot, shredded
1/2 cup fat-free mayonnaise	3 tablespoons bacon bits

In a small saucepan, combine vinegar, water, onion and garlic; simmer until the onion is tender, about 5 minutes. Add sugar; simmer until dissolved. Cool to room temperature. Stir in mayonnaise, sour cream and pepper. In a large salad bowl, toss greens, carrot and bacon bits; add dressing and toss to coat. Serve immediately. **Yield:** 8 servings.

Zucchini Orange Salad

Clarice Schweitzer, Sun City, Arizona

The ingredients in this recipe may surprise you, but not as much as the delightful flavor and refreshing crunch the blend produces! This salad feeds a crowd, so I often take it to potlucks and picnics.

2 medium zucchini, thinly sliced	1 can (15 ounces) mandarin oranges, drained
1 medium onion, thinly sliced	1 can (8 ounces) sliced water chestnuts, drained
1 cup chopped celery	1-1/2 cups sugar
1 can (16 ounces) green beans, drained	1 cup vinegar
1 can (16 ounces) wax beans, drained	1 tablespoon water

In a large bowl, toss zucchini, onion and celery. Cover with boiling water; let stand for 1 hour. Drain. Add beans, oranges and water chestnuts. Combine sugar, vinegar and water in a saucepan. Bring to a boil; boil for 1 minute. Pour over salad; cover and refrigerate 24 hours before serving. **Yield:** 20 servings.

Frozen Fruit Salad

Virginia Powell, Eureka, Kansas

I use this recipe to add a healthy twist to brown-bag lunches. I'm always in a hurry in the morning, so having a ready-made salad is a great help.

1 can (16 ounces) apricots in light syrup, drained
1 package (16 ounces) frozen sweetened sliced strawberries, thawed and drained
3 bananas, sliced

1 can (8 ounces) unsweetened pineapple tidbits, drained
1 can (6 ounces) frozen orange juice concentrate, thawed
3/4 cup water

In a food processor, chop apricots. In a pitcher or bowl, combine apricots, strawberries, bananas, pineapple, orange juice and water. Pour or ladle into muffin cups that have been sprayed with nonstick cooking spray. Freeze. When frozen, quickly remove salads to freezer bags or tightly covered storage containers. When packing a lunch, place salad in an individual storage container in a thermal lunch bag, and it will thaw by lunchtime. **Yield:** 24 salads.

NUTRITIONAL INFORMATION

Serving Size: 1 salad

Calories: 60
Total Fat: trace
Calories from Fat: 2%
Saturated Fat: trace
Cholesterol: 0
Sodium: 2 mg
Carbohydrate: 16 gm
Protein: 1 gm

Italian Salad Bowl

Carol Dalke, Elk Creek, Montana

With simple-to-prepare dishes like this, everyone in the family enjoys pitching in at dinnertime.

1 bunch leaf lettuce, torn
8 cherry tomatoes, halved
8 fresh mushrooms, sliced
4 radishes, sliced
1 small zucchini, thinly sliced

1/2 green, yellow *or* sweet red pepper, thinly sliced
1/4 cup shredded fat-free mozzarella cheese
1/3 cup fat-free Italian salad dressing

In a large salad bowl, toss all ingredients. Serve immediately. **Yield:** 4 servings.

NUTRITIONAL INFORMATION

Serving Size: 1/4 recipe

Calories: 58
Total Fat: 1 gm
Calories from Fat: 9%
Saturated Fat: trace
Cholesterol: 1 mg
Sodium: 270 mg
Carbohydrate: 10 gm
Protein: 5 gm

Quick Coleslaw

Linda Young, Longmont, Colorado

I figure I can enjoy more time cooking if I can rely on delicious, speedy recipes like this. Backyard picnics aren't complete without this coleslaw.

3 cups chopped cabbage
2 green onions, chopped
1 medium carrot, shredded
1/2 cup fat-free mayonnaise

1 tablespoon sugar
1 teaspoon celery seed
1/2 teaspoon ground mustard

In a medium bowl, combine cabbage, onions and carrot. Combine remaining ingredients; stir into vegetables. Chill until ready to serve. **Yield:** 4 servings.

NUTRITIONAL INFORMATION

Serving Size: 1/4 recipe

Calories: 59
Total Fat: trace
Calories from Fat: 7%
Saturated Fat: trace
Cholesterol: 0
Sodium: 228 mg
Carbohydrate: 13 gm
Protein: 1 gm

Creamy Sliced Tomatoes

Doris Smith, Woodbury, New Jersey

(Pictured above)

This is a family favorite that's also popular with friends. It's a pretty presentation, perfect as a side dish. The basil and cool creamy dressing make it tasty and refreshing.

1 cup fat-free mayonnaise
1/2 cup evaporated skim milk
3/4 teaspoon dried basil *or*
    1-1/2 teaspoons chopped
    fresh basil, *divided*

Lettuce leaves
  6 medium tomatoes, sliced
  1 medium red onion, thinly
    sliced into rings

In a small bowl, combine mayonnaise, milk and half of the basil; mix well. Refrigerate. Just before serving, arrange lettuce, tomatoes and onions on salad plates. Drizzle with dressing and sprinkle with remaining basil. **Yield:** 12 servings.

NUTRITIONAL INFORMATION

Serving Size: 1/12 recipe

Calories: 40
Total Fat: trace
Calories from Fat: 5%
Saturated Fat: trace
Cholesterol: trace
Sodium: 271 mg
Carbohydrate: 9 gm
Protein: 1 gm

Spinach Apple Salad

Darlis Wilfer, Phelps, Wisconsin

(Pictured above)

Whenever Mom made this salad, it was the first thing on my plate. With spinach, apples, raisins and a light dressing, this beautiful harvest salad is a feast for the eyes as well as the palate.

2 tablespoons unsweetened applesauce	1 cup diced unpeeled apple
2 tablespoons cider vinegar	1/4 cup chopped sweet onion
1 tablespoon vegetable oil	1/4 cup raisins
1/4 teaspoon sugar	2 cups torn fresh spinach
	2 cups torn romaine

In a small bowl, combine applesauce, vinegar, oil and sugar; mix well. Add apple, onion and raisins; toss lightly to coat. Cover and let stand for 10 minutes. Just before serving, combine spinach and romaine in a large salad bowl; add apple mixture and toss. **Yield:** 6 servings.

Raisin Slaw

Elaine Williams, Sebastopol, California

Bored with the same old salads? Turn to this flavorful unique version.

1/3 cup fat-free mayonnaise
2 teaspoons lemon juice
1 teaspoon sugar
1/2 teaspoon prepared
  mustard
1/4 teaspoon onion powder
  or dried minced onion

2 cups finely shredded
  cabbage
1 cup finely shredded carrot
1/2 cup shredded fat-free
  cheddar cheese
1/2 cup raisins

In a small bowl, combine mayonnaise, lemon juice, sugar, mustard and onion powder. In a large bowl, combine cabbage, carrot, cheese and raisins. Fold in dressing. Cover and refrigerate for at least 1 hour. **Yield:** 8 servings.

NUTRITIONAL INFORMATION

Serving Size: 1/8 recipe

Calories: 62
Total Fat: trace
Calories from Fat: 2%
Saturated Fat: trace
Cholesterol: 1 mg
Sodium: 138 mg
Carbohydrate: 13 gm
Protein: 3 gm

Orange and Onion Salad

Jean Ann Perkins, Newburyport, Maryland

Almonds give this salad real flair—it's very refreshing anytime of year.

1 head Boston lettuce,
  separated into leaves
1 medium red onion, thinly
  sliced into rings

1 can (11 ounces) mandarin
  oranges, drained
Fat-free salad dressing of
  your choice

Arrange lettuce, onion and oranges on salad plates. Serve with dressing of your choice. **Yield:** 6 servings.

NUTRITIONAL INFORMATION

Serving Size: 1/6 recipe
(calculated without dressing)

Calories: 30
Total Fat: trace
Calories from Fat: 3%
Saturated Fat: trace
Cholesterol: 0
Sodium: 5 mg
Carbohydrate: 7 gm
Protein: 1 gm

Luscious Raspberry Gelatin Salad

Bonnie Barclay, Custer, Michigan

Your family and friends alike will enjoy this colorful fruity salad.

1 package (6 ounces)
  raspberry gelatin
1 envelope unflavored
  gelatin
1 cup boiling water
2 cups cold water
1 pint fresh raspberries

2 large ripe bananas,
  mashed
1 can (20 ounces)
  unsweetened crushed
  pineapple with juice
1 cup (8 ounces) nonfat
  sour cream

In large mixing bowl, combine gelatins. Add boiling water and stir until dissolved. Stir in cold water. Add raspberries, bananas and pineapple; stir. Pour half into a glass serving bowl or 13-in. x 9-in. x 2-in. dish; chill until firm. (Let remaining half sit at room temperature.) When gelatin in serving bowl is firm, spread sour cream evenly on top, then carefully spoon remaining gelatin over the sour cream. Chill until firm. **Yield:** 16 servings.

NUTRITIONAL INFORMATION

Serving Size: 1/16 recipe

Calories: 100
Total Fat: trace
Calories from Fat: 1%
Saturated Fat: trace
Cholesterol: 1 mg
Sodium: 43 mg
Carbohydrate: 23 gm
Protein: 3 gm

Missouri Peach and Applesauce Salad

Bernice Morris, Marshfield, Missouri

Fresh peaches combine with applesauce in this tangy molded salad. This creamy-textured side dish is requested frequently by my family.

1 cup lemon-lime soda
1 package (3 ounces) peach gelatin
1 cup unsweetened applesauce

1/8 teaspoon ground nutmeg
2 cups light whipped topping
1 cup chopped peeled ripe peaches

In a saucepan, bring soda to a boil. Remove from the heat; stir in gelatin until dissolved. Add applesauce. Chill until mixture mounds slightly when dropped from a spoon. Stir nutmeg into whipped topping; fold into gelatin mixture along with the peaches. Transfer to a 1-1/2-qt. glass bowl. Chill until firm. **Yield:** 12 servings.

NUTRITIONAL INFORMATION

Serving Size: 1/12 recipe

Calories: 77
Total Fat: 1 gm
Calories from Fat: 12%
Saturated Fat: 1 gm
Cholesterol: 0
Sodium: 20 mg
Carbohydrate: 15 gm
Protein: 1 gm

Blueberry Gelatin Salad

Mildred Livingston, Phoenix, Arizona

I'm regularly asked to bring this dish along to potlucks. It can be served as either a salad or a dessert. Either way, it brings raves!

1 package (6 ounces) cherry gelatin
2 cups boiling water
1 can (15 ounces) blueberries in heavy syrup (not pie filling), undrained
1/2 cup sugar

1 package (8 ounces) fat-free cream cheese, softened
1 teaspoon vanilla extract
1 cup (8 ounces) nonfat sour cream
3 tablespoons chopped pecans

In a bowl, dissolve gelatin in boiling water; stir in blueberries. Pour into a 12-in. x 8-in. x 2-in. dish; chill until set. In a mixing bowl, beat sugar and cream cheese until smooth. Add vanilla and sour cream; mix well. Spread over gelatin; sprinkle with pecans. Chill several hours or overnight. **Yield:** 12 servings.

NUTRITIONAL INFORMATION

Serving Size: 1/12 recipe

Calories: 171
Total Fat: 1 gm
Calories from Fat: 7%
Saturated Fat: trace
Cholesterol: 3 mg
Sodium: 145 mg
Carbohydrate: 34 gm
Protein: 6 gm

Pineapple Coleslaw

Betty Follas, Morgan Hill, California

Sometimes I'll serve this salad with multicolored marshmallows sprinkled on top. They add a touch of sweetness without adding fat.

3/4 cup fat-free mayonnaise
2 tablespoons vinegar
2 tablespoons sugar
1 tablespoon skim milk
4 cups shredded cabbage

1 can (8 ounces) unsweetened pineapple tidbits, well drained
Paprika, optional

In a mixing bowl, combine mayonnaise, vinegar, sugar and milk. Place cabbage and pineapple in a large salad bowl; add dressing and toss. Chill. Sprinkle with paprika before serving if desired. **Yield:** 8 servings.

NUTRITIONAL INFORMATION

Serving Size: 1/8 recipe

Calories: 51
Total Fat: trace
Calories from Fat: 2%
Saturated Fat: trace
Cholesterol: trace
Sodium: 294 mg
Carbohydrate: 13 gm
Protein: 1 gm

German Cucumber Salad

Julie Koren, Kennesaw, Georgia

(Pictured above)

This salad is very cool and light with an exhilarating taste that's delicious anytime of the year, but especially when made with fresh-from-the-garden cucumbers and tomatoes.

2 medium cucumbers,
  thinly sliced
4 green onions, thinly
  sliced
3 small tomatoes, sliced
2 tablespoons snipped
  fresh parsley

1/4 cup nonfat sour cream
1/4 teaspoon prepared
  mustard
2 tablespoons minced fresh
  dill
1 tablespoon vinegar
1 tablespoon skim milk
1/8 teaspoon pepper

In a bowl, combine cucumbers, onions, tomatoes and parsley. Combine remaining ingredients; pour over cucumber mixture and toss gently. Cover and chill for at least 1 hour. **Yield:** 6 servings.

NUTRITIONAL INFORMATION

Serving Size: 1/6 recipe

Calories: 34
Total Fat: trace
Calories from Fat: 8%
Saturated Fat: trace
Cholesterol: trace
Sodium: 19 mg
Carbohydrate: 7 gm
Protein: 2 gm

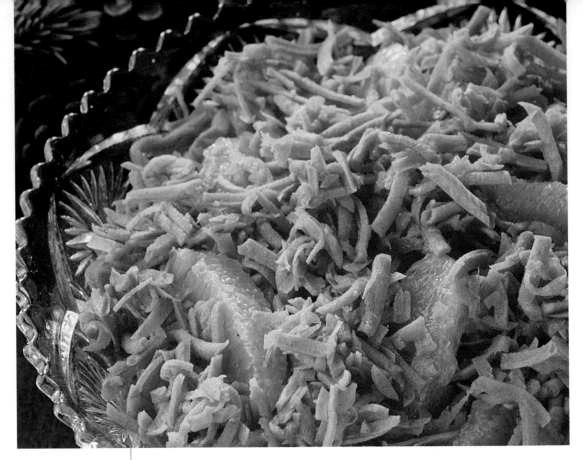

Orange Carrot Salad

Nancy Schmidt, Delhi, California

(Pictured above)

This is a refreshing salad that adds a little zip to a festive dinner. Our state produces a lot of oranges, so this dish truly represents my area.

3 cups shredded carrots
2 medium oranges, peeled
3 tablespoons lemon juice

1 tablespoon sugar
1 teaspoon ground cinnamon

Place carrots in a medium bowl. Section oranges into the bowl to catch juices. Add remaining ingredients and mix well. Cover and chill for several hours. **Yield:** 6 servings.

Lettuce with Sour Cream Dressing

Helen Bridges, Washington, Virginia

Though this dressing is very simple to make, the sweet-sour combination plus the tang of the onion convinces people there is some secret ingredient.

8 cups torn leaf or iceberg lettuce
1/2 cup sugar
1/4 cup vinegar

1/3 cup nonfat sour cream
2 tablespoons sliced green onions

Place lettuce in a large bowl. In a small bowl, stir together sugar, vinegar and sour cream until sugar dissolves and dressing is smooth. Stir in onions. Pour over lettuce and toss lightly; serve immediately. **Yield:** 6 servings.

NUTRITIONAL INFORMATION

Serving Size: 1/6 recipe

Calories: 55
Total Fat: trace
Calories from Fat: 3%
Saturated Fat: trace
Cholesterol: 0
Sodium: 21 mg
Carbohydrate: 14 gm
Protein: 1 gm

NUTRITIONAL INFORMATION

Serving Size: 1/6 recipe

Calories: 84
Total Fat: trace
Calories from Fat: 1%
Saturated Fat: trace
Cholesterol: 0
Sodium: 15 mg
Carbohydrate: 20 gm
Protein: 2 gm

Hidden Pear Salad

Sharon Mensing, Greenfield, Iowa

Light and fluffy, this colorful salad is a very flavorful family favorite. When I made it for my husband's family before we were married, we all joked about not being able to find any pears, so the name stuck.

1 can (16 ounces) pears, liquid drained and reserved
1 package (3 ounces) lime gelatin
3 ounces fat-free cream cheese, softened
1/4 teaspoon lemon juice
1 envelope whipped topping mix
1/2 cup skim milk
1/2 teaspoon vanilla extract
Lettuce leaves

In a saucepan, bring pear liquid to a boil. Stir in gelatin until dissolved. Remove from the heat and cool at room temperature until syrupy. Meanwhile, puree pears in a blender. In a mixing bowl, beat cream cheese and lemon juice until fluffy and smooth. Add pureed pears and mix well. Prepare whipped topping according to package directions using skim milk and vanilla; fold into pear mixture. Fold in cooled gelatin. Pour into a 4-1/2-cup mold coated with nonstick cooking spray. Chill overnight. Unmold onto a lettuce-lined platter. **Yield:** 8 servings.

NUTRITIONAL INFORMATION

Serving Size: 1/8 recipe

Calories: 73
Total Fat: trace
Calories from Fat: 1%
Saturated Fat: trace
Cholesterol: trace
Sodium: 100 mg
Carbohydrate: 15 gm
Protein: 3 gm

Make-Ahead Vegetable Medley

Ramona Hook Wysong, Barlow, Kentucky

I like experimenting with different combinations, and this is one of my most popular creations. I make it often for potlucks and seldom is there any left over.

1 can (16 ounces) kidney beans, rinsed and dained
1 can (15-1/4 ounces) lima beans, rinsed and drained
1 can (15 ounces) garbanzo beans, rinsed and drained
1 can (14-1/2 ounces) wax beans, drained
1 can (14-1/2 ounces) green beans, drained
1 can (15 ounces) small peas, drained
1 can (11 ounces) white shoepeg corn, drained
1-1/2 cups chopped onion
1/2 cup chopped green pepper
1 large cucumber, chopped
1 jar (2 ounces) diced pimientos, drained
2 cups cider vinegar
1-1/2 cups sugar
1/2 cup vegetable oil
1/2 teaspoon salt-free herb seasoning blend
1/2 teaspoon pepper
1/4 teaspoon garlic powder

In a large bowl, combine all of the beans, peas, corn, onion, green pepper, cucumber and pimientos. Combine the remaining ingredients; pour over vegetables and mix well. Cover and refrigerate overnight. **Yield:** 18 servings.

NUTRITIONAL INFORMATION

Serving Size: 3/4 cup

Calories: 250
Total Fat: 7 gm
Calories from Fat: 25%
Saturated Fat: 1 gm
Cholesterol: 0
Sodium: 328 mg
Carbohydrate: 41 gm
Protein: 6 gm

Better Than Potato Salad

Susan McCurdy, Elmhurst, Illinois

As soon as our family tried this delicious salad, it became a favorite, especially during the warmer months. It's a flavorful change of pace from traditional potato salad and it's simple to prepare.

NUTRITIONAL
INFORMATION

Serving Size: 2/3 cup

Calories: 130
Total Fat: 2 gm
Calories from Fat: 18%
Saturated Fat: 1 gm
Cholesterol: 71 mg
Sodium: 468 mg
Carbohydrate: 23 gm
Protein: 4 gm

4 cups cooked long grain rice	8 radishes, sliced
1 medium cucumber, seeded and chopped	4 hard-cooked eggs, chopped
2 cups thinly sliced celery	1-1/2 cups fat-free mayonnaise
1/2 cup chopped onion	3 tablespoons prepared mustard

In a large bowl, combine the first six ingredients. Combine mayonnaise and mustard; mix well. Pour over rice mixture and toss. Cover and refrigerate at least 1 hour. **Yield:** 12 servings.

Spinach Salad with Honey Dressing

Dee Simpson, Jefferson, Texas

This recipe is one of my favorite ways to use oranges—they pair nicely with the spinach and other vegetables. It's easy to make and quite refreshing.

NUTRITIONAL
INFORMATION

Serving Size: 2 cups

Calories: 96
Total Fat: 3 gm
Calories from Fat: 30%
Saturated Fat: trace
Cholesterol: 0
Sodium: 306 mg
Carbohydrate: 15 gm
Protein: 3 gm

1 package (10 ounces) fresh spinach, torn	1 medium cucumber, quartered and sliced
1 small head iceberg lettuce, torn	2 large oranges, cut into bite-size pieces
2 green onions, thinly sliced	1/2 cup sunflower seeds
3 tablespoons chopped green pepper	3/4 cup fat-free mayonnaise
	2 tablespoons honey
	1 tablespoon lemon juice

In a large bowl, combine the first seven ingredients. In a small bowl, stir mayonnaise, honey and lemon juice until smooth. Pour over the salad and toss to coat. Serve immediately. **Yield:** 10 servings.

Gala Crab Salad

Betty Follas, Morgan Hill, California

My family thinks this dish is just super, and it looks so nice after it's unmolded.

NUTRITIONAL
INFORMATION

Serving Size: 1/6 recipe

Calories: 198
Total Fat: 1 gm
Calories from Fat: 3%
Saturated Fat: trace
Cholesterol: 7 mg
Sodium: 791 mg
Carbohydrate: 41 gm
Protein: 7 gm

3 cups cooked rice	1/2 cup finely chopped onion
1-1/2 cups coarsely chopped imitation crab	1/2 cup finely chopped celery
1 cup fat-free mayonnaise	Leaf lettuce
1/2 cup finely chopped green pepper	Lemon slices *or* wedges, optional

In a bowl, combine rice, crab, mayonnaise, green pepper, onion and celery. Pack into a 6-cup mold coated with nonstick cooking spray. Chill 6 hours or overnight. Unmold onto a lettuce-lined platter. Garnish with lemon if desired. **Yield:** 6 servings.

Vegetable Pasta Salad

Kathy Crow, Cordova, Alaska

(Pictured below)

This light, multicolored salad is an original. When I serve it at potlucks, I'm always asked for the recipe.

12 ounces spiral pasta, cooked and drained
6 green onions, thinly sliced
1 medium zucchini, thinly sliced
2 cups frozen broccoli and cauliflower, thawed and drained
1-1/2 cups thinly sliced carrots, parboiled
1 cup thinly sliced celery
1 can (2-1/4 ounces) sliced ripe olives, drained
1/2 cup frozen peas, thawed
1 jar (6 ounces) marinated artichoke hearts, drained and quartered

DRESSING:
1/2 cup fat-free mayonnaise
1/2 cup fat-free Italian salad dressing
1/2 cup nonfat sour cream
1 tablespoon prepared mustard
1/2 teaspoon Italian seasoning

NUTRITIONAL INFORMATION

Serving Size: 1/2 cup

Calories: 111
Total Fat: 2 gm
Calories from Fat: 14%
Saturated Fat: trace
Cholesterol: 0
Sodium: 266 mg
Carbohydrate: 21 gm
Protein: 4 gm

In a large bowl, combine pasta, onions, zucchini, broccoli and cauliflower, carrots, celery, olives, peas and artichoke hearts. In a small bowl, combine dressing ingredients; mix well. Pour over salad and toss. Cover and refrigerate for at least 1 hour. **Yield:** 18 servings.

Marinated Slaw

Mary McGuire, Graham, North Carolina

(Pictured below)

This is a delectable dish that looks as good as it tastes. The best part is the mouth-watering dressing that even tempts you while it's cooking.

8 cups shredded cabbage (1-1/2 pounds)	3/4 cup chopped onion
2 tablespoons chopped pimientos	1 cup sugar
	1 cup vinegar
1/2 cup chopped green pepper	1/2 cup water
	1 tablespoon mustard seed

In a large bowl, combine the cabbage, pimientos, green pepper and onion. Toss lightly; set aside. Combine remaining ingredients in a medium saucepan; bring to a boil. Reduce heat; simmer, uncovered, for 20-25 minutes or until slightly thickened. Pour over cabbage mixture. Cover and refrigerate 4 hours or overnight. Slaw will keep in the refrigerator for several days. **Yield:** 10 servings.

Grandmother's Orange Salad

Ann Eastman, Greenville, California

(Pictured above)

This gelatin salad has a great citrus flavor. It adds beautiful color to any meal and appeals to appetites of all ages.

1 can (11 ounces)
  mandarin oranges
1 can (8 ounces)
  unsweetened crushed
  pineapple

1 package (6 ounces)
  orange gelatin
1 pint orange sherbet,
  softened
2 bananas, sliced

Drain oranges and pineapple, reserving juices. Set oranges and pineapple aside. Add water to juices to measure 2 cups. Place in a saucepan and bring to a boil; stir in gelatin until dissolved. Stir in sherbet until smooth. Chill until partially set (watch carefully). Fold in oranges, pineapple and bananas. Pour into a 6-cup mold coated with nonstick cooking spray. Chill until firm. **Yield:** 10 servings.

NUTRITIONAL INFORMATION

Serving Size: 1/10 recipe

Calories: 165
Total Fat: 1 gm
Calories from Fat: 5%
Saturated Fat: trace
Cholesterol: 2 mg
Sodium: 58 mg
Carbohydrate: 38 gm
Protein: 3 gm

Beet Salad

Lani Hasbrouck, Cascade, Idaho

This beet recipe came from a friend many years ago. It's a unique colorful salad that complements meat dishes.

1 can (16 ounces) diced *or*
  julienned beets
1 package (6 ounces)
  lemon gelatin
1-1/2 cups cold water
4 teaspoons vinegar

2 tablespoons finely
  chopped onion
1 tablespoon prepared
  horseradish
1-1/2 cups chopped celery
1/4 cup sliced stuffed olives

Drain beets, reserving liquid; set beets aside. Add water to reserved liquid to equal 2 cups; place in a saucepan and bring to a boil. Remove from the heat; stir in gelatin until dissolved. Add cold water, vinegar, onion and horseradish. Chill until partially set. Stir in the beets, celery and olives. Pour into an 8-in. square dish. Chill until firm, about 3 hours. Cut into squares. **Yield:** 9 servings.

NUTRITIONAL INFORMATION

Serving Size: 1/9 recipe

Calories: 97
Total Fat: 1 gm
Calories from Fat: 5%
Saturated Fat: trace
Cholesterol: 0
Sodium: 321 mg
Carbohydrate: 22 gm
Protein: 3 gm

Rosy Rhubarb Salad

Wanda Rader, Greeneville, Tennessee

(Pictured above)

I like to serve this salad with pork or poultry. It's just a little tart, so it rounds out rich food.

NUTRITIONAL INFORMATION

Serving Size: 1/8 recipe

Calories: 96
Total Fat: 1 gm
Calories from Fat: 12%
Saturated Fat: trace
Cholesterol: 0
Sodium: 42 mg
Carbohydrate: 21 gm
Protein: 2 gm

3 cups sliced fresh *or* frozen rhubarb
1 tablespoon sugar
1 package (3 ounces) raspberry gelatin
1 teaspoon lemon juice
1 cup unsweetened pineapple juice
1 cup diced peeled apples
1 cup diced celery
2 tablespoons chopped pecans

In a saucepan, cook and stir rhubarb and sugar over medium-low heat until rhubarb is soft and tender. Remove from the heat; add gelatin and stir until dissolved. Stir in lemon and pineapple juices. Chill until partially set. Stir in apples, celery and pecans. Pour into a 4-1/2-cup mold or glass bowl. Chill several hours or overnight. **Yield:** 8 servings.

Strawberry Spinach Salad

Jamie Stoneman, Winston-Salem, North Carolina

I love serving this salad to guests, who comment that it is very pretty. Not only that, it is also a tasty and nutritious dish!

NUTRITIONAL INFORMATION

Serving Size: 1/8 recipe

Calories: 125
Total Fat: 3 gm
Calories from Fat: 29%
Saturated Fat: trace
Cholesterol: 0
Sodium: 48 mg
Carbohydrate: 23 gm
Protein: 3 gm

8 cups fresh spinach, torn
1 pint fresh strawberries, sliced
1/2 cup sugar
2 tablespoons sesame seeds
1 tablespoon poppy seeds
1-1/2 teaspoons chopped onion
1/4 teaspoon Worcestershire sauce
1/4 teaspoon paprika
1/3 cup unsweetened applesauce
1/4 cup cider vinegar
1 tablespoon vegetable oil

Arrange spinach and berries on salad plates or in a large bowl. Place the next seven ingredients in a blender; with unit running, add vinegar and oil in a steady stream. Blend until thickened. Drizzle over salad; serve immediately. **Yield:** 8 servings.

Frozen Cranberry Banana Salad

Phylis Hoffmann, Conway, Arkansas

(Pictured below)

A luscious combination of sweet and tangy, crunchy and creamy, this pretty salad makes a great side dish or dessert. Its light pink color and delicate banana flavor make it perfect for a bridal shower or ladies' luncheon.

1 can (20 ounces) unsweetened pineapple tidbits
5 medium firm bananas, halved lengthwise and sliced
1/2 cup sugar
1 can (16 ounces) whole-berry cranberry sauce
1 carton (12 ounces) frozen light whipped topping, thawed
1/3 cup chopped walnuts

Drain pineapple juice into a medium bowl; set pineapple aside. Add bananas to the juice. In a large bowl, combine sugar and cranberry sauce. Remove bananas, discarding juice, and add to cranberry mixture. Stir in pineapple, whipped topping and nuts. Pour into a 13-in. x 9-in. x 2-in. dish. Freeze until solid. Remove from the freezer 15 minutes before cutting. **Yield:** 16 servings.

NUTRITIONAL INFORMATION

Serving Size: 1/16 recipe

Calories: 170
Total Fat: 4 gm
Calories from Fat: 21%
Saturated Fat: trace
Cholesterol: 1
Sodium: 25 mg
Carbohydrate: 34 gm
Protein: 1 gm

Cabbage Fruit Salad

Florence McNulty, Montebello, California

(Pictured below)

This salad goes well with all meats—it's especially good at barbecues and blends nicely with fish, too.

4 cups shredded cabbage
2 oranges, peeled and cut into bite-size pieces
2 red apples, chopped
1 cup seedless red grape halves
1/4 cup currants

1/2 cup fat-free mayonnaise
1/4 cup skim milk
1 tablespoon lemon juice
1 tablespoon sugar
1/3 cup chopped pecans, toasted

In a large bowl, toss cabbage, oranges, apples, grapes and currants; cover and refrigerate. In a small bowl, combine the mayonnaise, milk, lemon juice and sugar; cover and refrigerate. Just before serving, stir dressing and pecans into salad. **Yield:** 8 servings.

Minted Melon Salad

Terry Saylor, Vermillion, South Dakota

People can't resist digging into a salad made with colorful summer fruits. The unique dressing is what makes this salad a crowd-pleaser. I get compliments whenever I serve it, especially when I put it on the table in a melon boat. It's a warm-weather treat.

1 cup water	3 cups cubed cantaloupe
3/4 cup sugar	(1 medium melon)
3 tablespoons lime juice	3 cups cubed honeydew
1-1/2 teaspoons chopped fresh	(1 medium melon)
mint	2 cups sliced peaches
3/4 teaspoon aniseed	(2 peaches)
5 cups cubed watermelon	1 cup fresh blueberries
(1/2 medium melon)	

In a small saucepan, bring the first five ingredients to a boil. Boil for 2 minutes; remove from the heat. Cover and cool syrup completely. Combine the fruit in a large bowl; add syrup and stir to coat. Cover and chill for at least 2 hours, stirring occasionally. Drain before serving. **Yield:** 14 servings.

NUTRITIONAL INFORMATION

Serving Size: 1 cup

Calories: 102
Total Fat: trace
Calories from Fat: 4%
Saturated Fat: trace
Cholesterol: 0
Sodium: 10 mg
Carbohydrate: 25 gm
Protein: 1 gm

Four-Fruit Compote

Donna Long, Searcy, Arkansas

A beautiful side dish, this compote spotlights wonderful winter fruit like bananas, apples, oranges and pineapple. Of course, it can be made anytime of year. I'm sure you'll get as many smiles as I do when I bring out this refreshing salad at a potluck.

1 can (20 ounces)	1 tablespoon lemon juice
unsweetened pineapple	1 can (11 ounces)
chunks	mandarin oranges, drained
1/2 cup sugar	3 unpeeled apples, chopped
2 tablespoons cornstarch	2 bananas, sliced
1/3 cup orange juice	

Drain pineapple, reserving 3/4 cup juice. Set pineapple aside. In a saucepan, combine sugar and cornstarch. Add orange, lemon and pineapple juices. Cook and stir over medium heat until thickened and bubbly; cook and stir 1 minute longer. Remove from the heat. In a bowl, combine pineapple, oranges, apples and bananas. Pour warm sauce over the fruit; stir gently to coat. Cover and refrigerate. **Yield:** 16 servings.

NUTRITIONAL INFORMATION

Serving Size: 1/2 cup

Calories: 79
Total Fat: trace
Calories from Fat: 3%
Saturated Fat: trace
Cholesterol: 0
Sodium: 2 mg
Carbohydrate: 20 gm
Protein: 1 gm

Christmas Crunch Salad

Mary Anne McWhirter, Pearland, Texas

(Pictured above)

With its creamy dressing and colorful vegetables, this salad is both lovely and refreshing. Plus, since you make it ahead of time and it serves a lot, it's great for a party.

4 cups fresh broccoli florets
(3/4 pound)
4 cups fresh cauliflowerets
(3/4 pound)
1 medium red onion,
chopped
2 cups cherry tomatoes,
halved

DRESSING:
1 cup fat-free mayonnaise
1/2 cup nonfat sour cream
1 tablespoon sugar
1 tablespoon vinegar
Pepper to taste

In a large salad bowl, combine vegetables. Whisk the dressing ingredients until smooth; pour over vegetables and toss to coat. Cover and chill for at least 2 hours. **Yield:** 18 servings.

Pennsylvania Dutch Cucumbers

Shirley Helfenbein, Lapeer, Michigan

This is a Dutch dish Mom loved, and today it's my favorite garden salad …the blend of crisp cucumbers and homegrown tomatoes is wonderful!

3 small cucumbers
1/2 teaspoon salt, optional
1 medium onion, thinly sliced into rings
1/2 cup nonfat sour cream
2 tablespoons vinegar
1 tablespoon chopped fresh chives
1/2 teaspoon dill seed
1/4 teaspoon pepper
Pinch sugar, optional
Lettuce leaves
Sliced tomatoes

Peel cucumbers; slice paper-thin into a bowl. Sprinkle with salt if desired; cover and refrigerate for 3-4 hours. Rinse and drain cucumbers. Pat gently to press out excess liquid. Combine cucumbers and onion in a large bowl; set aside. In a small bowl, combine sour cream, vinegar, chives, dill seed, pepper and sugar if desired. Just before serving, add dressing to cucumbers and toss. Arrange lettuce and tomatoes in a serving bowl and spoon cucumbers into the middle. **Yield:** 6 servings.

NUTRITIONAL INFORMATION

Serving Size: 1/6 recipe
(calculated without salt and sugar)

Calories: 37
Total Fat: trace
Calories from Fat: 5%
Saturated Fat: trace
Cholesterol: 0
Sodium: 16 mg
Carbohydrate: 8 gm
Protein: 2 gm

Apricot Salad

Fae Fisher, Callao, Virginia

(Pictured below)

This colorful gelatin salad adds a spot of brightness to any table. Its smooth texture and delicate flavor blends well with many types of meals.

2 packages (3 ounces *each*) apricot gelatin
2 cups boiling water
1 package (8 ounces) fat-free cream cheese, softened
1 cup skim milk
1 can (20 ounces) crushed pineapple, undrained
1-1/2 cups whipped topping

Dissolve gelatin in boiling water and set aside. In a mixing bowl, beat cream cheese until smooth. Gradually beat in milk until smooth. Stir in gelatin. Add pineapple and mix well. Chill. When mixture begins to thicken, fold in whipped topping. Pour into a 2-1/2-qt. serving bowl. Chill for at least 2 hours. **Yield:** 8 servings.

NUTRITIONAL INFORMATION

Serving Size: 1/8 recipe

Calories: 198
Total Fat: 2 gm
Calories from Fat: 8%
Saturated Fat: 2 gm
Cholesterol: 6 mg
Sodium: 76 mg
Carbohydrate: 36 gm
Protein: 9 gm

Rave Reviews

When making fresh fruit salads, mix in some frozen seedless grapes just before serving. Everyone will comment on this clever, cool addition.

Raspberry Congealed Salad

Nancy Duty, Jacksonville, Florida

(Pictured above)

While growing up, my sisters and I especially enjoyed Mom's cool tangy salad, which looks so lovely on the table. The pineapple and raspberries are a delectable duo, and pecans add a little crunch.

1 can (8 ounces) unsweetened crushed pineapple
1 package (10 ounces) frozen unsweetened raspberries, thawed
1 package (3 ounces) raspberry gelatin
1 cup applesauce
3 tablespoons coarsely chopped pecans
Fat-free mayonnaise, optional

Drain pineapple and raspberries, reserving juices. Place fruit in a large bowl; set aside. Add enough water to the juice to measure 1 cup. Pour into a saucepan; bring to a boil. Remove from the heat; stir in gelatin until dissolved. Pour over fruit mixture. Add the applesauce and pecans. Pour into a 1-qt. bowl. Chill until set. Spoon into individual dessert dishes; top with a dollop of mayonnaise if desired. **Yield:** 6 servings.

Spring Rhubarb Salad

Joy Hansmeier, Waukon, Iowa

Each spring, we look forward to seeing the first rhubarb peeking out of the ground. Soon, I'll be making this salad, which is a family favorite.

4 cups diced fresh rhubarb
1-1/2 cups water
1/2 cup sugar
1 package (6 ounces) strawberry gelatin

1 cup orange juice
1 teaspoon grated orange peel
1 cup sliced fresh strawberries

Combine rhubarb, water and sugar in saucepan; cook and stir over medium heat until rhubarb is tender. Remove from the heat; add gelatin and stir until dissolved. Add orange juice and peel. Chill until syrupy. Add strawberries. Pour into 6-cup mold; chill until set. **Yield:** 10 servings.

NUTRITIONAL INFORMATION

Serving Size: 1/10 recipe

Calories: 130
Total Fat: trace
Calories from Fat: 1%
Saturated Fat: trace
Cholesterol: 0 mg
Sodium: 47 mg
Carbohydrate: 31 gm
Protein: 2 gm

Fiesta Corn Salad

Arlene Mawn, Holley, New York

We first had this salad in California. It's wonderful with a meat-and-potatoes dinner, or served for lunch with fresh French bread.

1 can (15-1/4 ounces) whole kernel corn, drained
1 cup chopped fresh tomato
1 cup chopped peeled cucumber

1/2 cup chopped celery
1/2 cup diced green or sweet red pepper
2 green onions, sliced
1/2 cup fat-free Italian salad dressing

Combine all ingredients. Cover and refrigerate for several hours before serving. **Yield:** 6 servings.

NUTRITIONAL INFORMATION

Serving Size: 1/6 recipe

Calories: 82
Total Fat: 1 gm
Calories from Fat: 5%
Saturated Fat: trace
Cholesterol: 0
Sodium: 489 mg
Carbohydrate: 19 gm
Protein: 2 gm

After-the-Holidays Salad

Gladys Kirsch, Mott, North Dakota

I'm always looking for new ways to use up our leftover holiday turkey. The fruit, nuts and seasonings give this salad a unique flavor.

2 cups diced cooked turkey breast
1 cup unsweetened pineapple chunks, well drained
1 cup diced celery
1 cup seedless green grapes
1/2 cup sliced green onions

1/4 cup reduced-fat honey-roasted peanuts
2/3 cup fat-free mayonnaise
2 tablespoons prepared chutney
1 tablespoon lime juice
1/2 teaspoon curry powder

In a bowl, toss the first six ingredients. In a small bowl, combine mayonnaise, chutney, lime juice and curry; pour over turkey mixture and mix gently. Chill. **Yield:** 4 servings.

NUTRITIONAL INFORMATION

Serving Size: 1/4 recipe

Calories: 236
Total Fat: 6 gm
Calories from Fat: 20%
Saturated Fat: 1 gm
Cholesterol: 63
Sodium: 361 mg
Carbohydrate: 23 gm
Protein: 26 gm

Black Bean and Corn Salad

Darlene Temple, Culpeper, Virginia

(Pictured above)

This recipe is a favorite with my husband and five boys, who are all hearty eaters. It's filling, economical and, best of all, easy to prepare.

1 can (15 ounces) black beans, rinsed and drained	3/4 cup thinly sliced celery
4 ounces reduced-fat Monterey Jack cheese, cut into 1/4-inch cubes	1 small sweet red pepper, diced
	3/4 cup picante sauce
1 can (8-3/4 ounces) whole kernel corn, drained	2 tablespoons olive *or* vegetable oil
1/4 cup sliced green onions with tops	2 tablespoons lemon juice
	1/2 teaspoon ground cumin
	1 garlic clove, minced

Combine all ingredients in a large bowl; mix well. Cover and chill several hours or overnight. **Yield:** 8 servings.

NUTRITIONAL INFORMATION

Serving Size: 1/8 recipe

Calories: 243
Total Fat: 7 gm
Calories from Fat: 25%
Saturated Fat: 2 gm
Cholesterol: 10 mg
Sodium: 401 mg
Carbohydrate: 36 gm
Protein: 13 gm

Broccoli Bacon Salad

Joyce Blakley, Windsor Locks, Connecticut

Try this salad at your next Sunday dinner. My family just loves it—especially my grandson—and friends rave about its taste, too!

1 large bunch broccoli, separated into florets	10 turkey bacon strips, cooked and crumbled
1 small red onion, coarsely chopped	3 tablespoons vinegar
	1/3 cup fat-free mayonnaise
1 cup raisins	1/3 cup sugar

In a large salad bowl, combine the broccoli, onion, raisins and bacon. In a small bowl, combine vinegar, mayonnaise and sugar; stir until smooth and sugar is dissolved. Pour over broccoli mixture; toss to coat. Serve immediately. **Yield:** 8 servings.

NUTRITIONAL INFORMATION

Serving Size: 1/8 recipe

Calories: 155
Total Fat: 4 gm
Calories from Fat: 21%
Saturated Fat: 1 gm
Cholesterol: 11 mg
Sodium: 401 mg
Carbohydrate: 28 gm
Protein: 6 gm

Fruited Wild Rice Salad

Larren Wood, Nevis, Minnesota

(Pictured below)

I created this salad recipe to feature wild rice, a state crop, plus other harvest ingredients like apples and pecans. I make bushels of it every year.

DRESSING:
- 3 tablespoons olive *or* vegetable oil
- 1/2 cup orange juice
- 2 tablespoons honey

SALAD:
- 1 cup uncooked wild rice
- 2 Golden Delicious apples, chopped
- Juice of 1 lemon
- 1 cup golden raisins
- 1 cup seedless red grapes, halved
- 2 tablespoons *each* minced fresh mint, parsley and chives
- Pepper to taste
- 1/3 cup chopped pecans

Combine dressing ingredients; set aside. Cook rice according to package directions; drain if needed and allow to cool. In a large bowl, toss apples with lemon juice. Add raisins, grapes, mint, parsley, chives and rice. Add dressing and toss. Season with pepper. Cover and chill several hours or overnight. Just before serving, top with pecans. **Yield:** 10 servings.

NUTRITIONAL INFORMATION

Serving Size: 3/4 cup

Calories: 207
Total Fat: 6 gm
Calories from Fat: 28%
Saturated Fat: 1 gm
Cholesterol: 0
Sodium: 5 mg
Carbohydrate: 37 gm
Protein: 3 gm

Layered Fruit Salad

Page Alexander, Baldwin City, Kansas

(Pictured below)

This colorful salad is a real eye-catcher, and it tastes as good as it looks. Fresh fruit is always a welcome side dish with a summer meal. The addition of oranges and grapefruit gives this salad a different twist.

NUTRITIONAL INFORMATION

Serving Size: 1/8 recipe
(calculated with fresh pineapple)

Calories: 135
Total Fat: 1 gm
Calories from Fat: 4%
Saturated Fat: trace
Cholesterol: 0
Sodium: 7 mg
Carbohydrate: 34 gm
Protein: 2 gm

1/2 cup orange juice
1/4 cup lemon juice
1/4 cup packed brown sugar
1/2 teaspoon grated orange peel
1/2 teaspoon grated lemon peel
1 cinnamon stick
2 cups fresh *or* drained canned unsweetened pineapple chunks
1 cup seedless red grapes
2 medium bananas, sliced
2 medium oranges, sectioned
1 medium grapefruit, sectioned
1 pint strawberries, sliced
2 kiwifruit, peeled and sliced

In a medium saucepan, combine the first six ingredients; bring to a boil. Reduce heat; simmer, uncovered, for 5 minutes. Remove from the heat; cool completely. Meanwhile, layer fruit in a glass serving bowl. Remove cinnamon stick from the sauce; pour sauce over fruit. Cover and chill for several hours. **Yield:** 8 servings.

Spiced Peach Salad

Karen Hamilton, Ludington, Michigan

This refreshing salad is my most requested recipe. A touch of cinnamon makes it taste like fresh peach pie.

1/2 cup sugar
3 tablespoons vinegar
2 cups water
1 tablespoon whole cloves
4 cinnamon sticks

1 package (6 ounces) peach gelatin
1 can (29 ounces) unsweetened peach halves

In a medium saucepan, combine sugar, vinegar and water. Tie cloves and cinnamon in a cheesecloth bag; place in the saucepan. Bring to a boil. Reduce heat; simmer, uncovered, for 10 minutes. Remove from the heat and discard spice bag. Add gelatin; stir until dissolved. Drain peaches, reserving syrup; set peaches aside. Add water to syrup to equal 2 cups. Add to gelatin mixture; stir well. Chill until slightly thickened. Thinly slice peaches; add to gelatin. Pour into a 2-qt. glass bowl; chill until firm. **Yield:** 10 servings. **Editor's Note:** If desired, 1/2 teaspoon ground cinnamon and 1/4 teaspoon ground cloves may be substituted for the whole spices; combine with the gelatin before adding to sugar mixture.

NUTRITIONAL INFORMATION

Serving Size: 3/4 cup

Calories: 143
Total Fat: trace
Calories from Fat: 1%
Saturated Fat: trace
Cholesterol: 0
Sodium: 50 mg
Carbohydrate: 36 gm
Protein: 2 gm

Roast Beef Pasta Salad

Sandy Shields, Mead, Washington

I made this salad one year when a neighbor came over to help my husband put up hay. On that hot, dusty day, this cool dish was well received.

1 package (16 ounces) spiral pasta
2 cups julienned cooked lean roast beef
1 cup chopped green pepper
1 cup sliced celery
3/4 cup chopped red onion
1/2 cup chopped sweet red pepper
1/3 cup chopped dill pickle
2 green onions, sliced

DRESSING:
2 tablespoons low-sodium beef bouillon granules
1/4 cup boiling water
1/2 cup skim milk
2 cups fat-free mayonnaise
1 cup (8 ounces) nonfat sour cream
1 teaspoon dill weed
Dash pepper

Cook the pasta according to package directions; drain and rinse in cold water. Place in a large bowl; add beef, green pepper, celery, red onion, red pepper, pickle and green onions. For dressing, dissolve bouillon in water. Add milk, mayonnaise, sour cream, dill and pepper; mix well. Toss with pasta mixture. Cover and refrigerate until ready to serve. **Yield:** 16 servings.

NUTRITIONAL INFORMATION

Serving Size: 1 cup

Calories: 206
Total Fat: 2 gm
Calories from Fat: 9%
Saturated Fat: 1 gm
Cholesterol: 10 mg
Sodium: 466 mg
Carbohydrate: 37 gm
Protein: 11 gm

OVEN-FRESH GOODIES. *Clockwise from top right: Sesame French Bread, Date Nut Bread (both recipes on page 83) and Oatmeal Carrot Muffins (recipe on page 84).*

Breads, Rolls & Muffins

Sesame French Bread

Peggy Van Arsdale, Trenton, New Jersey

(Pictured at left)

These easy-to-make loaves turn out golden and crunchy every time.

2 packages (1/4 ounce *each*) active dry yeast	6 to 6-1/2 cups all-purpose flour
2-1/2 cups warm water (110° to 115°)	2 tablespoons cornmeal
2 tablespoons sugar	1 egg white
2 tablespoons vegetable oil	1 tablespoon water
2 teaspoons salt	2 tablespoons sesame seeds

In a large mixing bowl, dissolve yeast in warm water. Add sugar, oil, salt and 4 cups of flour; beat until smooth. Add enough remaining flour to form a soft dough. Turn onto a floured surface; knead until smooth and elastic, about 6-8 minutes. Place in a bowl coated with nonstick cooking spray, turning once to grease top. Cover and let rise in a warm place until doubled, about 1 hour. Punch dough down. Divide in half. Roll each half into a 15-in. x 10-in. rectangle. Roll up from a long side; seal well. Place with seam side down on a baking sheet coated with non-stick cooking spray and sprinkled with cornmeal. Beat egg white and water; brush over loaves. Sprinkle with sesame seeds. Cover with plastic wrap sprayed with nonstick cooking spray; let rise until nearly doubled, about 30 minutes. With a very sharp knife, make four shallow diagonal cuts across top. Bake at 400° for 25 minutes or until lightly browned. Remove from pan and cool on a wire rack. **Yield:** 2 loaves (15 slices each).

NUTRITIONAL INFORMATION
Serving Size: 1 slice

Calories: 108
Total Fat: 1 gm
Calories from Fat: 12%
Saturated Fat: trace
Cholesterol: 0
Sodium: 145 mg
Carbohydrate: 20 gm
Protein: 3 gm

Date Nut Bread

Rosemary White, Oneida, New York

(Pictured at left)

My family likes the flavor of this bread...I like the fact it can be baked ahead!

1/4 cup shortening	2 teaspoons baking powder
1-1/2 cups sugar	1/4 teaspoon salt
2 eggs	1-1/2 cups orange juice
1-1/2 teaspoons vanilla extract	1-1/2 cups chopped dates
3 cups all-purpose flour	1/2 cup chopped walnuts
2 teaspoons baking soda	

In a mixing bowl, cream shortening and sugar. Add eggs and vanilla; beat until fluffy. Combine dry ingredients; add alternately to creamed mixture with orange juice. Blend well. Fold in dates and walnuts. Pour into two 8-in. x 4-in. x 2-in. loaf pans coated with nonstick cooking spray. Bake at 350° for 45-50 minutes or until a toothpick inserted near the center comes out clean. Cool in pans 10 minutes before removing to a wire rack. **Yield:** 2 loaves (14 slices each).

NUTRITIONAL INFORMATION
Serving Size: 1 slice

Calories: 158
Total Fat: 4 gm
Calories from Fat: 20%
Saturated Fat: 1 gm
Cholesterol: 15 mg
Sodium: 149 mg
Carbohydrate: 30 gm
Protein: 3 gm

Oatmeal Carrot Muffins

Jane Richter, Pompano Beach, Florida

(Pictured on page 82)

Just because you've started to reduce the amount of fat in your diet doesn't mean you can never munch a muffin again! With lots of hearty ingredients, these moist muffins are delicious!

1 cup old-fashioned oats	2 egg whites
1/2 cup raisins	1 teaspoon grated orange
1 cup skim milk	peel
1/2 cup shredded carrot	1/2 cup all-purpose flour
1/2 cup sugar	1/2 cup whole wheat flour
1/2 cup packed brown sugar	1 tablespoon baking powder
1/4 cup vegetable oil	1/2 teaspoon baking soda

In a large bowl, combine oats, raisins and milk; stir well. Cover and refrigerate 2 hours or overnight. Combine carrot, sugars, oil, egg whites and orange peel; stir into oat mixture. Combine dry ingredients; stir into the batter just until moistened. Coat muffin cups with nonstick cooking spray or use paper liners; fill cups two-thirds full. Bake at 400° for 20-25 minutes or until muffins test done. Cool in pan 10 minutes before removing to a wire rack. **Yield:** 10 muffins.

Southern Sweet Potato Bread

Judy Foss, Strum, Wisconsin

People are surprised to hear sweet potatoes are this bread's main ingredient.

1/4 cup margarine, softened	1/4 teaspoon ground nutmeg
1/2 cup packed brown sugar	2 tablespoons chopped
2 eggs	pecans
1 cup mashed sweet	**ORANGE CREAM SPREAD:**
potatoes	3 ounces fat-free cream
3 tablespoons skim milk	cheese, softened
1 teaspoon grated orange	1 teaspoon orange juice
peel	1 teaspoon grated orange
2 cups self-rising flour*	peel
1/4 teaspoon ground allspice	

In a mixing bowl, cream margarine and brown sugar. Add eggs; mix well. Add sweet potatoes, milk and orange peel; mix well. Combine flour, allspice and nutmeg. Add to creamed mixture; mix just until combined. Fold in nuts. Pour into a 9-in. x 5-in. x 3-in. loaf pan coated with nonstick cooking spray. Bake at 350° for 40-45 minutes or until bread tests done. Cool in pan for 10 minutes before removing to a wire rack. Cool completely. In a mixing bowl, combine spread ingredients; beat until smooth. Serve with bread. **Yield:** 1 loaf (16 slices).
*Editor's Note: 2 cups of all-purpose flour, 1 tablespoon baking powder and 1 teaspoon salt may be substituted for the self-rising flour.

Onion Herb Bread

Evette Nicksich, Bartlett, Nebraska

(Pictured above)

I've been making this easy bread for years. It goes great with soup or stew. I've taken it to many picnics and potluck suppers. Many people have asked for the recipe, and they're always delighted to see how simple it is to make!

1 package (1/4 ounce) active dry yeast	1 teaspoon dried rosemary, crushed
1/2 cup warm water (110° to 115°)	1/2 teaspoon salt
1/2 cup warm skim milk (110° to 115°)	1/2 teaspoon dill weed
1 tablespoon margarine	1/2 teaspoon garlic powder
1 tablespoon sugar	1/4 cup finely chopped onion
	2-1/4 cups all-purpose flour, *divided*

In a mixing bowl, dissolve yeast in water. Add milk, margarine, sugar, rosemary, salt, dill, garlic powder, onion and 1 cup of flour. Beat until smooth, about 1 minute. Add the remaining flour and stir for about 1 minute. Place in a bowl coated with nonstick cooking spray. Cover and let rise in a warm place until doubled, about 30 minutes. Stir down raised batter using 25 strokes. Spread into an 8-in. x 4-in. x 2-in. loaf pan coated with nonstick cooking spray. Cover and let rise in a warm place until almost doubled, about 15 minutes. Bake at 375° for 40-45 minutes. Remove from pan; serve warm. **Yield:** 1 loaf (14 slices).

NUTRITIONAL INFORMATION

Serving Size: 1 slice

Calories: 90
Total Fat: 1 gm
Calories from Fat: 10%
Saturated Fat: trace
Cholesterol: trace
Sodium: 92 mg
Carbohydrate: 17 gm
Protein: 3 gm

Jalapeno Bread

Mary Alice Watt, Upton, Wyoming

(Pictured below)

This bread is a big hit at our house and at potluck gatherings. Its unusual texture makes it a conversation piece, so almost everybody tries it.

NUTRITIONAL INFORMATION

Serving Size: 1 slice

Calories: 103
Total Fat: 2 gm
Calories from Fat: 15%
Saturated Fat: trace
Cholesterol: 8 mg
Sodium: 309 mg
Carbohydrate: 19 gm
Protein: 4 gm

2 loaves (1 pound *each*) frozen bread dough, thawed
1 can (8-3/4 ounces) whole kernel corn, drained
1 egg
1 can (3-1/2 ounces) whole jalapenos*, chopped
2 tablespoons taco seasoning mix
1 jar (2 ounces) sliced pimientos, drained
1-1/2 teaspoons vinegar

Cut bread dough into 1-in. pieces. Place all ingredients in a large bowl and toss to mix well. Spoon into two 8-in. x 4-in. x 2-in. loaf pans coated with nonstick cooking spray. Cover and let stand for 15 minutes. Bake at 350° for 35-40 minutes. Cool in pan 10 minutes before removing to a wire rack. Serve warm if desired. **Yield:** 2 loaves (14 slices each). *****Editor's Note:** Remove the seeds from the jalapenos before chopping for a milder bread.

Extra-Quick Yeast Rolls

Eleanor Paine, Junction City, Oregon

(Pictured on the front cover)

You'll never reach for packaged rolls again after trying these!

1 package (1/4 ounce) quick-rise yeast	3/4 cup warm water (110° to 115°)
1 tablespoon sugar	2-1/2 cups reduced-fat biscuit/ baking mix

Dissolve yeast and sugar in warm water. Stir in baking mix; turn onto a floured surface. Knead until smooth and elastic, about 5 minutes. Shape into dinner-size rolls. Place on a baking sheet coated with non-stick cooking spray. Cover and let rise in a warm place until doubled, about 30-45 minutes. Bake at 400° for 12-14 minutes or until golden brown. **Yield:** 2 dozen.

NUTRITIONAL INFORMATION

Serving Size: 1 roll

Calories: 50
Total Fat: 1 gm
Calories from Fat: 15%
Saturated Fat: trace
Cholesterol: 0
Sodium: 145 mg
Carbohydrate: 9 gm
Protein: 1 gm

Potato Biscuits

Jacqueline Thuma, Orange Park, Florida

I developed this recipe one evening while making "ordinary" biscuits. I had half a cup of potato flakes left in the box and I just added them to the dough.

1/2 cup instant mashed potato flakes	1/2 cup hot water
1 teaspoon sugar	1/3 cup cold water
2 tablespoons margarine, softened	3 cups reduced-fat biscuit/ baking mix

Combine potato flakes, sugar, margarine and hot water; mix well. Add cold water and baking mix, stirring until well blended. Add a little more cold water if necessary to make a soft dough. Turn onto a floured surface; knead about 10 times. Roll dough to 1/2- to 3/4-in. thickness; cut with a 2-in. biscuit cutter. Place on an ungreased baking sheet. Bake at 450° for 13 minutes or until lightly browned. **Yield:** 16 biscuits.

NUTRITIONAL INFORMATION

Serving Size: 1 biscuit

Calories: 104
Total Fat: 3 gm
Calories from Fat: 25%
Saturated Fat: 1 gm
Cholesterol: 0
Sodium: 277 mg
Carbohydrate: 17 gm
Protein: 2 gm

Mom's Corn Bread

Norma Erne, Albuquerque, New Mexico

Whenever Mom made chili, she always made a batch of corn bread, too.

2 eggs	3/4 cup all-purpose flour
1-1/4 cups skim milk	2 tablespoons sugar
1/4 cup shortening	2-1/4 teaspoons baking powder
1-1/2 cups yellow cornmeal	1 teaspoon salt

Combine eggs, milk and shortening. Sift together all remaining ingredients and add to egg mixture; stir only until blended. Pour into an 8-in. square baking pan coated with nonstick cooking spray. Bake at 400° for 20-25 minutes or until bread begins to pull away from sides of the pan and is browned on the edges. **Yield:** 9 servings.

NUTRITIONAL INFORMATION

Serving Size: 1/9 recipe

Calories: 210
Total Fat: 7 gm
Calories from Fat: 30%
Saturated Fat: 2 gm
Cholesterol: 48 mg
Sodium: 390 mg
Carbohydrate: 31 gm
Protein: 5 gm

Best-Ever Breadsticks

Carol Wolfer, Lebanon, Oregon

When time is short, try these fast, flavorful breadsticks. They'll satisfy your family's hunger for homemade bread in a hurry!

3/4 cup skim milk
1 tablespoon sugar
1 teaspoon salt
1 tablespoon margarine
1 package (1/4 ounce)
  quick-rise yeast

1/4 cup warm water
  (110° to 115°)
3 to 3-1/4 cups all-purpose
  flour
1 egg white
1 tablespoon water

In a saucepan, heat milk, sugar, salt and margarine. Cool to lukewarm. Dissolve yeast in warm water. Combine milk mixture, yeast and 1-1/2 cups flour; beat until smooth. Add enough remaining flour to form a stiff dough. Turn onto a floured surface and knead until smooth and elastic, about 6-8 minutes. Place in a bowl coated with nonstick cooking spray, turning once to grease top. Cover and let rise in a warm place until doubled, about 30 minutes. Punch dough down. Pinch off golf ball-size pieces; roll into pencil-size strips. Place 1 in. apart on baking sheets coated with nonstick cooking spray. Cover and let rise for 15 minutes. Beat egg white and water; brush over breadsticks. Bake at 400° for 10 minutes or until golden. **Yield:** 1-1/2 dozen.

Quick Blueberry Muffins

Katrina Shaner, Stronghurst, Illinois

My sister passed along this recipe for homemade muffins. It's as easy as using a box mix…but the muffins taste a whole lot better!

MUFFIN MIX:
2-1/2 cups all-purpose flour
2-1/2 cups whole wheat flour
1 cup wheat bran cereal
1 cup quick-cooking oats
1-1/2 cups sugar
2 tablespoons baking
  powder
2 teaspoons salt
BLUEBERRY MUFFINS:
3 cups Muffin Mix
  (recipe above)

2 tablespoons brown sugar
1 teaspoon ground
  cinnamon
1-1/4 cups fresh *or* frozen
  blueberries
1 cup skim milk
2 eggs
1/4 cup unsweetened
  applesauce
1 teaspoon vanilla extract

Combine all muffin mix ingredients in a large airtight container. Store at room temperature until ready to use. Stir well before measuring for the muffin recipe. **Yield:** 6 cups mix (2 batches of muffins). **To make blueberry muffins:** In a mixing bowl, combine mix, brown sugar and cinnamon. Stir in blueberries. In another bowl, beat milk, eggs, applesauce and vanilla; stir into blueberry mixture just until moistened. Coat muffin cups with nonstick cooking spray or use paper liners; fill cups two-thirds full. Bake at 425° for 15-18 minutes or until muffins test done. Cool in pan 10 minutes before removing to a wire rack. **Yield:** 1 dozen per batch.

New England Brown Bread

Rosemary Bouley, Worcester, Massachusetts

(Pictured below)

We New Englanders are noted for eating baked beans and brown bread on Saturday nights. I especially enjoy this recipe for brown bread. It was handed down to me by a cousin and I've made it many times over the years.

1/2 cup all-purpose flour
2 teaspoons baking soda
1 teaspoon salt
2 cups whole wheat flour

2 cups buttermilk
1/2 cup dark molasses
1 cup raisins

In a large bowl, combine all-purpose flour, baking soda and salt. In another bowl, combine whole wheat flour, buttermilk and molasses; add to flour mixture and mix well. Stir in raisins. Pour into two 5-1/4-in. x 3-3/4-in. coffee cans coated with nonstick cooking spray. Bake at 350° for 45-50 minutes or until breads test done. **Yield:** 2 loaves (9 slices each).

NUTRITIONAL INFORMATION

Serving Size: 1 slice

Calories: 112
Total Fat: 1 gm
Calories from Fat: 4%
Saturated Fat: trace
Cholesterol: 1 mg
Sodium: 297 mg
Carbohydrate: 25 gm
Protein: 3 gm

Festive Fruited Scones

Helen Carpenter, Marble Falls, Texas

(Pictured above)

I've found you don't need to put a thing on these scones…they're delicious plain and simple. I especially enjoy them in the wintertime with hot coffee or tea.

NUTRITIONAL INFORMATION

Serving Size: 1 scone

Calories: 148
Total Fat: 4 gm
Calories from Fat: 23%
Saturated Fat: 1 gm
Cholesterol: 1 mg
Sodium: 296 mg
Carbohydrate: 25 gm
Protein: 3 gm

2 cups all-purpose flour
1 tablespoon sugar
1 tablespoon baking powder
1/4 teaspoon baking soda
1/4 teaspoon salt
3 tablespoons cold margarine
1/2 cup diced dried fruit (apricots, apples *or* prunes)
1/2 teaspoon grated orange peel
3/4 cup buttermilk
1 tablespoon skim milk

In a bowl, combine flour, sugar, baking powder, baking soda and salt. Cut in margarine until the mixture resembles fine crumbs. Add fruit and orange peel. Stir in buttermilk until a soft dough forms. Turn onto a floured surface; knead gently for 2-3 minutes. Shape into a ball. Roll into a 7-in. circle. Cut into 10 wedges; place on a baking sheet coated with nonstick cooking spray. Brush with skim milk. Bake at 425° for 12-15 minutes or until lightly browned. Serve warm. **Yield:** 10 scones.

Pumpkin Spice Muffins

Michel Karkula, Chandler, Arizona

Years ago, I relied on recipes I could fix fast for my growing family. I still use this recipe today. These spicy, moist muffins can be prepared with little fuss from a baking mix, canned pumpkin and spices.

1/2 cup canned pumpkin
1/2 cup skim milk
1 egg
2 cups reduced-fat biscuit/ baking mix
1/4 cup sugar
1/2 teaspoon ground nutmeg
1/2 teaspoon ground cinnamon
1/2 teaspoon ground ginger

STREUSEL TOPPING:
1 tablespoon reduced-fat biscuit/baking mix
2 tablespoons sugar
1/4 teaspoon ground cinnamon
2 teaspoons margarine, softened

In a bowl, combine pumpkin, milk and egg with a fork. Combine the next five ingredients; add to pumpkin mixture and stir just until moistened. Coat muffin cups with nonstick cooking spray or use paper liners; fill cups two-thirds full. Combine streusel ingredients; sprinkle over muffins. Bake at 400° for 15 minutes or until golden brown. Serve warm. **Yield:** 1 dozen.

NUTRITIONAL INFORMATION

Serving Size: 1 muffin

Calories: 122
Total Fat: 2 gm
Calories from Fat: 18%
Saturated Fat: trace
Cholesterol: 18 mg
Sodium: 256 mg
Carbohydrate: 22 gm
Protein: 3 gm

Cranberry Orange Bread

Elaine Kremenak, Grants Pass, Oregon

This bread is a natural coming from Oregon, a state famous for its cranberries. I freeze berries and walnuts and have a ready supply all year long.

2 cups all-purpose flour
1-1/2 teaspoons baking powder
1 teaspoon baking soda
1/2 teaspoon salt
1 cup sugar
1 egg
1/2 cup orange juice
Grated peel of 1 orange

2 tablespoons margarine, melted
2 tablespoons hot water
1 cup fresh whole cranberries
1/2 cup coarsely chopped walnuts

Combine flour, baking powder, baking soda, salt and sugar; set aside. In a large bowl, mix egg, orange juice, peel, margarine and hot water. Fold in dry ingredients just until blended (do not beat). Gently fold in cranberries and walnuts. Spoon into a 9-in. x 5-in. x 3-in. loaf pan coated with nonstick cooking spray. Bake at 325° for 1 hour or until bread tests done. Cool on a wire rack for 15 minutes before removing from pan. **Yield:** 1 loaf (16 slices).

NUTRITIONAL INFORMATION

Serving Size: 1 slice

Calories: 153
Total Fat: 4 gm
Calories from Fat: 23%
Saturated Fat: 1 gm
Cholesterol: 13 mg
Sodium: 215 mg
Carbohydrate: 27 gm
Protein: 3 gm

Caraway Rolls

Ruth Hastings, Louisville, Illinois

Filled with caraway, these rolls are a nice addition to all of your meals. Cottage cheese helps make them nice and moist.

2 packages (1/4 ounce *each*) active dry yeast	1/2 teaspoon baking soda
1/2 cup warm water (110° to 115°)	1/4 cup sugar
2 tablespoons caraway seeds	2-1/2 teaspoons salt
2 cups (16 ounces) low-fat cottage cheese	2 eggs
	4-1/2 to 5 cups all-purpose flour
	1 tablespoon margarine, melted

In a large mixing bowl, dissolve yeast in water. Add caraway. In a small saucepan, heat cottage cheese until lukewarm; add baking soda and mix well. Stir into yeast mixture. Add sugar, salt and eggs; mix well. Gradually stir in enough flour to form a soft dough. Cover and let rise in a warm place until doubled, about 1 hour. Stir down. Turn onto a floured surface. Divide into 24 pieces. Place in muffin cups coated with nonstick cooking spray. Cover and let rise until doubled, about 35 minutes. Bake at 350° for 18-20 minutes. Remove to wire racks; brush with melted margarine. **Yield:** 2 dozen.

Cheesy Onion Burger Buns

Dolores Skrout, Summerhill, Pennsylvania

I've copied this recipe for many people—one of the nice things about it is that it also makes very good breadsticks.

5-3/4 to 6-3/4 cups flour	2 cups hot water (120° to 130°)
3 tablespoons sugar	1-1/2 cups shredded reduced-fat cheddar cheese
1-1/2 teaspoons salt	1/4 cup minced onion
2 packages (1/4 ounce *each*) active dry yeast	
2 tablespoons margarine, softened	

In a large mixing bowl, combine 2 cups flour, sugar, salt, yeast and margarine. Gradually add hot water. With electric mixer, beat 2 minutes on medium speed. Add 1 cup flour and mix on high speed 2 minutes. Stir in cheese, onion and enough of the remaining flour to form a soft dough. Turn onto a floured surface; knead until smooth and elastic, about 6-8 minutes. Place dough in a bowl coated with nonstick cooking spray, turning once to grease top. Cover and let rise in a warm place until doubled, about 1 hour. Punch dough down and turn onto a floured surface. Divide dough into 20 equal pieces; shape into smooth balls and place on baking sheets coated with nonstick cooking spray. Cover and let rise in a warm place until doubled, about 45 minutes. Bake at 400° for 15-20 minutes. Remove from the pans and cool on wire racks. **Yield:** 20 hamburger buns.

NUTRITIONAL INFORMATION

Serving Size: 1 roll

Calories: 122
Total Fat: 2 gm
Calories from Fat: 12%
Saturated Fat: trace
Cholesterol: 20 mg
Sodium: 319 mg
Carbohydrate: 21 gm
Protein: 5 gm

NUTRITIONAL INFORMATION

Serving Size: 1 bun

Calories: 172
Total Fat: 3 gm
Calories from Fat: 14%
Saturated Fat: 1 gm
Cholesterol: 5 mg
Sodium: 292 mg
Carbohydrate: 30 gm
Protein: 6 gm

Oatmeal Bread

Connie Moore, Medway, Ohio

(Pictured below)

I was raised on homemade bread, and this recipe couldn't be easier or more satisfying. Sometimes I'll add raisins and cinnamon for a different taste.

1 cup boiling water
1 cup plus 2 tablespoons old-fashioned oats, *divided*
1 package (1/4 ounce) active dry yeast
1/3 cup warm water (110° to 115°)

1/4 cup honey
1 tablespoon margarine
1 teaspoon salt
3 to 3-1/2 cups all-purpose flour
1 teaspoon margarine, melted

In a large mixing bowl, combine boiling water and 1 cup oats; let stand until warm (110°-115°). In a small bowl, dissolve yeast in warm water; add to oat mixture. Add honey, margarine, salt and 2 cups flour; beat until smooth. Add enough remaining flour to form a soft dough. Turn onto a floured surface; knead until smooth and elastic, about 6-8 minutes. Place in a bowl coated with nonstick cooking spray, turning once to grease top. Cover and let rise in a warm place until doubled, about 1 hour. Punch the dough down. Shape into a loaf; place in an 8-in. x 4-in. x 2-in. loaf pan coated with nonstick cooking spray. Brush with melted margarine. Sprinkle with remaining oats. Cover and let rise in a warm place until doubled, about 30 minutes. Bake at 350° for 50-55 minutes or until golden brown. **Yield:** 1 loaf (14 slices).

NUTRITIONAL INFORMATION

Serving Size: 1 slice

Calories: 176
Total Fat: 2 gm
Calories from Fat: 10%
Saturated Fat: trace
Cholesterol: 0
Sodium: 169 mg
Carbohydrate: 33 gm
Protein: 5 gm

Bread Basics

Most breads freeze beautifully. So if you're cooking for one or two, you can serve half a loaf and freeze the other half for later.

Instead of rolling out biscuit dough with a rolling pin, form the dough into a 2-in.-diameter log. Then just cut off slices and bake as usual.

Keep fresh-from-the-oven dinner rolls warmer longer by lining the bread basket with aluminum foil and covering it with a napkin.

Enhance the flavor of quick breads by storing them overnight before slicing and serving.

English Muffin Bread

Jane Zielinski, Rotterdam Junction, New York

(Pictured below)

Many years ago, a good friend gave me her mother's recipe for this delightful bread, and I've made it ever since. It's perfect for a hearty breakfast, especially when topped with your favorite jam.

NUTRITIONAL INFORMATION

Serving Size: 1 slice

Calories: 93
Total Fat: trace
Calories from Fat: 2%
Saturated Fat: trace
Cholesterol: trace
Sodium: 173 mg
Carbohydrate: 19 gm
Protein: 3 gm

5 cups all-purpose flour, *divided*
2 packages (1/4 ounce *each*) active dry yeast
1 tablespoon sugar
2 teaspoons salt
1/4 teaspoon baking soda

2 cups warm skim milk (120° to 130°)
1/2 cup warm water (120° to 130°)
2 tablespoons cornmeal, *divided*

In a large mixing bowl, combine 2 cups flour, yeast, sugar, salt and baking soda. Add warm milk and water; beat on low speed for 30 seconds, scraping bowl occasionally. Beat on high for 3 minutes. Stir in remaining flour (batter will be stiff). *Do not knead.* Coat two 8-in. x 4-in. x 2-in. loaf pans with nonstick cooking spray. Sprinkle pans with cornmeal. Spoon batter into the pans and sprinkle cornmeal on top. Cover and let rise in a warm place until doubled, about 45 minutes. Bake at 375° for 35 minutes or until golden brown. Remove from pans immediately and cool on wire racks. Slice and toast. **Yield:** 2 loaves (14 slices each).

Buttermilk Biscuits

Jean Parsons, Sarver, Pennsylvania

(Pictured above)

These biscuits are made from a recipe that's been in our family for years. They're simple to make and smell so good when baking!

2 cups all-purpose flour
1/2 teaspoon baking soda
2 teaspoons baking powder
1 teaspoon salt
1/4 cup cold shortening
3/4 cup buttermilk

Sift together dry ingredients. Cut in shortening until mixture resembles coarse crumbs. Add buttermilk; stir just until the dough clings together. On a floured surface, knead dough gently, about 10-12 strokes. Roll to 1/2-in. thickness; cut with a 2-in. round biscuit cutter. Place on a baking sheet coated with nonstick cooking spray. Bake at 450° for 12-15 minutes or until lightly browned. **Yield:** 20 biscuits.

NUTRITIONAL INFORMATION

Serving Size: 1 biscuit

Calories: 71
Total Fat: 3 gm
Calories from Fat: 33%
Saturated Fat: 1 gm
Cholesterol: trace
Sodium: 196 mg
Carbohydrate: 10 gm
Protein: 2 gm

Icebox Rolls

Jean Fox, Welch, Minnesota

Although these rolls take a little time to prepare, they're really not all that difficult to make. And there's nothing in the stores that can compare!

1 package (1/4 ounce)
   active dry yeast
2-1/2 cups water, *divided*
1/2 cup shortening
2 eggs
1-1/2 teaspoons salt
1/2 cup sugar
7-1/2 to 8 cups all-purpose
   flour

Dissolve yeast in 1/2 cup warm water (110°-115°). In a large mixing bowl, combine 1 cup boiling water and shortening. Add eggs, salt, sugar, yeast mixture and remaining water. Stir in 1 cup of flour at a time, mixing well after each addition. Add enough flour to form a soft dough. Turn onto a floured surface and knead until smooth and elastic, about 6-8 minutes. Place in a bowl coated with nonstick cooking spray, turning once to grease top. Cover and refrigerate overnight. When ready to bake, form dough into cloverleaf rolls and place in muffin cups coated with nonstick cooking spray. Cover and let rise in a warm place until doubled, about 1 hour. Bake at 375° for 15-20 minutes. **Yield:** 3 dozen.

NUTRITIONAL INFORMATION

Serving Size: 1 roll

Calories: 135
Total Fat: 3 gm
Calories from Fat: 22%
Saturated Fat: 1 gm
Cholesterol: 12 mg
Sodium: 93 mg
Carbohydrate: 23 gm
Protein: 3 gm

Low-Fat Banana Muffins

Marcia Lane, Hemet, California

Instead of oil, this recipe calls for unsweetened applesauce. So not only are these muffins moist and delicious, they're low in fat.

2-1/2 cups all-purpose flour
  2 teaspoons baking powder
  1 teaspoon baking soda
  1 teaspoon ground
    cinnamon
  1 cup sugar

1/2 cup unsweetened
  applesauce
3 egg whites
3 to 4 medium ripe
  bananas, mashed (2 cups)
1 teaspoon vanilla extract

In a large bowl, combine flour, baking powder, baking soda and cinnamon. Combine remaining ingredients; stir into dry ingredients just until moistened. Coat muffin cups with nonstick cooking spray or use paper liners; fill cups two-thirds full. Bake at 350° for 20-25 minutes or until muffins test done. Cool in pan 10 minutes before removing to a wire rack. **Yield:** 15 muffins.

Breakfast Buns

Dorothy McGinnis, West Haven, Connecticut

(Pictured below)

My grandmother taught me to bake these breakfast buns 70 years ago. The batter is like a biscuit dough and can be made up in a short time.

  2 cups all-purpose flour
3/4 cup sugar, *divided*
  1 tablespoon baking powder
  3 tablespoons margarine
  2 eggs

1 teaspoon vanilla extract
1/2 cup skim milk
1 cup raisins
1/2 teaspoon ground
  cinnamon

In a mixing bowl, stir together flour, 1/2 cup sugar and baking powder; cut in margarine. Combine eggs, vanilla and milk; add to dry ingredients and stir just until moistened. Add raisins. Drop by tablespoonfuls onto a baking sheet coated with nonstick cooking spray. Combine the cinnamon and remaining sugar; sprinkle over buns. Bake at 325° for 20-25 minutes or until light golden brown. Serve warm. **Yield:** 16 buns.

Caraway Rye Bread

Millie Feather, Baroda, Michigan

(Pictured above)

It was probably 45 years ago when the thrashers came to dinner at our house and Mother served this bread. Today, every time I bake it, I get nostalgic for those days. My parents had emigrated from Czechoslovakia and couldn't speak English very well. The thrashers hardly talked anyway—they were too busy enjoying Mother's delicious food!

2 packages (1/4 ounce *each*) active dry yeast	1 tablespoon vegetable oil
2 cups warm water (110° to 115°), *divided*	2 teaspoons salt
1/4 cup packed brown sugar	2-1/2 cups rye flour
1 tablespoon caraway seeds	2-3/4 to 3-1/4 cups all-purpose flour

In a large mixing bowl, dissolve yeast in 1/2 cup warm water. Add brown sugar, caraway, oil, salt and remaining water; mix well. Stir in rye flour and 1 cup all-purpose flour; beat until smooth. Add enough remaining all-purpose flour to form a soft dough. Turn onto a floured surface; knead until smooth and elastic, about 6-8 minutes. Place in a bowl coated with nonstick cooking spray, turning once to grease top. Cover and let rise in a warm place until doubled, about 1 hour. Punch dough down; divide in half. Shape each half into a ball; place in two 8-in. round cake pans coated with nonstick cooking spray. Flatten balls to a 6-in. diameter. Cover and let rise until nearly doubled, about 30 minutes. Bake at 375° for 25-30 minutes or until golden brown. **Yield:** 2 loaves.

NUTRITIONAL INFORMATION

Serving Size: 1/8 loaf

Calories: 159
Total Fat: 1 gm
Calories from Fat: 8%
Saturated Fat: trace
Cholesterol: 0
Sodium: 270 mg
Carbohydrate: 33 gm
Protein: 4 gm

FLAVORFUL FINGER FOOD. *Top to bottom: Pork Poor Boy and Picadillo in Pita Bread (both recipes on page 99).*

Hot & Cold Sandwiches

Pork Poor Boy

Fran Sprain, Westfield, Wisconsin

(Pictured at left)

A wealth of flavor stacks up in this stellar sandwich, featuring thin-sliced pork loin roast and a garden medley of fresh spinach, sprouts, cucumber and other toppings. Use leftover roast or fix one especially for this recipe. It's a nice change of pace from ordinary sandwiches.

1 boneless pork loin roast (1 pound), trimmed	1 medium cucumber, thinly sliced
1/2 teaspoon pepper	1 medium green pepper, cut into strips
1 loaf (1 pound) French *or* Italian bread	1/4 pound alfalfa sprouts
4 ounces fresh spinach	1/4 cup fat-free Italian salad dressing
1 medium tomato, sliced	

Rub roast with pepper; place in a shallow roasting pan. Roast, uncovered, at 325° for 45-60 minutes or until meat is no longer pink. Let stand 10 minutes; slice thin. Slice bread lengthwise. On bottom half of bread, layer spinach, meat, tomato, cucumber, green pepper and alfalfa sprouts. Drizzle with dressing. Replace top of bread; slice and serve immediately. **Yield:** 6 servings.

Picadillo in Pita Bread

Shirley Smith, Orange, California

(Pictured at left)

It's fun to watch the expressions of people when they first taste this. Each bite is both sweet and tart! I made many one-dish, top-of-the-stove meals like this while raising three children. After working all day, there wasn't much time to cook.

1 pound ground round	1/2 teaspoon ground cinnamon
1 garlic clove, minced	1/2 teaspoon ground cumin
1/2 medium onion, chopped	1/4 cup raisins
1 small apple, peeled and chopped	3 tablespoons sliced almonds, optional
1/4 cup low-sodium beef broth	3 pita breads, halved
1 tablespoon vinegar	1/2 cup nonfat sour cream
1 can (8 ounces) tomato sauce	Chopped chives, optional

In a large skillet over medium heat, cook beef, garlic and onion until beef is browned and onion is tender; drain. Stir in apple, broth, vinegar, tomato sauce, cinnamon and cumin; simmer, stirring occasionally, until the liquid is absorbed, about 15 minutes. Stir in raisins and almonds if desired. To serve, fill each pita half with beef mixture and top with a dollop of sour cream; sprinkle with chives if desired. **Yield:** 6 sandwiches.

Mexican Carnitas

Patricia Collins, Imbler, Oregon

(Pictured above)

These easy-to-make pork crisps are very popular in Mexico. The secret to this recipe is the citrus and quick frying. In addition to cooking and canning, I enjoy fishing, gardening and crafting.

NUTRITIONAL INFORMATION

Serving Size: 1/16 recipe
(calculated without
cheese and salsa)

Calories: 220
Total Fat: 4 gm
Calories from Fat: 18%
Saturated Fat: 2 gm
Cholesterol: 37 mg
Sodium: 364 mg
Carbohydrate: 28 gm
Protein: 16 gm

1 boneless pork loin roast
(3 pounds), trimmed and
cut into 1-inch cubes
6 large garlic cloves,
minced
1/2 cup fresh cilantro,
chopped
Pepper to taste
3 large oranges, *divided*
1 large lemon
16 fat-free flour tortillas,
warmed
Salsa and shredded fat-free
cheddar cheese, optional

Place meat in a medium-size roasting pan coated with nonstick cooking spray. Sprinkle with garlic, cilantro and pepper. Squeeze the juice from one orange and the lemon over the meat. Slice the remaining oranges and place over the meat. Cover and bake at 350° for about 2 hours or until meat is very tender. With a slotted spoon, remove meat and drain well on paper towels. In a skillet coated with nonstick cooking spray, cook meat 1 lb. at a time until brown and crispy. Serve warm in flour tortillas; garnish with salsa and cheese if desired. **Yield:** 16 servings.

Open-Faced Tuna Sandwiches

Christine Eliza, Miami, Florida

A pantry standby, tuna takes on a new dimension in this appealing open-faced sandwich, and chopped apple adds a nice crunch.

1 can (6-1/8 ounces) light
   tuna in water, drained
   and flaked
1 cup chopped unpeeled
   apple
3 tablespoons finely
   chopped onion

1/4 cup light mayonnaise
2 teaspoons lemon juice
1/8 teaspoon pepper
4 slices bread, toasted
4 thin slices (2 ounces)
   Monterey Jack cheese

In a bowl, combine tuna, apple, onion, mayonnaise, lemon juice and pepper. Spread on bread; top with a cheese slice. Broil 4 in. from the heat for 4 minutes or until cheese is melted. **Yield:** 4 sandwiches.

NUTRITIONAL INFORMATION

Serving Size: 1 sandwich

Calories: 255
Total Fat: 11 gm
Calories from Fat: 39%
Saturated Fat: 4 gm
Cholesterol: 29 mg
Sodium: 493 mg
Carbohydrate: 21 gm
Protein: 17 gm

Top-Dog Hot Dogs

Kathy Burggraaf, Plainfield Township, Michigan

Our sons came up with this tasty recipe when they were 10 and 7. It's easy to get them to eat when they plan the menu!

8 fat-free hot dogs
8 hot dog buns, split
1 jar (10 ounces) hot dog
   relish
1 small green pepper,
   chopped

1 small onion, chopped
1 small tomato, chopped
   and seeded
Shredded part-skim mozzarella
   cheese, optional

Cook hot dogs according to package directions. Place in buns; top with relish, green pepper, onion and tomato. Sprinkle with mozzarella cheese if desired. **Yield:** 8 sandwiches.

NUTRITIONAL INFORMATION

Serving Size: 1 sandwich
(calculated without cheese)

Calories: 199
Total Fat: 3 gm
Calories from Fat: 12%
Saturated Fat: 1 gm
Cholesterol: 20 mg
Sodium: 892 mg
Carbohydrate: 34 gm
Protein: 11 gm

Waldorf Sandwiches

Darlene Sutton, Arvada, Colorado

The fresh fruity filling for this sandwich is a nice variation of a classic. My clan loves the cool and creamy combination, so I serve these often.

1 can (20 ounces) crushed
   unsweetened pineapple
3 cups cubed cooked
   chicken breast
1 medium red apple,
   chopped
1 medium green apple,
   chopped

1 cup sliced celery
1 cup light mayonnaise
1 tablespoon poppy seeds
1 teaspoon sugar
1 teaspoon grated lemon
   peel
1/2 teaspoon vanilla extract
16 hard rolls, split

Drain pineapple, pressing out excess juice and reserving 1/4 cup. In a large bowl, combine pineapple, chicken, apples and celery. In a small bowl, combine mayonnaise, poppy seeds, sugar, lemon peel, vanilla and reserved pineapple juice. Pour over chicken mixture and toss well. Chill. Serve on rolls. **Yield:** 16 sandwiches.

NUTRITIONAL INFORMATION

Serving Size: 1 sandwich

Calories: 268
Total Fat: 9 gm
Calories from Fat: 31%
Saturated Fat: 2 gm
Cholesterol: 16 mg
Sodium: 394 mg
Carbohydrate: 35 gm
Protein: 10 gm

Curried Chicken Pita Pockets

Vicky Whitehead, Norman, Oklahoma

I like to prepare these sandwiches for special luncheons. Everyone who tries them raves about the refreshing combination of tender chicken, flavorful curry and cool grapes.

3/4 cup fat-free mayonnaise
1 teaspoon soy sauce
1 teaspoon lemon juice
1/2 teaspoon curry powder
1 small onion, finely chopped

2-1/2 cups cubed cooked chicken breast
1-1/2 cups halved seedless green grapes
3/4 cup chopped celery
1/4 cup sliced almonds
10 pita breads, halved

In a large bowl, combine the first five ingredients. Stir in chicken, grapes and celery; refrigerate. Just before serving, add almonds. Stuff about 1/4 cup into each pita half. **Yield:** 10 servings.

NUTRITIONAL INFORMATION

Serving Size: 2 halves

Calories: 251
Total Fat: 4 gm
Calories from Fat: 13%
Saturated Fat: 1 gm
Cholesterol: 21 mg
Sodium: 504 mg
Carbohydrate: 42 gm
Protein: 12 gm

Open-Faced Turkey Sandwiches

Debra Rae, Franklin, Wisconsin

These special sandwiches are great for lunch or supper. I enjoy being creative with simple meals. Time spent in the kitchen is kept to a minimum when this entree is on the menu.

4 teaspoons light cream cheese, softened
2 slices whole wheat bread, toasted
2 slices (1 ounce *each*) reduced-fat cheddar cheese

4 ounces thinly sliced cooked turkey breast
6 fresh spinach leaves, shredded

Spread cream cheese on toast. Layer cheese, turkey and spinach over cream cheese. Broil until cheese is melted. Serve immediately. **Yield:** 2 sandwiches.

NUTRITIONAL INFORMATION

Serving Size: 1 sandwich

Calories: 293
Total Fat: 12 gm
Calories from Fat: 38%
Saturated Fat: 6 gm
Cholesterol: 68 mg
Sodium: 468 mg
Carbohydrate: 16 gm
Protein: 30 gm

"Humpty-Dumpty" Sandwiches

Cheryl Miller, Fort Collins, Colorado

Instead of ordinary egg salad, spark up lunches with this hearty sandwich.

1 hard-cooked egg, chopped
1 celery rib, chopped
1/3 cup low-fat cottage cheese
1/4 cup shredded fat-free cheddar cheese

1-1/2 teaspoons spicy brown mustard
1/8 teaspoon pepper
4 slices whole wheat bread
Lettuce leaves, optional

Combine the first six ingredients; spread on two slices of bread. Top with lettuce if desired and remaining bread. **Yield:** 2 sandwiches.

NUTRITIONAL INFORMATION

Serving Size: 1 sandwich

Calories: 268
Total Fat: 6 gm
Calories from Fat: 20%
Saturated Fat: 2 gm
Cholesterol: 109 mg
Sodium: 729 mg
Carbohydrate: 35 gm
Protein: 20 gm

Italian Beef Sandwiches

Marjorie Libby, Madison, Wisconsin

(Pictured below)

I love having friends over for a "winter picnic" each year, and these sandwiches are really a hit with potato salad and baked beans. The beef freezes well, which makes it handy to have on hand for last-minute meals.

1 beef sirloin tip roast
   (4 pounds)
3 onions, thinly sliced
1/4 teaspoon onion powder
1/4 teaspoon garlic powder
1 teaspoon dried oregano
2 teaspoons Italian
   seasoning
1 teaspoon salt-free
   seasoning blend
1 teaspoon dried basil
3 low-sodium beef bouillon
   cubes
7 hot banana peppers,
   seeded and sliced
24 hard rolls, split

In a deep baking pan, place roast and 1 in. of water. Cover with onions. Bake, covered, at 350° for 1-1/2 hours or until meat is tender. Remove meat from baking pan; reserve and chill broth. Refrigerate meat until firm. Skim fat from broth. In a medium saucepan, combine broth and remaining ingredients except rolls. Bring to a boil; reduce heat and simmer 10 minutes. Meanwhile, cut meat into thin slices; place in a 13-in. x 9-in. x 2-in. baking pan. Pour broth mixture over meat. Cover and refrigerate for 24 hours. Reheat, covered, at 325° for 1 hour. Serve on hard rolls. **Yield:** 24 sandwiches.

NUTRITIONAL INFORMATION

Serving Size: 1 sandwich

Calories: 286
Total Fat: 6 gm
Calories from Fat: 19%
Saturated Fat: 2 gm
Cholesterol: 50 mg
Sodium: 400 mg
Carbohydrate: 29 gm
Protein: 27 gm

Scrum-Delicious Burgers

Wendy Sommers, West Chicago, Illinois

(Pictured below)

I'm not sure where this recipe originated, but it's one of my family's summertime favorites. I usually serve these juicy burgers when we have company. The guests rave about the flavorful cheesy topping. It's fun to serve a burger that's a little more special.

1-1/2 pounds ground round
3 tablespoons finely chopped onion
Dash garlic powder
1/2 teaspoon pepper
6 turkey bacon strips, cooked and crumbled
1/3 cup canned sliced mushrooms
1 cup (4 ounces) shredded reduced-fat cheddar cheese
1/4 cup reduced-fat mayonnaise
8 hamburger buns, split
Lettuce leaves and tomato slices, optional

In a medium bowl, combine beef, onion, garlic powder and pepper; mix well. Shape into eight patties, 3/4 in. thick. In a small bowl, combine the bacon, mushrooms, cheese and mayonnaise; refrigerate. Grill burgers over medium-hot coals for 8-10 minutes or until no longer pink, turning once. During the last 3 minutes, spoon a scant 1/4 cup of the cheese mixture onto each burger. Serve on buns with lettuce and tomato if desired. **Yield:** 8 sandwiches.

Salsa Sloppy Joes

Mary Banninga, Austin, Minnesota

I was looking for a way to spice up my already quick-and-easy sloppy joe recipe. So I decided to add a little salsa. Everyone who's tried this recipe really likes the results.

3 pounds ground round
1 cup chopped onion
1 jar (16 ounces) salsa

1 can (15 ounces) sloppy
  joe sauce
20 hamburger buns, split

In a large skillet, brown beef and onion; drain. Stir in salsa and sloppy joe sauce; bring to a boil. Reduce heat; cover and simmer for 20 minutes. Spoon about 1/2 cup onto each bun. **Yield:** 20 sandwiches.

Hot Chicken Salad Sandwiches

Mary Jo Vander West, Grant, Michigan

Adding light process American cheese to chicken salad and heating in the oven makes these sandwiches extra special.

2 cups diced cooked
  chicken breast
1/4 pound light process
  American cheese, diced
1 tablespoon pickle relish
1/4 cup light mayonnaise

2 tablespoons chopped
  onion
2 tablespoons chopped
  green pepper
8 kaiser rolls, split

In a bowl, combine the first six ingredients; mix well. Spoon about 1/3 cup onto each roll. Wrap each tightly in foil. Bake at 300° for 20-30 minutes or until heated through. **Yield:** 8 sandwiches.

Sausage and Cabbage Sandwiches

Elaine Fenton, Prescott, Arizona

For a country-style lunch that's sure to satisfy hearty appetites, try these sandwiches. Folks love the tasty combination of ingredients.

1 pound bulk turkey
  sausage
7 cups shredded cabbage
1 medium onion, chopped
1 medium sweet red pepper,
  thinly sliced

1/2 cup water
1/2 teaspoon sugar
1/4 cup light sour cream
12 pita breads, halved

In a large skillet, brown sausage; drain. Add cabbage, onion, red pepper, water and sugar; mix well. Cover and cook for 20 minutes or until the vegetables are tender, stirring occasionally. Stir in sour cream and heat through. Spoon into pita halves. **Yield:** 12 servings.

Poor Boy Sandwich

Violet Beard, Marshall, Illinois

The original poor boy sandwiches called for oysters. But I made this meal more healthy and economical by substituting tuna instead. The horseradish in this recipe really wakes up an ordinary tuna sandwich.

2 French *or* submarine rolls
2 tablespoons fat-free margarine
1/4 teaspoon celery seed
1 can (6 ounces) light tuna in water, drained and flaked
1/4 cup chopped celery

1/4 cup chopped fresh parsley
3 tablespoons fat-free mayonnaise
1 tablespoon horseradish
1/2 teaspoon grated lemon peel
1/8 teaspoon pepper

Cut a thin slice off top of roll; set aside. Hollow out center, reserving 1/2 cup of bread and leaving a 1/4-in. shell. Combine margarine and celery seed; spread over inside of roll and on cut surface of top. Combine remaining ingredients and reserved bread; spoon into roll. Replace top. **Yield:** 2 sandwiches.

Potluck Pockets

Debbie Jones, California, Maryland

My husband taught me how to make these fun tasty sandwiches. They take little time to prepare, and we enjoy them all through the year. They don't last long on a buffet table.

1 pound ground round
1/2 cup chopped onion
1/2 cup chopped green pepper
2 tablespoons Worcestershire sauce
2 tablespoons light soy sauce
2 teaspoons garlic powder
1 teaspoon ground cumin
1/2 teaspoon Italian seasoning
6 pita breads, halved

2 medium tomatoes, diced
3 cups shredded lettuce
SAUCE:
1/2 cup light soy sauce
1/4 cup vinegar
2 tablespoons Worcestershire sauce
1/2 teaspoon onion powder
1/2 teaspoon garlic powder
1/2 teaspoon Italian seasoning
Dash pepper

In a skillet, brown beef, onion and green pepper; drain. Add Worcestershire sauce, soy sauce, garlic powder, cumin and Italian seasoning; mix well. Simmer for 5-10 minutes. In a small saucepan, bring all the sauce ingredients to a boil. Reduce heat and simmer for 5-10 minutes. Spoon meat mixture into pita halves; top with sauce, tomatoes and lettuce. **Yield:** 12 servings.

Chicken Pita Sandwiches

Glenda Schwarz, Morden, Manitoba

(Pictured above)

When company is coming for lunch, this is my favorite sandwich to make, since it looks and tastes a bit fancy. Even kids like it because of the crunchy green pepper and onions and creamy filling.

1 package (8 ounces)
   fat-free cream cheese,
   softened
3 tablespoons skim milk
1 tablespoon lemon juice
2 cups cubed cooked
   chicken breast
1/2 cup chopped green pepper

2 tablespoons chopped
   green onions
1 teaspoon ground mustard
1/2 teaspoon dried thyme
1/8 teaspoon pepper
3 tablespoons chopped
   walnuts, optional
3 pita breads, halved
Alfalfa sprouts

In a mixing bowl, beat cream cheese, milk and lemon juice until smooth. Stir in the chicken, green pepper, onions, mustard, thyme and pepper; refrigerate. Just before serving, stir in the walnuts if desired. Spoon about 1/2 cup filling into each pita half; top with alfalfa sprouts. **Yield:** 6 servings.

NUTRITIONAL INFORMATION

Serving Size: 1 half
(calculated without walnuts)

Calories: 187
Total Fat: 2 gm
Calories from Fat: 9%
Saturated Fat: trace
Cholesterol: 31 mg
Sodium: 419 mg
Carbohydrate: 20 gm
Protein: 20 gm

Santa Fe Chicken Heroes

Bonnie Link, Goose Creek, South Carolina

(Pictured above)

My son discovered this recipe and shared it with me because he knows I'm fond of easy and tasty meals from the grill. The Southwestern seasonings make these sandwiches spicy and very flavorful.

6 boneless skinless chicken breast halves
1/4 teaspoon pepper
1/4 teaspoon crushed red pepper flakes
1/4 teaspoon chili powder
6 slices part-skim mozzarella cheese

6 French *or* Italian rolls, split
2 tablespoons fat-free margarine
Lettuce leaves and tomato slices
Salsa *or* picante sauce, optional

Pound chicken breasts slightly to flatten evenly. Spray both sides with nonstick cooking spray. Combine seasonings; sprinkle on both sides of chicken. Grill over medium-hot coals for 6-8 minutes; turn and grill 4-6 minutes more or until chicken is tender and no longer pink. Top with cheese; allow to melt, about 2 minutes. Grill rolls just until toasted; spread with margarine. Place chicken on rolls; top with lettuce, tomato and salsa or picante sauce if desired. **Yield:** 6 sandwiches.

Salmon Salad Sandwiches

Yvonne Shust, Shoal Lake, Manitoba

These are perfect to pack in your kids' lunch boxes when they can't face another boring sandwich. We love the salmon, cream cheese and dill tucked inside a crusty roll. The carrot and celery add a nice crunch.

3 ounces fat-free cream
  cheese, softened
1 tablespoon fat-free
  mayonnaise
1 tablespoon lemon juice
1 teaspoon dill weed
1/8 teaspoon pepper

1 can (6 ounces) pink
  salmon, drained, skin
  and bones removed
1/2 cup shredded carrot
1/2 cup chopped celery
Lettuce leaves, optional
2 whole wheat buns,
  split

In a mixing bowl, beat cream cheese, mayonnaise, lemon juice, dill and pepper until smooth. Add the salmon, carrot and celery; mix well. Place a lettuce leaf if desired and about 1/2 cup salmon salad on each bun. **Yield:** 2 sandwiches.

NUTRITIONAL INFORMATION

Serving Size: 1 sandwich

Calories: 263
Total Fat: 9 gm
Calories from Fat: 29%
Saturated Fat: 2 gm
Cholesterol: 57 mg
Sodium: 757 mg
Carbohydrate: 22 gm
Protein: 26 gm

Cool Cucumber Sandwich

Denise Baumert, Dalhart, Texas

This is one of my favorite summertime sandwiches. It's refreshing and a great way to use crisp garden cucumbers sliced very thin.

1 tablespoon fat-free ranch
  salad dressing
2 slices whole wheat bread,
  toasted

12 thin cucumber slices
2 bacon strips, cooked and
  drained
1 tomato slice

Spread salad dressing on one side of each slice of toast. Layer cucumber, bacon and tomato on one slice; top with second slice. **Yield:** 1 sandwich.

NUTRITIONAL INFORMATION

Serving Size: 1 sandwich

Calories: 269
Total Fat: 9 gm
Calories from Fat: 30%
Saturated Fat: 3 gm
Cholesterol: 11 mg
Sodium: 703 mg
Carbohydrate: 38 gm
Protein: 11 gm

Dilly Roast Beef Sandwich

Betsey Bishop, Jeffersonton, Virginia

The seasoned cream cheese spread is a nice change from ordinary mustard and makes this sandwich something extra special.

2 tablespoons fat-free
  cream cheese, softened
Pinch *each* dill weed, garlic
  powder and pepper
2 slices whole wheat bread

1-1/2 ounces thinly sliced
  cooked lean roast beef
3 tomato slices
Alfalfa sprouts

Combine cream cheese, dill, garlic powder and pepper; spread on one slice of bread. Top with beef, tomato, sprouts and remaining bread. **Yield:** 1 sandwich.

NUTRITIONAL INFORMATION

Serving Size: 1 sandwich

Calories: 289
Total Fat: 6 gm
Calories from Fat: 17%
Saturated Fat: 2 gm
Cholesterol: 32 mg
Sodium: 561 mg
Carbohydrate: 37 gm
Protein: 25 gm

Dandy Ham Sandwiches

Mrs. Wallace Carlson, Two Harbors, Minnesota

With its nutty flavor, caraway perks up regular ham salad sandwiches.

2 cups (8 ounces) shredded reduced-fat cheddar cheese
1-1/2 cups ground fully cooked low-fat ham
1/2 cup finely chopped onion
1/3 cup fat-free French salad dressing
2 tablespoons prepared mustard
4 teaspoons caraway seeds
5 hamburger buns, split

Combine the first six ingredients; mix well. Spread over cut side of buns. Place on a baking sheet coated with nonstick cooking spray. Bake at 350° for 15-20 minutes or until the cheese is melted. **Yield:** 10 sandwiches.

Hearty Beef Sandwiches

Peggy Pruska, Hales Corners, Wisconsin

Perfect for summer, these beefy rolls are a winner whenever you serve them. A zesty cream cheese-horseradish filling cheers on flavorful roast beef.

1 small apple, finely chopped
2 teaspoons lemon juice
3 ounces fat-free cream cheese, softened
1 tablespoon skim milk
1 tablespoon prepared horseradish
2 tablespoons chopped walnuts
6 kaiser rolls, split
6 lettuce leaves
12 ounces thinly sliced cooked lean roast beef
2 tablespoons sliced green onions

Toss apple with lemon juice. In a small bowl, combine cream cheese, milk and horseradish; add apple and walnuts and mix well. Spread onto cut side of roll tops. On each roll bottom, place the lettuce, roast beef and green onions; replace tops. **Yield:** 6 sandwiches.

Pronto Pizza Burgers

Karen Kruse, Gahanna, Ohio

These zesty, satisfying sandwiches have a true pizza taste my family loves.

1 pound ground turkey breast
1/3 cup grated Parmesan cheese
1 tablespoon chopped onion
1 tablespoon tomato paste
1 teaspoon dried oregano
1/4 teaspoon pepper
4 English muffins, split
8 tomato slices
1 cup (4 ounces) shredded part-skim mozzarella cheese
Additional oregano, optional

In a bowl, mix turkey, Parmesan cheese, onion, tomato paste, oregano and pepper just until combined. Toast the muffins in broiler until lightly browned. Divide meat mixture among muffins. Broil 4 in. from the heat for 8-10 minutes or until meat is cooked. Top with tomato and cheese. Return to broiler until cheese is melted. Sprinkle with oregano if desired. Serve immediately. **Yield:** 4 servings.

Cajun Burgers

Julie Culbertson, Bensalem, Pennsylvania

(Pictured below)

I found the original recipe for these burgers in a cookbook, then added and subtracted ingredients until they suited my family's taste for spicy foods. These are always on the menu for backyard cookouts.

CAJUN SEASONING BLEND:
- 3 tablespoons ground cumin
- 3 tablespoons dried oregano
- 1 tablespoon garlic powder
- 1 tablespoon paprika
- 1 teaspoon cayenne pepper

BURGERS:
- 1 pound ground round
- 1/4 cup finely chopped onion
- 1 teaspoon Cajun Seasoning Blend (at left)
- 1/2 teaspoon hot pepper sauce
- 1/2 teaspoon dried thyme
- 1/4 teaspoon dried basil
- 1 garlic clove, minced
- 4 hamburger buns, split
- Sauteed onions, optional

Combine all seasoning blend ingredients in a small bowl or resealable plastic bag; mix well. In a bowl, combine the first seven burger ingredients; shape into four patties. Cook in a skillet or grill over medium-hot coals for 4-5 minutes per side or until burgers reach desired doneness. Serve on buns; top with sauteed onions if desired. Store remaining seasoning blend in an airtight container. **Yield:** 4 sandwiches.

NUTRITIONAL INFORMATION

Serving Size: 1 sandwich
(calculated without sauteed onions)

Calories: 335
Total Fat: 9 gm
Calories from Fat: 25%
Saturated Fat: 3 gm
Cholesterol: 78 mg
Sodium: 445 mg
Carbohydrate: 24 gm
Protein: 37 gm

Ham and Cheese Calzones

Shelby Marino, Neptune Beach, Florida

(Pictured below)

This sort of inside-out pizza is something I concocted one evening when I had leftover baked ham and needed to fix something quick and simple. My husband loved it—so did all his friends when he took some to work for lunch.

NUTRITIONAL INFORMATION

Serving Size: 1/8 recipe
(calculated without Parmesan
cheese and spaghetti sauce)

Calories: 314
Total Fat: 8 gm
Calories from Fat: 22%
Saturated Fat: trace
Cholesterol: 32 mg
Sodium: 938 mg
Carbohydrate: 35 gm
Protein: 24 gm

2 tubes (10 ounces *each*) refrigerated pizza crust
1 cup light ricotta cheese
2 cups diced fully cooked low-fat ham
2 cups (8 ounces) shredded part-skim mozzarella cheese

Dried basil
Shredded Parmesan cheese, optional
Meatless spaghetti sauce, warmed, optional

Unroll one pizza crust, stretching gently to make a 14-in. x 11-in. rectangle. Spread half of the ricotta on half of the dough lengthwise, to within 1 in. of the edges. Sprinkle with half of the ham and mozzarella. Fold unfilled side of dough over filled half and press edges together firmly to seal. Transfer to a baking sheet coated with nonstick cooking spray. Repeat with remaining crust and filling ingredients. Bake at 400° for 20-25 minutes or until golden brown. Sprinkle with basil and Parmesan if desired. Slice into serving-size pieces. Serve with spaghetti sauce for dipping if desired. **Yield:** 8 servings.

Pepper Lovers' BLT

Carol Reaves, San Antonio, Texas

One of my family's favorite sandwiches is a BLT, and they especially love this one because it combines the tantalizing tastes of bacon, fresh tomatoes and hot peppers.

1/4 cup fat-free mayonnaise	6 tablespoons shredded fat-free sharp cheddar cheese
1 tablespoon diced pimientos	
1/8 teaspoon coarsely ground pepper	4 pickled jalapeno peppers thinly sliced
1/4 teaspoon hot pepper sauce	6 turkey bacon strips, cooked and drained
8 slices sourdough bread, toasted	8 tomato slices
	4 lettuce leaves
4 teaspoons Dijon-mayonnaise blend	8 ounces thinly sliced cooked chicken breast

In a small bowl, combine mayonnaise, pimientos, pepper and hot pepper sauce; mix well. Chill for at least 1 hour. Spread four slices of toast with Dijon-mayonnaise blend. Sprinkle with cheese; top with jalapenos, bacon, tomato, lettuce and chicken. Spread mayonnaise mixture on remaining slices of toast; place over chicken. **Yield:** 4 sandwiches.

Stroganoff Sandwich

Gretchen Kuipers, Platte, South Dakota

This sandwich can easily be prepared at a moment's notice. It gives tried-and-true ground beef a tasty new zing! I often serve this to my husband when he comes in from working in the field.

1 pound ground round	1 loaf (1 pound) French bread, halved lengthwise
1/4 cup chopped onion	
1/4 teaspoon garlic powder	2 medium tomatoes, thinly sliced
Pepper to taste	
1 teaspoon Worcestershire sauce	1 medium green pepper, cut into rings
1 can (4 ounces) sliced mushrooms, drained	1 cup (4 ounces) shredded reduced-fat cheddar cheese
1 cup (8 ounces) light sour cream	

In a skillet coated with nonstick cooking spray, cook beef with onion; drain. Add garlic powder, pepper and Worcestershire sauce. Remove from the heat and stir in mushrooms and sour cream; set aside. Place bread with the cut side up on a baking sheet; broil until light golden brown. Reset oven to 375°. Spread beef mixture over bread; top with tomatoes, pepper rings and cheese. Bake for 5 minutes or until the cheese melts. Serve immediately. **Yield:** 8 servings.

Speedy Beef Sandwiches

Ruth Page, Hillsborough, North Carolina

I keep the ingredients for these simple sandwiches on hand so that I can whip up a snack in a matter of minutes.

4 slices French bread
(3/4 inch thick)
Prepared mustard, optional
1/2 pound ground round
1/4 cup skim milk

1 tablespoon minced onion
1 tablespoon steak sauce
Dash garlic powder
1/4 teaspoon pepper

In a broiler, toast one side of the bread. Spread untoasted sides with mustard if desired. In a small bowl, combine remaining ingredients; spread evenly over mustard side of bread. Broil 6 in. from the heat for 5-7 minutes or until beef reaches desired doneness. **Yield:** 2 servings.

Calico Burgers

Maryann Bondonese, Nazareth, Pennsylvania

On summer Sundays when our children were young, we'd often invite guests for cookouts. These unique burgers were always a hit. They're still a family favorite throughout the week!

1-1/2 pounds ground round
1/2 cup cooked rice
1/4 cup chopped onion
1/4 cup chopped green pepper
1 tablespoon dried parsley
flakes
1/4 teaspoon garlic powder
Dash pepper

2/3 cup water
1/4 cup ketchup
3 tablespoons chili sauce
1 teaspoon Worcestershire
sauce
1/4 teaspoon dried basil
6 hamburger buns, split

In bowl, combine the first seven ingredients; mix well. Shape into six patties. Grill over hot coals until meat is no longer pink, about 15-20 minutes. In a saucepan, combine water, ketchup, chili sauce, Worcestershire sauce and basil; simmer for 15 minutes. Serve burgers on buns with sauce. **Yield:** 6 servings.

Scrumptious Turkey Sandwich

Linda Nilsen, Anoka, Minnesota

Making brown-bag lunches interesting and tasty can be a challenge. This flavorful recipe is just the way to do it!

2 tablespoons jellied
cranberry sauce
2 slices whole wheat bread
1 ounce thinly sliced
cooked turkey breast

1/3 cup alfalfa sprouts
2 tablespoons softened
fat-free cream cheese

Spread cranberry sauce on one slice of bread; top with turkey and alfalfa sprouts. Spread cream cheese on the other slice of bread and place over sprouts. **Yield:** 1 sandwich.

Barbecued Hot Dogs

Joyce Koehler, Watertown, Wisconsin

(Pictured above)

I grew up in a large family, and we never complained if Mom made these terrific hot dogs often for birthday parties and other family gatherings. You'll find that kids and grown-ups devour these…good thing they're easy to make.

NUTRITIONAL INFORMATION

Serving Size: 1 sandwich

Calories: 216
Total Fat: 4 gm
Calories from Fat: 16%
Saturated Fat: 1 gm
Cholesterol: 25 mg
Sodium: 1,051 mg
Carbohydrate: 32 gm
Protein: 13 gm

3/4 cup chopped onion
1-1/2 cups chopped celery
1-1/2 cups ketchup
3/4 cup water
1/3 cup lemon juice
3 tablespoons brown sugar
3 tablespoons vinegar
1 tablespoon Worcestershire sauce
1 tablespoon prepared mustard
20 reduced-fat hot dogs
20 hot dog buns, split

In a saucepan coated with nonstick cooking spray, saute onion over medium heat until tender. Add celery, ketchup, water, lemon juice, sugar, vinegar, Worcestershire sauce and mustard; bring to a boil. Reduce heat; cover and simmer for 30 minutes. Cut three 1/4-in.-deep slits on each side of hot dogs; place in a 2-1/2-qt. baking dish coated with nonstick cooking spray. Pour the sauce over the hot dogs. Cover and bake at 350° for 40-45 minutes or until heated through. Serve on buns. **Yield:** 20 sandwiches.

Oregon Muffaleta

Marilou Robinson, Portland, Oregon

Traditional muffaleta is made extra special with the addition of apples, blueberries and cranberries. This is a meaty make-ahead meal that's perfect for picnics and potlucks.

1 small tart apple, chopped
1/2 cup fresh blueberries
1/2 cup thinly sliced celery
1/2 cup dried cranberries
1/2 cup thinly sliced green onions
1/2 cup orange juice
2 tablespoons vegetable oil
2 tablespoons cider vinegar
1/2 teaspoon pepper
1/8 teaspoon salt
1 round loaf (2 pounds) Italian bread
3/4 pound thinly sliced fully cooked low-fat ham, *divided*
1/2 pound thinly sliced reduced-fat cheddar cheese

In a large bowl, combine the first 10 ingredients; chill for at least 8 hours, stirring occasionally. Cut a thin slice off the top of the bread; hollow out the bottom half, leaving a 1-in. shell. (Discard removed bread or save for another use.) Drain 1/4 cup liquid from the fruit mixture; brush on inside of bread shell. In bottom of bread shell, layer half of the ham, 1-1/4 cups fruit mixture, cheese, remaining fruit mixture and remaining ham. Replace bread top and wrap tightly with plastic wrap. Chill for at least 2 hours. Remove from the refrigerator 30 minutes before serving. Cut into wedges. **Yield:** 10 servings.

Chicken Burgers

Myrna Huebert, Tofield, Alberta

I love to cook and rarely work from any recipes. My family always wonders what's cooking in the kitchen! They really enjoy these herb-flavored chicken burgers.

1/2 cup chopped onion
1-1/2 pounds cooked chicken breast, ground *or* finely chopped
1-1/2 cups dry bread crumbs
1/2 cup grated Parmesan cheese
Egg substitute equivalent to 3 eggs
2 tablespoons dried parsley flakes
1 teaspoon *each* poultry seasoning, dried thyme and ground mustard
1/2 teaspoon rubbed sage
1/2 teaspoon pepper
3/4 cup skim milk
2 teaspoons cooking oil
8 hamburger buns, split
Lettuce leaves and sliced tomatoes

In a large skillet coated with nonstick cooking spray, saute onion until tender. Place in a large bowl. Add chicken, crumbs, Parmesan, egg substitute, herbs and seasonings; mix well. Stir in milk. Shape into eight patties. In the same skillet, cook patties in oil for 5 minutes or until browned on each side and heated through. Serve on buns with lettuce and tomatoes. **Yield:** 8 sandwiches.

Barbecued Beef Sandwiches

Denise Marshall, Bagley, Wisconsin

(Pictured below)

The great thing about this recipe—especially for non-cabbage lovers!—is that you can't taste the cabbage in the meat. Yet, at the same time, it adds a nice heartiness and moistness to it.

2 pounds boneless round
   steak, trimmed and cubed
2 cups water
4 cups shredded cabbage
1/2 cup barbecue sauce
1/2 cup ketchup
1/3 cup Worcestershire sauce
1 tablespoon prepared
   horseradish
1 tablespoon prepared
   mustard
10 hamburger buns, split

In a covered Dutch oven or saucepan, simmer beef in water for 1-1/2 hours or until tender. Drain cooking liquid, reserving 3/4 cup. Cool beef; shred and return to the Dutch oven. Add cabbage, barbecue sauce, ketchup, Worcestershire sauce, horseradish, mustard and the reserved cooking liquid. Cover and simmer for 1 hour. Serve warm on buns. **Yield:** 10 sandwiches.

NUTRITIONAL INFORMATION

Serving Size: 1 sandwich

Calories: 279
Total Fat: 7 gm
Calories from Fat: 22%
Saturated Fat: 2 gm
Cholesterol: 51 mg
Sodium: 716 mg
Carbohydrate: 32 gm
Protein: 21 gm

Reuben Loaf

Elizabeth Eissler, Osage City, Kansas

(Pictured above)

When I make this bread, I always have to bake two loaves so that everyone gets a taste! It's especially good in winter, served along with a hearty soup as the main course. It looks so pretty sliced and arranged on a platter, too.

3-1/4 to 3-3/4 cups all-purpose
    flour
  1 package (1/4 ounce)
    quick-rise yeast
  1 tablespoon sugar
  1 tablespoon margarine,
    softened
  1 teaspoon salt
  1 cup warm water
    (120° to 130°)

1/4 cup reduced-fat
    Thousand Island salad
    dressing
  6 ounces thinly sliced
    reduced-fat corned beef
  4 ounces sliced reduced-fat
    Swiss cheese
  1 can (8 ounces)
    sauerkraut, drained
  1 egg white, beaten
Caraway seeds, optional

NUTRITIONAL INFORMATION

Serving Size: 1/8 recipe

Calories: 298
Total Fat: 6 gm
Calories from Fat: 18%
Saturated Fat: 2 gm
Cholesterol: 32 mg
Sodium: 835 mg
Carbohydrate: 45 gm
Protein: 16 gm

In a mixing bowl, combine 2-1/4 cups flour, yeast, sugar, margarine and salt. Stir in warm water; mix until a soft dough forms. Add remaining flour if necessary. Turn onto a lightly floured surface; knead until smooth, about 4 minutes. On a baking sheet coated with nonstick cooking spray, roll dough to a 14-in. x 10-in. rectangle. Spread dressing down center third of dough. Top with layers of beef, cheese and sauerkraut. Make cuts from filling to edges of dough 1 in. apart on both sides of the filling. Alternating sides, fold the strips at an angle across filling. Cover dough and let rise in a warm place for 15 minutes. Brush with egg white and sprinkle with caraway seeds if desired. Bake at 400° for 25 minutes or until lightly browned. Serve immediately; refrigerate leftovers. **Yield:** 8 servings.

Tomato Cheese Melt

Suzanne Winters, Middletown, Delaware

I love this as a late-night snack, but it also goes great with a bowl of soup at lunch. The cayenne pepper gives it just a bit of zip. It tastes and looks great.

1 English muffin, split	2 tomato slices
1/4 cup shredded reduced-fat cheddar cheese	1 tablespoon shredded Parmesan cheese
1/8 teaspoon cayenne pepper	

On each muffin half, sprinkle half of the cheddar cheese and cayenne. Top with a tomato slice and Parmesan cheese. Broil 6 in. from the heat for 4-5 minutes or until cheese is bubbly. **Yield:** 2 sandwiches.

NUTRITIONAL INFORMATION

Serving Size: 1 sandwich

Calories: 131
Total Fat: 5 gm
Calories from Fat: 31%
Saturated Fat: 3 gm
Cholesterol: 12 mg
Sodium: 192 mg
Carbohydrate: 14 gm
Protein: 9 gm

Philly Steak Sandwiches

Sheryl Christian, Watertown, Wisconsin

Even though everyone in our family's always coming and going, I feel it's important to sit down together to a meal like this once a week.

1/2 pound fresh mushrooms, sliced	6 hoagie rolls, split
2 medium onions, thinly sliced	6 slices (6 ounces) part-skim mozzarella cheese
1 medium green pepper, sliced	4 low-sodium beef bouillon cubes
12 ounces thinly sliced cooked lean roast beef	2 cups water

In a skillet coated with nonstick cooking spray, saute mushrooms, onions and green pepper until tender. Divide beef among rolls. Top with vegetables and cheese; replace roll tops. Place on an ungreased baking sheet; cover with foil. Bake at 350° for 15 minutes or until heated through. In a small saucepan, heat bouillon and water until cubes are dissolved; serve as a dipping sauce. **Yield:** 6 servings. **Editor's Note:** Sandwiches may be heated in the microwave on high for 1 minute instead of baking.

NUTRITIONAL INFORMATION

Serving Size: 1/6 recipe

Calories: 523
Total Fat: 10 gm
Calories from Fat: 17%
Saturated Fat: 4 gm
Cholesterol: 22 mg
Sodium: 948 mg
Carbohydrate: 83 gm
Protein: 24 gm

Mexican Beef Burgers

Stanny Barta, Pisek, North Dakota

One night for dinner, when half the family requested hamburgers and the others wanted tacos, my daughter-in-law and I came up with this compromise to satisfy everyone's tastes. It's become our most-requested burger recipe.

2 eggs
2 cans (4 ounces *each*) chopped green chilies
1/4 cup minced onion
1/3 cup salsa
1/2 teaspoon pepper
1 garlic clove, minced
3/4 cup finely crushed baked tortilla chips

2 pounds ground round
10 fat-free flour tortillas (10 inches), warmed
TOPPINGS:
Chopped tomatoes
Chopped ripe olives
Shredded fat-free cheddar cheese
Shredded lettuce

In a bowl, combine the first six ingredients. Add chips and beef; mix well. Shape into 10 patties. Pan-fry, grill or broil until no longer pink. Wrap burgers and desired toppings in tortillas. **Yield:** 10 servings.

Spinach Bacon Loaf

Jeanette Hios, Brooklyn, New York

My cousin introduced me to this sandwich years ago. Not only is it quick and easy, it's a guaranteed crowd-pleaser. Try it at your next potluck and see for yourself.

3 garlic cloves, minced
2 packages (10 ounces *each*) frozen chopped spinach, thawed and squeezed dry
1/4 teaspoon pepper
6 turkey bacon strips, cooked and crumbled

1-1/2 cups (6 ounces) shredded part-skim mozzarella cheese
1 loaf (1 pound) Italian bread
1/4 cup shredded Parmesan cheese

In a large skillet coated with nonstick cooking spray, saute garlic over medium heat. Add spinach and pepper; cook, stirring occasionally, until heated through. Remove from the heat; cool for 5 minutes. Add bacon and mozzarella; mix well. Slice bread horizontally. Spread about 2-1/4 cups spinach mixture on each half. Sprinkle with Parmesan. Bake at 450° for 6-8 minutes or until cheese is melted. **Yield:** 10 servings.

All-American Barbecue Sandwiches

Sue Gronholz, Columbus, Wisconsin

(Pictured above)

I came up with this delicious recipe on my own. It's my husband's favorite and a big hit with family and friends who enjoy it at our Fourth of July picnics.

4-1/2 pounds ground round
1-1/2 cups chopped onion
2-1/4 cups ketchup
   3 tablespoons prepared
      mustard

  3 tablespoons
     Worcestershire sauce
  2 tablespoons vinegar
  2 tablespoons sugar
  1 tablespoon pepper
18 hamburger buns, split

In a Dutch oven, cook beef and onion until meat is browned and onion is tender; drain. Combine ketchup, mustard, Worcestershire, vinegar, sugar and pepper; stir into beef mixture. Heat through. Serve on buns.
Yield: 18 sandwiches.

NUTRITIONAL INFORMATION

Serving Size: 1 sandwich

Calories: 375
Total Fat: 9 gm
Calories from Fat: 22%
Saturated Fat: 3 gm
Cholesterol: 78 mg
Sodium: 746 mg
Carbohydrate: 35 gm
Protein: 38 gm

Nutritional Information

Serving Size: 1/6 recipe

Calories: 375
Total Fat: 12 gm
Calories from Fat: 28%
Saturated Fat: 4 gm
Cholesterol: 42 mg
Sodium: 1,062 mg
Carbohydrate: 48 gm
Protein: 20 gm

"Mock Guac"

To make your favorite guac-amole recipe lower in fat, replace the avocado with cooked, drained and pu-reed broccoli or asparagus. For every 2 cups of "mock" guacamole, stir in 1/4 cup fat-free mayonnaise.

Sausage-Stuffed Loaf

Mary Koehler, Portland, Oregon

(Pictured above)

I love to serve this hearty sandwich of sausage and ground round in a zesty spaghetti sauce stuffed inside a loaf of French bread. Topped with melted cheese, it's a real crowd-pleaser every time.

2 turkey Italian sausages	1/2 teaspoon sugar
1/2 pound ground round	1/4 teaspoon aniseed
1/2 cup chopped onion	1/8 teaspoon garlic powder
1/4 cup chopped green pepper	1 loaf (1 pound) French
1 medium tomato, chopped	bread
1 can (15 ounces) chunky	1/4 cup grated Parmesan
Italian-style tomato sauce	cheese
1/2 teaspoon dried basil	Coarsely ground pepper
1/2 teaspoon dried oregano	

In a skillet, cook sausages until no longer pink. Remove and set aside. In the same skillet, cook beef, onion and green pepper until beef is no longer pink; drain. Stir in tomato, tomato sauce and seasonings. Cut sausages in half lengthwise and slice; add to meat sauce. Cut a wedge out of the top of the bread, about 2 in. wide and three-fourths of the way through the loaf. Fill loaf with meat sauce. Sprinkle with Parme-san cheese and pepper. Wrap in heavy-duty foil. Bake at 400° for 15-20 minutes or until heated through. **Yield:** 6 servings.

Turkey Burritos

Chris Bakewell, Glendale, Arizona

When my husband and I were married almost 30 years ago, my biggest challenge was learning to cook. Now I struggle to find filling lunches for our son.

1 pound ground turkey breast
1/2 cup chopped onion
1 can (14-1/2 ounces) diced tomatoes, undrained
1 can (16 ounces) fat-free refried beans with green chilies
1 can (4 ounces) chopped green chilies
1 can (2-1/4 ounces) sliced ripe olives, drained
1 envelope taco seasoning mix
1/4 cup frozen corn
1/4 cup uncooked instant rice
12 fat-free flour tortillas

In a large nonstick saucepan, brown turkey and onion; drain. Add the next six ingredients; bring to a boil. Reduce heat; cover and simmer for 15 minutes. Return to a boil. Stir in rice; remove from the heat. Cover; let stand for 5 minutes. Spoon about 1/2 cup down the center of each tortilla; fold in sides. **Yield:** 12 servings.

Paul's Burgers on the Grill

Paul Miller, Green Bay, Wisconsin

I've enjoyed cooking foods like these hearty burgers since I was a boy.

1 pound ground round
1/4 cup ketchup
1/4 cup finely chopped onion
2 teaspoons Italian seasoning
1 teaspoon garlic powder
6 hamburger buns, split

Combine the first five ingredients in a medium bowl; mix well. Shape into six patties. Grill over medium coals for 4-5 minutes per side or until no longer pink. Serve on buns. **Yield:** 6 sandwiches.

Snappy Barbecue Beef Sandwiches

Patricia Throlsen, Hawick, Minnesota

This is a great recipe—put it in the oven and forget about it 'til dinnertime!

4 pounds flank steak, trimmed
1 cup ketchup
1 cup barbecue sauce
4 cups chopped celery
2 cups water
1 cup chopped onion
2 tablespoons vinegar
2 tablespoons brown sugar
2 tablespoons Worcestershire sauce
1 teaspoon chili powder
1 teaspoon garlic powder
24 French rolls, split

Place beef in a Dutch oven. Combine all remaining ingredients except the rolls; pour over beef. Cover and bake at 350° for 5 hours or until very tender, turning beef occasionally. Shred beef with a fork. Serve on rolls. **Yield:** 24 sandwiches.

Big Sandwich

Margaret Yost, Tipp City, Ohio

(Pictured below)

I have served this impressive sandwich many times for casual lunches and suppers. The tall layers prompt people to ask how they're supposed to eat it. I encourage them to simply dig in and enjoy!

NUTRITIONAL INFORMATION

Serving Size: 1/10 recipe

Calories: 307
Total Fat: 11 gm
Calories from Fat: 30%
Saturated Fat: 3 gm
Cholesterol: 41 mg
Sodium: 853 mg
Carbohydrate: 27 gm
Protein: 24 gm

1 unsliced round loaf of bread (8 inches)
2 tablespoons prepared horseradish
1/2 pound thinly sliced cooked lean roast beef
2 tablespoons prepared mustard
1/4 pound thinly sliced fully cooked low-fat ham
1/4 pound thinly sliced cooked turkey breast
4 slices reduced-fat Swiss cheese
2 tablespoons light mayonnaise
1 small tomato, thinly sliced
6 turkey bacon strips, cooked and drained
4 slices fat-free process American cheese
1 small onion, thinly sliced
2 tablespoons margarine, melted
1 tablespoon sesame seeds
Dash onion powder

Slice bread horizontally into five equal layers. Spread bottom layer with horseradish; top with roast beef. Place the next slice of bread over beef; spread with mustard and top with ham, turkey and Swiss cheese. Add the next slice of bread; spread with mayonnaise and top with tomato and bacon. Add the next slice of bread; top with American cheese and onion. Cover with remaining bread. Combine margarine, sesame seeds and onion powder; brush over top and sides of loaf. Place on a baking sheet; loosely tent with heavy-duty foil. Bake at 400° for 15-20 minutes or until heated through. Carefully slice into wedges. **Yield:** 10 servings.

French Dip

Margaret McNeil, Memphis, Tennessee

(Pictured above)

For a sandwich with more pizzazz than the traditional French dip, give this recipe a try. The seasonings give the broth a wonderful flavor, and the meat cooks up tender and juicy.

1 beef top round roast (3 pounds), trimmed	1 teaspoon dried thyme
2 cups water	1 teaspoon garlic powder
1/2 cup light soy sauce	1 bay leaf
1 teaspoon dried rosemary	3 whole peppercorns
	8 French rolls, split

Place roast in a slow cooker. Add water, soy sauce and seasonings. Cover and cook on high for 5-6 hours or until beef is tender. Remove meat from broth; thinly slice or shred and keep warm. Strain broth; skim off fat. Pour broth into small cups for dipping. Serve beef on rolls. **Yield:** 8 servings.

NUTRITIONAL INFORMATION

Serving Size: 1/8 recipe

Calories: 461
Total Fat: 12 gm
Calories from Fat: 24%
Saturated Fat: 4 gm
Cholesterol: 117 mg
Sodium: 884 mg
Carbohydrate: 29 gm
Protein: 56 gm

Pork Tenderloin Sandwiches

Margarete Muhle, Pewaukee, Wisconsin

Chutney and pears add a distinctive touch to these sandwiches, making them perfect for special luncheons. Best of all, they're simple to make.

1 pork tenderloin (1 pound), trimmed	3 tablespoons mango chutney
1 teaspoon salt-free seasoning blend	1 can (15 ounces) unsweetened sliced pears, drained
1/2 teaspoon pepper	6 slices light process American cheese
6 thick slices sourdough bread	

Cut pork crosswise into six slices; sprinkle with seasoning blend and pepper. Flatten to 1/4-in. thickness; heat a large skillet coated with nonstick cooking spray over medium heat. Cook pork for about 4 minutes per side or until no longer pink. Meanwhile, toast bread and spread each slice with about 1-1/2 teaspoons chutney. Top each slice with tenderloin, pears and cheese. Place on an ungreased baking sheet. Bake at 300° for 2-3 minutes or until cheese is melted. **Yield:** 6 sandwiches.

NUTRITIONAL INFORMATION

Serving Size: 1 sandwich

Calories: 269
Total Fat: 6 gm
Calories from Fat: 21%
Saturated Fat: 3 gm
Cholesterol: 41 mg
Sodium: 584 mg
Carbohydrate: 34 gm
Protein: 19 gm

Oriental Chicken Grill

Rosemary Splittgerber, Mesa, Arizona

Since my husband and I are empty nesters, this recipe is great for just the two of us. We both love these tasty sandwiches.

1/2 cup orange juice
2 tablespoons honey
2 tablespoons light soy sauce
1 teaspoon lemon-pepper seasoning
1 teaspoon ground ginger
1/2 teaspoon garlic powder
2 boneless skinless chicken breast halves
2 hamburger buns, split
Lettuce leaves and tomato slices

In a small bowl, combine the first six ingredients; mix well. Set aside 1/4 cup for basting chicken; cover and refrigerate. Pound chicken breasts to 3/8-in. thickness. Place in a resealable plastic bag or glass bowl; pour remaining marinade over chicken. Close bag or cover and refrigerate overnight. Drain, discarding marinade. Grill chicken, uncovered, over medium coals for 6-8 minutes per side or until juices run clear, basting several times with reserved marinade. Serve on buns with lettuce and tomato. **Yield:** 2 sandwiches.

Fantastic Beef Fajitas

Marla Brenneman, Goshen, Indiana

The first time I made this dish, my family couldn't get enough of it. The next time, I had to make a double batch so everyone had enough. This is a favorite evening meal for me because it fixes up quick.

1 pound top sirloin steak trimmed and cut across the grain into 1/4-inch strips
2 tablespoons water
2 tablespoons lemon juice
1 tablespoon vegetable oil
1 teaspoon dried oregano
1 garlic clove, minced
1/4 teaspoon salt
1/4 teaspoon pepper
1/2 medium onion, sliced
1 medium sweet red pepper, sliced into thin strips
6 fat-free flour tortilla shells, warmed
Salsa and nonfat sour cream, optional

In a bowl or resealable plastic bag, combine the first seven ingredients; add beef and toss. Cover and refrigerate 3-6 hours or overnight, stirring several times. Drain meat, discarding marinade. In a skillet coated with nonstick cooking spray, saute onion and red pepper until crisp-tender; remove. In the same skillet, saute meat until no longer pink, about 4 minutes. Return vegetables to pan and heat through. Spoon onto tortillas; top with salsa and sour cream if desired. Roll tortilla around filling. **Yield:** 6 servings.

Barbecued Pork Sandwiches

Karla Labby, Otsego, Michigan

(Pictured above)

When our office held a bridal shower for a co-worker, we presented the future bride with a collection of our favorite recipes. I included this one. I like serving this savory pork as an alternative to a typical ground beef barbecue.

2 boneless pork loin roasts (2-1/2 pounds *each*)	1/3 cup steak sauce
1 cup water	1/4 cup packed brown sugar
2 cups ketchup	1/4 cup vinegar
2 cups diced celery	2 teaspoons lemon juice
	25 hamburger buns, split

Place roasts in an 8-qt. Dutch oven; add water. Cover and cook on medium-low heat for 2-1/2 hours or until meat is tender. Remove roasts and shred with a fork; set aside. Skim fat from cooking liquid and discard. Drain all but 1 cup cooking liquid. Add meat, ketchup, celery, steak sauce, brown sugar, vinegar and lemon juice. Cover and cook on medium-low heat for 1-1/2 hours. Serve on buns. **Yield:** 25 sandwiches.

NUTRITIONAL INFORMATION

Serving Size: 1 sandwich

Calories: 258
Total Fat: 7 gm
Calories from Fat: 25%
Saturated Fat: 2 gm
Cholesterol: 40 mg
Sodium: 560 mg
Carbohydrate: 30 gm
Protein: 18 gm

ONE-POT MEALS. *Top to bottom: Corn Chowder, Quick Beef Stew (both recipes on page 129) and Harvest Chicken Soup (recipe on page 130).*

Soups & Stews

Corn Chowder

Muriel Lerdal, Humboldt, Iowa

(Pictured at left)

Fresh corn gives wonderful appeal to this full-bodied soup. It's also satisfying on a chilly fall or winter day.

3/4 cup chopped onion
1 cup diced cooked peeled
   potatoes
1 cup diced fully cooked
   ham
2 cups fresh *or* frozen
   sweet corn
1 cup cream-style corn
1 can (10-3/4 ounces)
   low-fat condensed cream
   of mushroom soup,
   undiluted
2-1/2 cups skim milk
Pepper to taste
1 tablespoon chopped fresh
   parsley

In a heavy saucepan coated with nonstick cooking spray, saute the onion until tender. Add remaining ingredients; bring to a boil. Reduce heat; simmer, uncovered, for 20-30 minutes. **Yield:** 8 servings (2 quarts).

NUTRITIONAL INFORMATION

Serving Size: 1 cup

Calories: 152
Total Fat: 2 gm
Calories from Fat: 12%
Saturated Fat: 1 gm
Cholesterol: 13 mg
Sodium: 546 mg
Carbohydrate: 26 gm
Protein: 9 gm

Quick Beef Stew

Laura McCormick, Lebanon, Missouri

(Pictured at left)

When my family has a craving for stew at the last minute, I can count on this recipe. This stew is prepared in the microwave, so it's fast and flavorful.

5 medium red potatoes,
   diced
2 cups water
2 pounds ground round
1 medium onion, chopped
1 package (16 ounces)
   frozen mixed vegetables
1 can (8 ounces) no-salt-
   added tomato sauce
1 can (14-1/2 ounces)
   no-salt-added tomatoes,
   diced and undrained
1 can (10 ounces) diced
   tomatoes with green
   chilies, undrained
1/2 teaspoon chili powder
1/4 teaspoon garlic powder

Place the potatoes and water in a microwave-safe dish; microwave on high until almost tender, about 12-14 minutes. Set aside (do not drain). In a 3-qt. microwave-safe dish, cook beef and onion on medium until beef is browned, about 14 minutes; drain. Add potatoes and remaining ingredients. Cover and microwave on medium for 20 minutes or until potatoes are tender and vegetables are heated through. **Yield:** 12 servings.

NUTRITIONAL INFORMATION

Serving Size: 1-1/2 cups

Calories: 201
Total Fat: 6 gm
Calories from Fat: 28%
Saturated Fat: 2 gm
Cholesterol: 24 mg
Sodium: 168 mg
Carbohydrate: 20 gm
Protein: 16 gm

Harvest Chicken Soup

Bob Crabb, Scio, Oregon

(Pictured on page 128)

When I retired, I decided to cook up some fun by volunteering to take over for my wife in the kitchen. I've gone from tackling basic recipes to more complex ones. This soup is made with a colorful and tasty mix of vegetables.

3 medium onions	1 can (14-1/2 ounces) no-salt-added tomatoes, diced and undrained
3 chicken breast halves (bone in), skinned	
4 cups water	4 teaspoons low-sodium chicken bouillon granules
3 celery ribs, halved	
1/8 teaspoon pepper	1 small zucchini, halved and thinly sliced
3 medium carrots, thinly sliced	
	1 cup frozen peas

Chop one onion; set aside. Quarter the other two; place in a Dutch oven with chicken, water, celery and pepper. Cover and simmer for 2 hours or until chicken is tender. Remove chicken; set aside. Discard celery and onion. To broth, add the carrots, tomatoes, bouillon and chopped onion. Cover and simmer for 30 minutes or until the carrots are tender. Debone and cube chicken; add to soup with zucchini and peas. Cover and simmer for 10 minutes or until zucchini is tender. **Yield:** 8 servings (2 quarts).

NUTRITIONAL INFORMATION

Serving Size: 1 cup

Calories: 84
Total Fat: 1 gm
Calories from Fat: 11%
Saturated Fat: trace
Cholesterol: 13 mg
Sodium: 68 mg
Carbohydrate: 13 gm
Protein: 8 gm

Black Bean Soup

Mrs. Albert Lopez, Riverside, California

This should be a thick soup, but I often add water if too much liquid has boiled away. It has a nice consistency, and the topping adds flavor.

2 cups dry black beans, rinsed	1 can (6 ounces) tomato paste
2 quarts water	Optional toppings: thinly sliced radishes, finely shredded cabbage, minced fresh chili peppers and nonfat sour cream
1 medium onion, chopped	
1/2 pound lean pork, cubed	
3 garlic cloves, minced	
1 teaspoon dried oregano	

In a Dutch oven, combine beans and water; bring to a boil. Reduce heat; cover and simmer until beans wrinkle and crack, about 1-1/2 hours. Add onion, pork, garlic and oregano. Simmer, covered, 1-1/2 to 2 hours, or until beans and pork are tender. Stir in tomato paste; heat through. If desired, top individual servings with radishes, cabbage, peppers and/or sour cream. **Yield:** 8 servings (2 quarts).

NUTRITIONAL INFORMATION

Serving Size: 1 cup
(calculated without toppings)

Calories: 225
Total Fat: 3 gm
Calories from Fat: 11%
Saturated Fat: 1 gm
Cholesterol: 17 mg
Sodium: 181 mg
Carbohydrate: 34 gm
Protein: 17 gm

Grandma's Tomato Soup

Gerri Sysun, Narragansett, Rhode Island

(Pictured below)

This recipe is my grandmother's. Originally she even made the tomato juice in it from scratch! Every time I return to Massachusetts for a visit, Gram has this delicious soup simmering on the stove.

1 tablespoon margarine
1 tablespoon all-purpose
  flour
2 cups low-sodium tomato
  juice

1/2 cup water
2 tablespoons sugar
3/4 cup cooked wide egg
  noodles

In a saucepan over medium heat, melt margarine. Add flour; stir to form a smooth paste. Gradually add tomato juice and water, stirring constantly; bring to a boil. Cook and stir for 2 minutes or until thickened. Add sugar. Stir in egg noodles and heat through. **Yield:** 2 servings.

NUTRITIONAL INFORMATION

Serving Size: 1/2 recipe

Calories: 210
Total Fat: 7 gm
Calories from Fat: 30%
Saturated Fat: 7 gm
Cholesterol: 16 mg
Sodium: 94 mg
Carbohydrate: 36 gm
Protein: 4 gm

Pasta Meatball Stew

Pat Jelinek, Kitchener, Ontario

(Pictured above)

Growing up on the farm, I participated in 4-H club cooking activities. Nowadays, I like to visit Mom, Dad and their varied animals...including a llama.

1 pound ground turkey breast
1 egg
1/4 cup dry bread crumbs
1/4 cup skim milk
1/2 teaspoon ground mustard
1/2 teaspoon pepper
1 cup chopped onion
2 garlic cloves, minced
2 tablespoons all-purpose flour
1-1/2 cups low-sodium beef broth
2 tablespoons no-salt-added tomato paste
1 can (14-1/2 ounces) no-salt-added tomatoes, diced and undrained
1 bay leaf
3/4 teaspoon dried thyme
1-1/2 cups sliced carrots
1-1/2 cups chopped zucchini
1 cup chopped green pepper
1 cup chopped sweet red pepper
1 tablespoon minced fresh parsley
2 cups cooked pasta

Combine the first six ingredients; mix well. Shape into 1-in. balls. In a Dutch oven coated with nonstick cooking spray, brown meatballs over medium heat; drain and set aside. In the same pan, cook onion and garlic until onion is tender. Stir in flour. Gradually add broth, stirring constantly; bring to a boil. Cook and stir 1-2 minutes or until thickened. Add tomato paste, tomatoes, bay leaf and thyme; mix well. Add meatballs and carrots; bring to a boil. Reduce heat; cover and simmer 30 minutes. Add zucchini and peppers; bring to a boil. Reduce heat; cover and simmer 10-15 minutes or until vegetables are tender. Add parsley and pasta; heat through. Remove bay leaf. **Yield:** 8 servings.

Skimming Off the Top

Before freezing homemade soup, refrigerate it until the fat rises to the surface. Skim off the fat and discard any bones. Then freeze the soup in serving-size portions for easy meals anytime.

Stuffed Roast Pepper Soup

Betty Vig, Viroqua, Wisconsin

After sampling a similar soup at a resort, my daughter and I invented this version. Using a colorful variety of peppers makes it especially appealing.

2 pounds ground round
1/2 medium onion, chopped
6 cups water
8 low-sodium beef
   bouillon cubes
1/2 teaspoon pepper
1/2 teaspoon paprika

2 cans (28 ounces *each*)
   diced tomatoes,
   undrained
2 cups cooked rice
3 green, yellow *or* sweet
   red peppers, seeded
   and chopped

In a soup kettle, cook beef and onion until the meat is browned and the onion is tender; drain. Add water, bouillon, pepper, paprika, tomatoes and rice; bring to a boil. Reduce heat; cover and simmer for 1 hour. Add peppers; cook, uncovered, for 10-15 minutes or just until tender. **Yield:** 16 servings (4 quarts).

NUTRITIONAL INFORMATION

Serving Size: 1 cup

Calories: 147
Total Fat: 5 gm
Calories from Fat: 29%
Saturated Fat: 2 gm
Cholesterol: 18 mg
Sodium: 201 mg
Carbohydrate: 14 gm
Protein: 12 gm

Turkey Vegetable Soup

Bonnie Smith, Clifton, Virginia

(Pictured below)

This is one of my tried-and-true recipes that I make after Thanksgiving.

6 cups low-sodium chicken
   broth
3 medium potatoes, peeled
   and chopped
2 carrots, chopped
2 celery ribs, chopped
2 medium onions, chopped

2 cans (15 ounces *each*)
   cream-style corn
2 cans (8-1/2 ounces *each*)
   lima beans, drained
1 cup chopped cooked
   turkey breast
1/2 teaspoon chili powder

In a soup kettle, combine broth, potatoes, carrots, celery and onions; bring to a boil. Reduce heat; cover and simmer for 30 minutes or until vegetables are tender. Add corn, beans, turkey and chili powder. Cover and simmer 10 minutes longer. **Yield:** 14 servings (3-1/2 quarts).

NUTRITIONAL INFORMATION

Serving Size: 1 cup

Calories: 136
Total Fat: 2 gm
Calories from Fat: 11%
Saturated Fat: 1 gm
Cholesterol: 8 mg
Sodium: 316 mg
Carbohydrate: 26 gm
Protein: 7 gm

Clam Chowder

Rosemary Peterson, Archie, Missouri

This recipe pleasantly proves you can enjoy good food without a lot of fat.

2 cans (6-1/2 ounces *each*)
    minced clams
1-1/2 cups water
  6 potatoes, peeled and diced
  6 carrots, diced
1/2 cup chopped onion
1/4 cup margarine

2 cans (10-3/4 ounces
    each) low-fat condensed
    mushroom soup, undiluted
2 cans (12 ounces *each*)
    evaporated skim milk
1/2 teaspoon pepper

Drain clams, reserving liquid. Set the clams aside. In a large kettle, combine clam juice, water, potatoes, carrots, onion and margarine; cook over medium heat for 15 minutes or until the vegetables are tender. Stir in soup, milk and pepper; simmer until heated through. Stir in clams. **Yield:** 12 servings (3 quarts).

Quick Vegetable Soup

Faye Johnson, Connersville, Indiana

This recipe uses leftover chicken for an economical entree in no time.

1 quart low-sodium
  chicken broth
1 can (14-1/2 ounces)
  diced tomatoes, undrained
1/2 cup chopped onion
1/2 cup chopped cabbage
1 package (10 ounces)
  frozen mixed vegetables,
  thawed

1/2 teaspoon dried basil
1/8 teaspoon pepper
Dash sugar
1/4 cup uncooked elbow
  macaroni
1 cup cubed cooked
  chicken

In a large saucepan, bring broth, tomatoes, onion, cabbage, vegetables and seasonings to a boil. Add macaroni; simmer for 10 minutes or until tender. Add chicken and heat through. **Yield:** 6 servings.

German Potato Soup

Carolyn Ringer, North Little Rock, Arkansas

My family always requests this soup when they're feeling under the weather.

6 cups cubed peeled
  potatoes
1-1/4 cups sliced celery
1/2 cup chopped onion
5 cups water
1/8 teaspoon pepper

DROP DUMPLINGS:
  1 egg
1/3 cup water
1/2 teaspoon salt
3/4 cup all-purpose flour
Chopped fresh parsley

In a kettle, combine the first five ingredients; bring to a boil. Reduce heat and simmer until vegetables are tender, about 1 hour. With a potato masher, mash most of the vegetables. For dumplings, combine egg, water, salt and flour. Stir until smooth and stiff. Drop by teaspoonsful into the boiling soup. Cover and simmer until the dumplings are cooked through, about 10-15 minutes. Sprinkle with parsley. **Yield:** 6 servings.

NUTRITIONAL INFORMATION

Serving Size: 1 cup

Calories: 219
Total Fat: 6 gm
Calories from Fat: 25%
Saturated Fat: 1 gm
Cholesterol: 18 mg
Sodium: 392 mg
Carbohydrate: 31 gm
Protein: 2 gm

NUTRITIONAL INFORMATION

Serving Size: 1/6 recipe

Calories: 126
Total Fat: 3 gm
Calories from Fat: 23%
Saturated Fat: 1 gm
Cholesterol: 24 mg
Sodium: 234 mg
Carbohydrate: 15 gm
Protein: 12 gm

NUTRITIONAL INFORMATION

Serving Size: 1/6 recipe

Calories: 208
Total Fat: 1 gm
Calories from Fat: 5%
Saturated Fat: trace
Cholesterol: 35 mg
Sodium: 218 mg
Carbohydrate: 44 gm
Protein: 6 gm

Potluck Minestrone Soup

Lana Rutledge, Shepherdsville, Kentucky

(Pictured above)

Here's the perfect summertime soup to put all those fresh garden vegetables to good use! It's great for a light meal served with a salad and warm bread. Take it to a potluck and watch people go back for seconds.

1 beef chuck roast
(4 pounds), trimmed
1 gallon water
2 bay leaves
2 medium onions, diced
2 cups sliced carrots
2 cups sliced celery
1 can (28 ounces) diced
tomatoes, undrained
1 can (15 ounces) tomato
sauce
1/4 cup chopped fresh parsley
Pepper to taste

4 teaspoons dried basil
1 teaspoon garlic powder
1 package (16 ounces)
frozen peas
2 cans (16 ounces
each) kidney beans,
rinsed and drained
2 packages (9 ounces *each*)
frozen cut green beans
2 packages (7 ounces *each*)
shell macaroni, cooked
and drained

NUTRITIONAL INFORMATION

Serving Size: 1 cup

Calories: 150
Total Fat: 3 gm
Calories from Fat: 16%
Saturated Fat: 1 gm
Cholesterol: 30 mg
Sodium: 200 mg
Carbohydrate: 17 gm
Protein: 14 gm

Place beef roast, water and bay leaves in a large kettle or Dutch oven; bring to a boil. Reduce heat; cover and simmer until meat is tender, about 3 hours. Remove meat from broth; cool. Add onions, carrots and celery to broth; cook for 20 minutes or until vegetables are tender. Cut meat into bite-size pieces; add to broth. Add tomatoes, tomato sauce, parsley, seasonings, peas and beans. Cook until vegetables are done, about 10 minutes. Add macaroni and heat through. Remove bay leaves. **Yield:** 40 servings (10 quarts).

135

Hearty Beef Stew

Virginia Brown, Hudson, Florida

(Pictured below)

This recipe is a lifesaver when you have out-of-town company. Put it in the oven, forget it and be gone for the day with your guests. When you return home, fix a salad, warm some bread and dinner will be ready.

NUTRITIONAL INFORMATION

Serving Size: 1/8 recipe

Calories: 338
Total Fat: 8 gm
Calories from Fat: 22%
Saturated Fat: 3 gm
Cholesterol: 70 mg
Sodium: 646 mg
Carbohydrate: 42 gm
Protein: 25 gm

2 pounds lean beef stew meat
6 medium potatoes, peeled and cut into 1-1/2-inch pieces
2 medium onions, cut into wedges
8 medium carrots, cut into 1-inch pieces
4 celery ribs, cut into 1-inch pieces
1 can (4 ounces) sliced mushrooms, drained
1/3 cup quick-cooking tapioca
1 low-sodium beef bouillon cube
1 teaspoon sugar
2 bay leaves
1-1/2 teaspoons dried thyme
3 cups tomato juice

In a 4-qt. Dutch oven or baking dish, layer the first 11 ingredients; pour tomato juice over all. Cover and bake at 300° for 3 hours, stirring occasionally, or until the meat and vegetables are tender. Remove bay leaves before serving. **Yield:** 8 servings.

Southwestern Bean Soup

Grace Nordang, Methow, Washington

My daughter gave me this hearty soup recipe, and I'm glad she did—it's become a family favorite. You can't beat it on a cold winter day!

4 turkey bacon strips
3/4 cup chopped onion
3/4 cup chopped celery
1/8 teaspoon garlic powder
1 can (16 ounces) fat-free refried beans

1/4 cup picante sauce
1 can (14-1/2 ounces) low-sodium chicken broth
1 tablespoon chopped fresh parsley

In a medium saucepan coated with nonstick cooking spray, cook bacon until crisp; remove to paper towel to drain. Crumble and set aside. In the same saucepan, saute onion and celery; sprinkle with garlic powder. Cover and simmer for 10 minutes or until vegetables are tender. Add beans, picante sauce, broth, parsley and bacon; bring to a boil. Reduce heat and simmer, uncovered, for 5-10 minutes. **Yield:** 4 servings.

Italian Chicken Soup

John Croce, Yarmouthport, Massachusetts

Here's a real comforting dish on a chilly day. A blend of spices makes this stand out from traditional chicken soup.

4 chicken breast halves (bone in), skinned
1 large onion, halved
1 large carrot, quartered
3 celery ribs with leaves, chopped
3-1/2 cups low-sodium chicken broth
2 cups water
2 teaspoons low-sodium chicken bouillon granules
2 bay leaves
1 can (14-1/2 ounces) diced tomatoes, undrained

6 green onions, thinly sliced
1/2 cup chopped fresh parsley
1/4 cup ketchup
1 teaspoon dried rosemary, crushed
1/2 teaspoon dried basil
2 garlic cloves, minced
1/2 teaspoon pepper
2 cans (15-1/2 ounces *each*) kidney beans, rinsed and drained
1/4 cup grated Romano cheese

In a 5-qt. Dutch oven, combine the first eight ingredients; bring to a boil. Reduce heat; leaving cover ajar, simmer for 1-1/2 hours. Remove chicken; strain and reserve broth. Discard vegetables and bay leaves. When the chicken is cool enough to handle, remove bones; discard. Cut chicken into bite-size pieces; set aside. Return broth to kettle; add tomatoes, onions, parsley, ketchup, rosemary, basil, garlic and pepper; bring to a boil. Reduce heat; leaving cover ajar, simmer for 45 minutes. Add beans, cheese and chicken; heat through. **Yield:** 14 servings (3-1/2 quarts).

Vegetable Beef Soup

Nancy Soderstrom, Roseville, Minnesota

When my family comes in from playing in the snow, I serve this hearty soup. It really takes the chill away.

2-1/2 pounds beef round steak, trimmed
4 quarts water
1 cup pearl barley
1-1/2 cups chopped onion
1-1/2 cups chopped celery
1 teaspoon pepper
1-1/2 cups chopped carrots
1 can (28 ounces) diced tomatoes, undrained
1 package (16 ounces) frozen mixed vegetables
1/4 cup minced fresh parsley
1/2 teaspoon dried basil
1/4 teaspoon dried thyme
Dash garlic powder

Place beef in a large Dutch oven or soup kettle. Add water, barley, onion, celery and pepper; bring to a boil. Reduce heat; cover and simmer for 1 hour and 15 minutes or until meat is tender. Remove meat; cool. Cut into bite-size pieces. Skim fat from broth. Add beef and remaining ingredients; bring to a boil. Reduce heat; cover and simmer for 45 minutes or until vegetables are tender. **Yield:** 20 servings (6-1/4 quarts).

NUTRITIONAL INFORMATION

Serving Size: 1-1/4 cups

Calories: 163
Total Fat: 4 gm
Calories from Fat: 24%
Saturated Fat: 1 gm
Cholesterol: 41 mg
Sodium: 213 mg
Carbohydrate: 15 gm
Protein: 17 gm

Mom's Chicken Noodle Soup

Marlene Doolittle, Story City, Iowa

My mother did a lot of cooking for potlucks. This recipe's one she created herself. I serve it frequently to my husband and our four children.

3 boneless skinless chicken breast halves
2 quarts water
1 medium onion, chopped
2 low-sodium chicken bouillon cubes
2 celery ribs, diced
2 carrots, diced
2 medium potatoes, peeled and cubed
1-1/2 cups fresh *or* frozen cut green beans
1/4 teaspoon pepper
NOODLES:
1 cup all-purpose flour
1 egg
1/2 teaspoon salt
1 teaspoon margarine, softened
1/4 teaspoon baking powder
2 tablespoons skim milk

Place chicken and water in a soup kettle; bring to a boil. Reduce heat; cover and simmer until chicken is tender. Cool broth and skim off fat. Cut chicken into bite-size pieces; return to broth. Add the next seven ingredients; bring to a boil. Reduce heat; simmer, uncovered, for 50-60 minutes or until vegetables are tender. Meanwhile, for noodles, place flour on a pastry board or countertop and make a well in the center. Stir together remaining ingredients; pour into well. Gradually fold flour into wet ingredients with hands until dough can be rolled into a ball. Knead for 5-6 minutes. Cover and let rest for 10 minutes. On a floured surface, roll dough out to a square, 1/16 to 1/8 in. thick, and cut into 1/4-in.-wide strips. Cook noodles in boiling water for 2-3 minutes or until done. Drain and add to soup just before serving. **Yield:** 6 servings (1-1/2 quarts).

NUTRITIONAL INFORMATION

Serving Size: 1 cup

Calories: 237
Total Fat: 3 gm
Calories from Fat: 13%
Saturated Fat: 1 gm
Cholesterol: 72 mg
Sodium: 94 mg
Carbohydrate: 32 gm
Protein: 19 gm

Confetti Chowder

Rose Bomba, Lisbon, New Hampshire

(Pictured above)

Grandma's philosophy was, "Add a little color to your food, and folks will eat up a storm!" This delightful golden chowder was one of her favorite recipes, and the broccoli, carrots and zucchini in it add flavor as well as color.

1 cup diced carrots
1 cup diced zucchini
1 cup broccoli florets
1/2 cup chopped onion
1/2 cup chopped celery
1/4 cup all-purpose flour
1/2 teaspoon pepper
1/4 teaspoon sugar
3 cups skim milk
1 cup low-sodium chicken broth

1 cup frozen whole kernel corn, thawed
1 cup diced fully cooked low-fat ham
1/2 cup frozen peas, thawed
1 jar (2 ounces) sliced pimientos, drained
1 cup (4 ounces) shredded reduced-fat cheddar cheese

NUTRITIONAL INFORMATION

Serving Size: 1 cup

Calories: 163
Total Fat: 5 gm
Calories from Fat: 24%
Saturated Fat: 3 gm
Cholesterol: 21 mg
Sodium: 341 mg
Carbohydrate: 18 gm
Protein: 15 gm

In a Dutch oven coated with nonstick cooking spray, saute carrots, zucchini, broccoli, onion and celery for about 5 minutes or until crisp-tender. Sprinkle flour, pepper and sugar over vegetables; mix well. Stir in milk and broth; cook and stir until thickened and bubbly. Add corn, ham, peas and pimientos; cook and stir until heated through. Remove from the heat; stir in cheese until melted. **Yield:** 8 servings (2 quarts).

NUTRITIONAL INFORMATION

Serving Size: 1 cup

Calories: 156
Total Fat: 4 gm
Calories from Fat: 21%
Saturated Fat: 1 gm
Cholesterol: 2 mg
Sodium: 747 mg
Carbohydrate: 26 gm
Protein: 7 gm

Round Steak Chili

Linda Goshorn, Bedford, Virginia

(Pictured above)

The addition of round steak gives this chili recipe a nice change of pace. Everyone in my family just loves it!

1 pound beef round steak, trimmed and cut into 1/2-inch cubes	1 bay leaf
1 large onion, chopped	2 tablespoons chili powder
2 garlic cloves, minced	1 teaspoon dried oregano
1 can (46 ounces) V-8 juice	1 teaspoon brown sugar
1 can (28 ounces) crushed tomatoes	1/2 teaspoon *each* celery seed, paprika, ground mustard and cumin
2 cups sliced celery	1/4 teaspoon cayenne pepper
1 medium green pepper, chopped	1/4 teaspoon dried basil
	1 can (16 ounces) kidney beans, rinsed and drained

In a large kettle or Dutch oven coated with nonstick cooking spray, brown meat, onion and garlic. Add V-8, tomatoes, celery, green pepper and seasonings; bring to a boil. Reduce heat; simmer, uncovered, for 3 hours. Add kidney beans; heat through. Remove bay leaf before serving. **Yield:** 10 servings (2-1/2 quarts).

Santa Fe Stew

Patti Henson, Linden, Texas

This recipe came with me from New Mexico, where I lived years ago. It's been a hit at everything from a simple family supper to a church fellowship.

1 boneless beef chuck roast (2 pounds), trimmed and cut into 1/2-inch cubes
2 medium onions, sliced
1 can (10 ounces) tomatoes with jalapenos* *or* 1 can (14-1/2 ounces) diced tomatoes, undrained
2 cans (4 ounces *each*) chopped green chilies
1 can (10-1/2 ounces) low-sodium condensed beef broth
1 tablespoon sugar
1 garlic clove, minced
1 teaspoon ground cumin
1 medium green pepper, chopped
1 cup water
1 can (15 ounces) pinto beans, rinsed and drained

In a Dutch oven coated with nonstick cooking spray, brown roast on all sides over medium-high heat. Add the next nine ingredients; bring to a boil. Reduce heat; simmer for 1-1/2 hours or until the meat is tender. Add pinto beans and heat through. **Yield:** 8 servings. ***Editor's Note:** Look for tomatoes with jalapenos in the ethnic food section of your grocery store.

NUTRITIONAL INFORMATION

Serving Size: 1/8 recipe

Calories: 252
Total Fat: 7 gm
Calories from Fat: 26%
Saturated Fat: 2 gm
Cholesterol: 78 mg
Sodium: 450 mg
Carbohydrate: 15 gm
Protein: 30 gm

Spinach Garlic Soup

Marilyn Paradis, Woodburn, Oregon

During the years I owned and operated a deli, this was one of the most popular soups I served. I hope you enjoy it, too.

1 package (10 ounces) fresh spinach, trimmed and coarsely chopped
4 cups low-sodium chicken broth, *divided*
1/2 cup shredded carrot
1/2 cup chopped onion
8 garlic cloves, minced
1/4 cup all-purpose flour
3/4 cup evaporated skim milk
1/4 cup skim milk
1/2 teaspoon pepper
1/8 teaspoon ground nutmeg

In a 5-qt. Dutch oven, bring spinach, 3-1/2 cups broth and carrot to a boil. Reduce heat; simmer for 5 minutes, stirring occasionally. Remove from the heat; cool to lukewarm. Meanwhile, in a skillet coated with nonstick cooking spray, saute onion and garlic until onion is soft, about 5 minutes. Combine flour and remaining broth until smooth. Add to skillet; cook and stir over low heat for 3-5 minutes. Add to spinach mixture. Puree in small batches in a blender or food processor until finely chopped. Place in a large saucepan. Add evaporated milk, milk, pepper and nutmeg; heat through but do not boil. **Yield:** 6 servings.

NUTRITIONAL INFORMATION

Serving Size: 1/6 recipe

Calories: 84
Total Fat: trace
Calories from Fat: 4%
Saturated Fat: trace
Cholesterol: trace
Sodium: 425 mg
Carbohydrate: 14 gm
Protein: 6 gm

Grandmother's Chicken 'n' Dumplings

Cynthis Carroll, Cary, North Carolina

When I was growing up, my grandmother could feed our whole big family with a single chicken—and lots of dumplings.

1 large chicken (5 pounds), cut up and skin removed
4 quarts water
2 tablespoons vinegar
1 large onion, sliced
2 carrots, chopped
2 celery ribs, sliced

DUMPLINGS:
2 cups all-purpose flour
1 teaspoon salt
1 egg
1/4 to 1 cup reserved chicken broth
Pepper to taste

Place chicken, water, vinegar, onion, carrots and celery in a large soup kettle; add more water if necessary to cover chicken. Bring to a boil. Reduce heat; cover and simmer until meat nearly falls off the bones. Strain broth and return to kettle. Reserve chicken meat; remove and discard bones and vegetables. Cut meat into bite-size pieces; set aside. Reserve 1 cup broth; cool to lukewarm. For dumplings, combine flour and salt. Make a well in flour; add egg. Gradually mix 1/4 cup broth into egg, stirring until all flour is incorporated into dough. Add additional broth as needed so dough is consistency of pie dough. Pour any unused reserved broth back into kettle. Turn dough onto floured surface; knead in additional flour to make a stiff dough. Allow to rest for 15 minutes. Roll out dough on a floured surface into a 17-in. square. Cut into 1-in. square pieces. Dust with additional flour; set aside to dry for 30-60 minutes. Skim fat from broth; bring to a boil (there should be about 4 qts.). Drop dough into boiling broth; reduce heat. Cover and simmer for 10 minutes. Uncover; cook until dumplings test done, about 30 minutes. Add pepper and chicken; heat through. **Yield:** 10 servings.

Gazpacho

Sharon Balzer, Phoenix, Arizona

This gazpacho is simple, inexpensive, healthy and delicious. It works well as an appetizer, brunch dish or accompaniment to any meat entree.

2 cans (14-1/2 ounces *each*) tomatoes, minced and undrained
2 cups reduced-sodium V-8 juice
2 tablespoons red wine vinegar
1 garlic clove, minced
1/2 teaspoon pepper

8 drops hot pepper sauce
1 package (6 ounces) seasoned croutons
1 medium cucumber, peeled and diced
1 medium green pepper, diced
1 bunch green onions with tops, sliced

In a large bowl, combine the first six ingredients. Cover and refrigerate overnight. Stir well. Ladle into bowls; garnish with croutons, cucumber, green pepper and onions. **Yield:** 8 servings.

Golden Squash Soup

Nancy McFadyen, Smiths Falls, Ontario

(Pictured above)

I served this unusual soup one Thanksgiving and received rave reviews—even people who don't usually like squash enjoyed its hearty flavor. To dress it up, I sometimes add a dollop of nonfat yogurt on top.

3 cups coarsely chopped onion
1/4 teaspoon ground nutmeg
1/4 teaspoon ground cinnamon
1/4 teaspoon dried thyme
2 bay leaves
1-1/2 cups water

2 celery ribs, chopped
1 medium carrot, chopped
2 cups mashed cooked butternut squash, *divided*
1-1/2 cups tomato juice, *divided*
1 cup apple juice, *divided*
1 cup orange juice, *divided*
Pepper to taste

In a large saucepan or Dutch oven coated with nonstick cooking spray, saute onion with nutmeg, cinnamon, thyme and bay leaves until onion is tender. Add water, celery and carrot; cover and simmer until carrot is tender. Discard bay leaves. In a blender container, place half of the squash and half of the tomato, apple and orange juices; add half of the vegetable mixture. Puree; return to pan. Repeat with the remaining squash, juices and vegetable mixture; return to pan. Add pepper; heat through. **Yield:** 8 servings (2 quarts).

NUTRITIONAL INFORMATION

Serving Size: 1 cup

Calories: 86
Total Fat: trace
Calories from Fat: 0%
Saturated Fat: trace
Cholesterol: 0
Sodium: 190 mg
Carbohydrate: 21 gm
Protein: 2 gm

Split Pea Vegetable Soup

Maureen Ylitalo, Wahnapitae, Ontario

(Pictured below)

This recipe originated with the master chef of our family—my father-in-law. It freezes so well that frequently I'll cook up a double batch.

NUTRITIONAL INFORMATION

Serving Size: 1 cup

Calories: 139
Total Fat: 1 gm
Calories from Fat: 7%
Saturated Fat: trace
Cholesterol: 6 mg
Sodium: 217 mg
Carbohydrate: 25 gm
Protein: 8 gm

1-1/2 cups dry split peas, rinsed
2-1/2 quarts water
   7 whole allspice, tied in a cheesecloth bag
1/2 teaspoon pepper
1/2 medium head cabbage, shredded

6 large potatoes, peeled and cut into 1/2-inch cubes
6 carrots, chopped
2 medium onions, chopped
2 cups cubed fully cooked low-fat ham

In a large kettle, combine peas, water, allspice and pepper; bring to a boil. Reduce heat; cover and simmer for 1 hour. Stir in cabbage, potatoes, carrots, onions and ham; bring to a boil. Reduce heat; cover and simmer for 30 minutes or until vegetables are tender, stirring occasionally. Discard allspice. **Yield:** 20 servings (5 quarts).

Skillet Chicken Stew

Valerie Jordan, Kingmont, West Virginia

It's been more than 20 years now since I adapted this from a recipe for beef stew. We like it so much that, in all that time, I have never changed any ingredients or amounts—unless it was to double them! My family often requests this stew when the weather turns cooler.

1-1/2 pounds boneless skinless chicken breasts, cut into 1-inch chunks
1 medium onion, sliced
3 celery ribs, sliced
Dash pepper
2 medium potatoes, peeled and cut into 3/4-inch cubes
3 medium carrots, sliced 1/4 inch thick
1 cup low-sodium chicken broth
1/2 teaspoon dried thyme
1 tablespoon ketchup
1 tablespoon cornstarch

In a large skillet coated with nonstick cooking spray, brown chicken. Add onion, celery and pepper; cook for 3 minutes. Stir in potatoes and carrots. Combine broth, thyme, ketchup and cornstarch; stir into skillet. Bring to a boil. Reduce heat; cover and simmer for 15-20 minutes or until the vegetables are tender. **Yield:** 6 servings.

NUTRITIONAL INFORMATION

Serving Size: 1/6 recipe

Calories: 198
Total Fat: 3 gm
Calories from Fat: 14%
Saturated Fat: 1 gm
Cholesterol: 63 mg
Sodium: 136 mg
Carbohydrate: 17 gm
Protein: 25 gm

Cabbage and Beef Soup

Ethel Ledbetter, Canton, North Carolina

When I was a little girl, I helped my parents work the fields of their small farm. At lunchtime, Mother would often pick vegetables from the garden and simmer them in a big soup pot. This down-home soup reminds me of those days.

1 pound lean ground round
1/2 teaspoon garlic powder
1/4 teaspoon pepper
2 celery ribs, chopped
1 can (16 ounces) kidney beans, undrained
1/2 medium head cabbage, chopped
2 cans (14-1/2 ounces *each*) no-salt-added tomatoes, diced and undrained
3 cups water
4 low-sodium beef bouillon cubes

In a Dutch oven coated with nonstick cooking spray, brown beef. Add remaining ingredients; bring to a boil. Reduce heat; cover and simmer for 1 hour. **Yield:** 12 servings (3 quarts).

NUTRITIONAL INFORMATION

Serving Size: 1 cup

Calories: 122
Total Fat: 4 gm
Calories from Fat: 28%
Saturated Fat: 1 gm
Cholesterol: 14 mg
Sodium: 179 mg
Carbohydrate: 11 gm
Protein: 11 gm

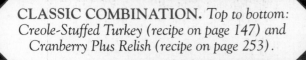

CLASSIC COMBINATION. Top to bottom:
Creole-Stuffed Turkey (recipe on page 147) and
Cranberry Plus Relish (recipe on page 253).

Chicken & Turkey

Creole-Stuffed Turkey

Sandy Szwarc, Albuquerque, New Mexico

(Pictured at left)

Some of my family's favorite dishes came about because of my passion for experimenting with recipes. This is one of them. It originated when my sister from Texas and her family—who love Southern cooking—were here one Thanksgiving.

4 cups cubed corn bread
2 cups cubed crustless day-old whole wheat bread
1 cup chopped fully cooked low-fat ham
3/4 cup chopped low-fat turkey kielbasa
1/2 cup chopped sweet red pepper
1/2 cup chopped green pepper
1/4 cup chopped celery
3 tablespoons chopped onion
2-1/2 teaspoons Creole seasoning*
2 eggs
1 to 1-1/2 cups low-sodium chicken broth
1 turkey (10 pounds)

In a large bowl, combine the first 10 ingredients; add enough broth to moisten. Just before baking, stuff the turkey. Skewer openings; tie drumsticks together. Place on a rack in a roasting pan. Bake at 325° for 3-1/2 to 4 hours or until meat thermometer reads 185°. When the turkey begins to brown, cover lightly with a tent of aluminum foil. Remove all stuffing. **Yield:** 10 servings. *(You may substitute the following spices for the Creole seasoning: 1 teaspoon *each* paprika and garlic powder, and 1/4 teaspoon *each* cayenne pepper, dried thyme and ground cumin.) **Editor's Note:** Stuffing may be baked in a 2-qt. covered baking dish coated with nonstick cooking spray at 325° for 70 minutes (uncover during the last 10 minutes). Stuffing yields 6 cups.

NUTRITIONAL INFORMATION

Serving Size: 3 ounces skinless turkey and 2/3 cup dressing)
(calculated with 1 cup broth)

Calories: 255
Total Fat: 7 gm
Calories from Fat: 25%
Saturated Fat: 2 gm
Cholesterol: 126 mg
Sodium: 742 mg
Carbohydrate: 19 gm
Protein: 29 gm

No-Fuss Chicken

Marilyn Dick, Centralia, Missouri

This recipe could hardly be simpler to prepare. The chicken gets a wonderful tangy taste, and no one will know you used convenient ingredients like a bottle of salad dressing and onion soup mix...unless you tell them.

1 bottle (16 ounces) reduced-fat Russian salad dressing
2/3 cup apricot preserves
2 envelopes dry onion soup mix
16 boneless skinless chicken breast halves (4 pounds)

In a bowl, combine dressing, preserves and soup mix. Place chicken in two ungreased 11-in. x 7-in. x 2-in. baking pans; top with dressing mixture. Cover and bake at 350° for 20 minutes; baste. Bake, uncovered, 20 minutes longer or until chicken juices run clear. **Yield:** 16 servings.

NUTRITIONAL INFORMATION

Serving Size: 1/16 recipe

Calories: 217
Total Fat: 4 gm
Calories from Fat: 18%
Saturated Fat: 1 gm
Cholesterol: 75 mg
Sodium: 396 mg
Carbohydrate: 17 gm
Protein: 27 gm

Southwest Roll-Ups

Dean Schrock, Jacksonville, Florida

Taste buds tingle when I serve these tempting tortillas stuffed with a zesty mixture of chicken, refried beans, salsa and jalapeno peppers.

2 tablespoons salsa
1 jalapeno pepper, seeded
1 garlic clove
2 tablespoons chopped onion
1 can (16 ounces) fat-free refried beans
1/2 teaspoon ground cumin
1 tablespoon chopped fresh cilantro, optional
1 cup cubed cooked chicken breast
1 cup (4 ounces) shredded reduced-fat cheddar cheese, *divided*
12 fat-free flour tortillas
Nonfat sour cream and additional salsa, optional

Place the first eight ingredients and 1/2 cup cheese in a food processor; blend until smooth. Spread evenly over tortillas. Roll up and place seam side down in a 13-in. x 9-in. x 2-in. baking dish coated with non-stick cooking spray. Cover and bake at 350° for 20 minutes or until heated through. Sprinkle with remaining cheese; let stand until cheese melts. Serve with sour cream and salsa if desired. **Yield:** 12 servings.

Marinated Italian Chicken

Jean Brenneman, Cedar Rapids, Iowa

After our baby girl was born, our schedules became even more hectic. So I developed this simple recipe for extra-quick dinners.

4 boneless skinless chicken breast halves (1 pound)
1/2 cup low-fat Italian salad dressing

Place chicken in a shallow pan; pour dressing over. Marinate for 15 minutes; drain. Place chicken on broiler pan rack. Broil for 5-7 minutes on each side or until juices run clear. **Yield:** 4 servings.

Turkey Minute Steaks

Barbara Powell, Laramie, Wyoming

Family and friends rave about these minute steaks made with turkey instead of the traditional beef.

3/4 cup Italian-seasoned bread crumbs
1/4 cup grated Parmesan cheese
1/2 teaspoon dried basil
Pepper to taste
1-1/2 pounds uncooked sliced turkey breast tenderloin
1 egg, beaten
2 tablespoons margarine

In a shallow bowl, combine the bread crumbs, Parmesan cheese, basil and pepper; mix well. Dip turkey in egg, then in crumb mixture, coating both sides. Melt margarine in a skillet over medium-high heat. Cook turkey for 2-3 minutes on each side or until golden brown and juices run clear. **Yield:** 8 servings.

Tarragon Chicken Casserole

Bob Breno, Strongsville, Ohio

(Pictured above)

For a quick, hearty main dish that's ideal when the weather's warm, try this casserole. With cooked chicken, it bakes in just half an hour. People love the tasty sauce and cheese on top.

2 cans (10-3/4 ounces each) low-fat condensed cream of chicken soup, undiluted
2 cups evaporated skim milk
4 teaspoons dried tarragon
1/2 teaspoon pepper
1 package (16 ounces) linguine *or* spaghetti, cooked and drained
6 cups cubed cooked chicken breast
1/3 cup grated Parmesan cheese
Paprika, optional

In a large bowl, combine soup, evaporated milk, tarragon and pepper. Stir in the linguine and chicken. Transfer to an ungreased 4-qt. baking dish. Sprinkle with the Parmesan cheese and paprika if desired. Bake, uncovered, at 350° for 30 minutes or until heated through. **Yield:** 12 servings.

NUTRITIONAL INFORMATION

Serving Size: 1/12 recipe

Calories: 248
Total Fat: 5 gm
Calories from Fat: 17%
Saturated Fat: 1 gm
Cholesterol: 50 mg
Sodium: 373 mg
Carbohydrate: 31 gm
Protein: 20 gm

Old-Fashioned Cabbage Rolls

Florence Krantz, Bismarck, North Dakota

(Pictured below)

It was an abundance of dill in my garden that led me to try this. My family liked the taste so much that, from then on, I made my cabbage rolls with dill.

1 medium head cabbage (3 pounds)
1 pound ground turkey breast
1 can (15 ounces) tomato sauce, *divided*
1 small onion, chopped
1/2 cup uncooked long grain rice
1 tablespoon dried parsley flakes
1/2 teaspoon dill weed
1/8 teaspoon cayenne pepper
1 can (14-1/2 ounces) diced tomatoes, undrained
1/2 teaspoon sugar

Remove core from cabbage. In a large kettle or Dutch oven, cook cabbage in boiling water for 2-3 minutes. Remove outer leaves when softened; return to boiling water as necessary to obtain 12 leaves. Drain; remove thick center vein from leaves. In a bowl, combine turkey, 1/2 cup tomato sauce, onion, rice, parsley, dill and cayenne pepper; mix well. Place about 1/4 cup meat mixture on each cabbage leaf. Fold in sides; starting at unfolded edge, roll up to completely enclose filling. Slice the remaining cabbage; place in a large kettle or Dutch oven. Arrange the cabbage rolls, seam side down, over cabbage. Combine tomatoes, sugar and remaining tomato sauce; pour over cabbage rolls. Cover and bake at 350° for 1-1/2 hours. **Yield:** 6 servings.

Orange Barbecued Turkey

Lynn Zukas, Spencer, Massachusetts

Entertaining is one of my favorite things to do, especially when I can rely on easy recipes that always taste delicious.

5 turkey breast steaks
(1-1/4 pounds)
1/2 cup orange juice
1 teaspoon grated orange
peel
2 teaspoons cooking oil

2 teaspoons Worcestershire
sauce
1 teaspoon ground mustard
1/2 teaspoon pepper
1/8 teaspoon garlic powder

Place turkey in a shallow glass baking dish. Combine all remaining ingredients and pour over turkey. Cover and refrigerate, turning occasionally, 4-6 hours or overnight. Remove turkey; discard marinade. Grill or broil turkey until juices run clear, about 3-5 minutes per side. Do not overcook. **Yield:** 5 servings.

NUTRITIONAL INFORMATION

Serving Size: 1/5 recipe

Calories: 139
Total Fat: 2 gm
Calories from Fat: 16%
Saturated Fat: 1 gm
Cholesterol: 54 mg
Sodium: 99 mg
Carbohydrate: 2 gm
Protein: 27 gm

Dilled Turkey Breast

Nancy Bohlen, Brookings, South Dakota

A nice light cream sauce is a fast yet fancy way to dress up leftover turkey.

1 can (10-3/4 ounces)
low-fat condensed cream
of mushroom soup,
undiluted
3/4 cup light sour cream

3/4 cup low-sodium chicken
broth
1 tablespoon dill weed
1-1/2 pounds sliced cooked
turkey breast, warmed

In a saucepan, combine soup, sour cream, broth and dill. Cook until heated through (do not boil). Arrange turkey slices on a platter; pour sauce over and serve immediately. **Yield:** 8 servings.

NUTRITIONAL INFORMATION

Serving Size: 1/8 recipe

Calories: 170
Total Fat: 4 gm
Calories from Fat: 20%
Saturated Fat: 2 gm
Cholesterol: 82 mg
Sodium: 218 mg
Carbohydrate: 5 gm
Protein: 28 gm

Italian Chicken

Nancy Tafoya, Fort Collins, Colorado

Unfortunately, I have little time for leisure cooking. But this dish proves you don't have to sacrifice flavor when serving "fast foods".

1/2 cup grated Parmesan
cheese
2 tablespoons dried oregano
1 tablespoon minced fresh
parsley
1/4 teaspoon pepper

Dash garlic powder
4 boneless skinless chicken
breast halves (1 pound)
2 egg whites, beaten
1 tablespoon margarine,
melted

In a shallow bowl, combine Parmesan cheese, oregano, parsley, pepper and garlic powder. Brush chicken with egg whites, then coat with Parmesan mixture. Place in a 9-in. square baking dish coated with non-stick cooking spray. Drizzle with margarine. Bake, uncovered, at 425° for 15-20 minutes or until juices run clear. **Yield:** 4 servings.

NUTRITIONAL INFORMATION

Serving Size: 1/4 recipe

Calories: 240
Total Fat: 10 gm
Calories from Fat: 38%
Saturated Fat: 4 gm
Cholesterol: 83 mg
Sodium: 349 mg
Carbohydrate: 2 gm
Protein: 34 gm

Cranberry Chicken

Dorothy Bateman, Carver, Massachusetts

(Pictured above)

My husband loves chicken when it's nice and moist, like it is in this hearty recipe. I serve it over hot fluffy rice for a complete meal. The ruby-red sauce has a tart cinnamony flavor.

1/2 cup all-purpose flour	1 cup fresh *or* frozen
1/4 teaspoon pepper	cranberries
6 boneless skinless chicken	1/2 cup packed brown sugar
breast halves (1-1/2	Dash ground nutmeg
pounds)	1 tablespoon red wine
3 tablespoons margarine	vinegar, optional
1 cup water	Hot cooked rice, optional

In a shallow dish, combine flour and pepper; dredge chicken. In a skillet, melt margarine over medium heat. Brown the chicken on both sides. Remove and keep warm. In the same skillet, combine water, cranberries, brown sugar, nutmeg and vinegar if desired. Cook and stir until the berries burst, about 5 minutes. Return chicken to skillet. Cover and simmer for 20-30 minutes or until chicken is tender, basting occasionally with the sauce. Serve over rice if desired. **Yield:** 6 servings.

Creamy Nutmeg Chicken

Candi Ondracek, West Sacramento, California

As a way to cut costs in the kitchen, I've been experimenting with chicken recipes. I actually wanted to make another dish but didn't have all the ingredients, so I substituted a few and came up with this recipe.

6 boneless skinless chicken breast halves (1-1/2 pounds)
1/4 cup chopped onion
1/4 cup minced fresh parsley
2 cans (10-3/4 ounces *each*) low-fat condensed cream of mushroom soup, undiluted

1/2 cup light sour cream
1/2 cup skim milk
1 tablespoon ground nutmeg
1/4 teaspoon rubbed sage
1/4 teaspoon dried thyme
1/4 teaspoon dried rosemary, crushed
Additional nutmeg, optional

In a large skillet coated with nonstick cooking spray, brown chicken. Remove chicken and set aside. In the drippings, saute onion and parsley until onion is tender. Add soup, sour cream, milk, nutmeg, sage, thyme and rosemary; mix well. Return chicken to the skillet and spoon sauce over pieces. Simmer, uncovered, for 25-30 minutes or until chicken is tender and juices run clear. Baste occasionally. Sprinkle with nutmeg if desired. **Yield:** 6 servings.

NUTRITIONAL INFORMATION

Serving Size: 1/6 recipe

Calories: 242
Total Fat: 7 gm
Calories from Fat: 28%
Saturated Fat: 3 gm
Cholesterol: 88 mg
Sodium: 480 mg
Carbohydrate: 11 gm
Protein: 31 gm

Turkey Stroganoff

Karen Ann Bland, Gove, Kansas

This tasty new spin on ordinary Stroganoff teams up turkey and broccoli for unbeatable flavor. And microwave-cooking allows me to get dinner on the table in a jiffy.

2 cups frozen cut broccoli
1 tablespoon water
1/4 cup chopped onion
3 tablespoons all-purpose flour
1 can (10-3/4 ounces) condensed low-sodium chicken broth, undiluted

2 cups cubed cooked turkey breast
1 cup (8 ounces) light sour cream
1 can (4 ounces) sliced mushrooms, drained
1/2 teaspoon dried rosemary, crushed
1/4 teaspoon pepper

Cook broccoli according to package directions; drain and set aside. In a 2-qt. microwave-safe casserole, combine water and onion; cover and cook on high until tender. Add flour and blend well. Whisk in broth; cook on high for 4-6 minutes or until thickened and bubbly, stirring every 2 minutes. Add remaining ingredients. Cook on high for 2-3 minutes or until heated through, stirring once. **Yield:** 4 servings.

NUTRITIONAL INFORMATION

Serving Size: 1/4 recipe

Calories: 187
Total Fat: 6 gm
Calories from Fat: 27%
Saturated Fat: 4 gm
Cholesterol: 40 mg
Sodium: 422 mg
Carbohydrate: 16 gm
Protein: 19 gm

Spaghetti with Turkey Sausage

Ginger Harrell, El Dorado, Arkansas

With fresh garden peppers and onion, this dish is not only quick but economical, too. It's a great summertime supper.

1 pound low-fat smoked turkey sausage, cut into 1/4-inch slices
2 medium green peppers, thinly sliced
2 medium sweet red peppers, thinly sliced
1 medium onion, halved and thinly sliced
2 cans (14-1/2 ounces *each*) diced tomatoes, undrained
3 garlic cloves, minced
6 drops hot pepper sauce
1 teaspoon paprika
1/4 teaspoon cayenne pepper
1/2 cup low-sodium chicken broth
2 tablespoons cornstarch
1 package (12 ounces) spaghetti, cooked and drained

In a Dutch oven, brown sausage. Add peppers and onion; saute for 2 minutes. Add tomatoes, garlic, hot pepper sauce, paprika and cayenne; cook and stir until the vegetables are tender. Combine broth and cornstarch; add to sausage mixture. Bring to a boil; cook and stir until thickened. Add spaghetti; heat through, stirring occasionally. **Yield:** 8 servings.

Herbed Chicken

Marshall Simon, Grand Rapids, Michigan

I've enjoyed cooking up dishes like this since I was a teen. It's a great meal.

1 medium onion, chopped
1 green *or* sweet red pepper, chopped
6 large fresh mushrooms, thinly sliced
1/3 cup low-sodium chicken broth
2 tablespoons red wine vinegar
3 cups no-salt-added tomato sauce
2 garlic cloves, minced
1 teaspoon sugar
1/4 teaspoon pepper
1 pound boneless skinless chicken breasts, cut into chunks
2 tablespoons chopped fresh basil *or* 2 teaspoons dried basil
1 tablespoon chopped fresh sage *or* 1 teaspoon rubbed sage
1 package (16 ounces) linguine, cooked and drained
2 tablespoons grated Parmesan cheese
2 tablespoons chopped fresh parsley

In a skillet coated with nonstick cooking spray, saute onion, pepper and mushrooms over medium-high heat until tender. Add broth and vinegar; bring to a boil. Boil 2 minutes. Add tomato sauce, garlic, sugar and pepper; return to a boil. Reduce heat; cover and simmer for 25 minutes. Add chicken, basil and sage. Cook, uncovered, 15 minutes more or until chicken is tender and sauce is slightly thickened. Serve chicken and sauce over linguine. Sprinkle with cheese and parsley. **Yield:** 4 servings.

Orange Turkey Stir-Fry

Anne Frederick, New Hartford, New York

(Pictured above)

This dish can be ready to serve in no more than 30 minutes. One of my favorite hobbies is cooking, but because I lead a busy life, it's essential to be able to fix a good meal quickly. The citrus sauce and colorful orange slices will give you a "sunshine feeling" when you sit down to eat this after a busy day!

3/4 cup orange juice
1/4 cup orange marmalade
2 tablespoons light soy
   sauce
2 tablespoons cornstarch
1/8 teaspoon ground ginger
1/8 teaspoon hot pepper
   sauce
1 pound turkey tenderloin,
   trimmed and cut into
   1-inch strips

1/4 cup all-purpose flour
2 teaspoons cooking oil
4 green onions, cut into
   1-inch pieces
1/2 cup coarsely chopped
   green pepper
1 seedless orange, peeled,
   sliced and halved
Hot cooked rice, optional

In a small bowl, combine the first six ingredients; set aside. Dredge turkey in flour; shake off excess. In a 10-in. skillet, heat oil over medium-high heat. Cook turkey in three batches until tender and lightly browned on all sides. Remove and keep warm. Add onions and green pepper to the skillet; cook and stir for 1 minute. Stir in orange juice mixture. Bring to a boil; reduce heat and simmer for 3 minutes. Add turkey and oranges; heat through. Serve over rice if desired. **Yield:** 4 servings.

NUTRITIONAL INFORMATION

Serving Size: 1/4 recipe
(calculated without rice)

Calories: 289
Total Fat: 4 gm
Calories from Fat: 13%
Saturated Fat: 1 gm
Cholesterol: 54 mg
Sodium: 353 mg
Carbohydrate: 35 gm
Protein: 30 gm

Scalloped Chicken

Rosella Bauer, Cissna Park, Illinois

(Pictured above)

For easy preparation, make everything but the topping a day ahead and then refrigerate it. The next day, remove from the refrigerator 30 minutes before baking and add the topping.

8 slices white bread, cubed	2 tablespoons chopped
1-1/2 cups low-sodium cracker crumbs, *divided*	onion
	3 cups cubed cooked chicken breast
3 cups low-sodium chicken broth	1 can (8 ounces) sliced mushrooms, drained
3 eggs	
3/4 cup diced celery	2 teaspoons margarine

In a bowl, combine bread cubes and 1 cup cracker crumbs. Stir in broth, eggs, celery, onion, chicken and mushrooms. Spoon into a 2-qt. baking dish coated with nonstick cooking spray. In a saucepan, melt margarine; brown remaining cracker crumbs. Sprinkle over casserole. Bake at 350° for 1 hour. **Yield:** 8 servings.

Autumn Casserole

Joan Hoch, Boyertown, Pennsylvania

My family agrees that fall is the perfect time of year for this hearty casserole to make an appearance on the dinner table. You'll love the flavor!

2 cans (15 ounces *each*) sweet potatoes, drained	2 tablespoons brown sugar
	1 pound low-fat smoked turkey sausage, sliced
5 medium tart apples, peeled and quartered	1 inch thick

In a 2-1/2-qt. baking dish coated with nonstick cooking spray, layer sweet potatoes and apples. Sprinkle with sugar. Top with sausage. Cover and bake at 375° for 30 minutes or until the apples are tender. **Yield:** 8 servings.

Curry Chicken Dinner

Marilyn Ausland, Columbus, Georgia

(Pictured below)

This chicken dish was originated by a woman from our town for a special party in honor of President Franklin D. Roosevelt. I really enjoy treating out-of-town relatives and friends to this dish when they come to visit.

8 boneless skinless chicken breast halves (2 pounds)
1/2 cup all-purpose flour
2 tablespoons cooking oil
2 medium onions, chopped
2 medium green peppers, chopped
1 garlic clove, minced
2 teaspoons curry powder
1/2 teaspoon white pepper
2 cans (14-1/2 ounces *each*) diced tomatoes, undrained
1 teaspoon chopped fresh parsley
1/2 teaspoon dried thyme
1 cup water
3 tablespoons raisins
Hot cooked rice, optional

Dust chicken with flour. In a Dutch oven over medium heat, brown the chicken in oil. Remove chicken and set aside. Add onions, green peppers and garlic to drippings; saute for 3-4 minutes or until tender. Add curry and pepper; mix well. Return chicken to the pan. Add tomatoes, parsley, thyme and water. Cover and bake at 375° for 45-50 minutes or until chicken is tender and juices run clear. Stir in raisins. Serve over rice if desired. **Yield:** 8 servings.

NUTRITIONAL INFORMATION

Serving Size: 1/8 recipe
(calculated without rice)

Calories: 230
Total Fat: 6 gm
Calories from Fat: 25%
Saturated Fat: 1 gm
Cholesterol: 63 mg
Sodium: 233 mg
Carbohydrate: 17 gm
Protein: 25 gm

Turkey Primavera

Zita Wilensky, North Miami Beach, Florida

(Pictured above)

We grow herbs and vegetables in our garden, so I incorporate them into recipes whenever possible. This creation has tender turkey and mushrooms, onions and green pepper covered in a zippy tomato sauce.

NUTRITIONAL INFORMATION

Serving Size: 1/6 recipe
(calculated without pasta)

Calories: 196
Total Fat: 4 gm
Calories from Fat: 19%
Saturated Fat: 1 gm
Cholesterol: 54
Sodium: 411 mg
Carbohydrate: 10 gm
Protein: 30 gm

1/4 cup all-purpose flour
2 teaspoons minced fresh parsley
1-1/2 pounds turkey tenderloin, trimmed and cubed
1 tablespoon olive *or* vegetable oil
1/2 cup low-sodium chicken broth
1 cup sliced fresh mushrooms
1 medium onion, chopped
4 garlic cloves, minced
1/2 medium green pepper, chopped
1-3/4 cups low-sodium beef broth
3/4 cup tomato puree
1/2 teaspoon dried thyme
1/2 teaspoon dried rosemary, crushed
1/2 teaspoon dried basil
1 bay leaf
1/8 teaspoon pepper
Hot cooked fettuccine *or* spaghetti, optional

Combine flour and parsley; toss with turkey. In a skillet, brown turkey in oil; remove with a slotted spoon and set aside. In the same skillet, combine chicken broth, mushrooms, onion, garlic and green pepper; cook and stir for 3-4 minutes. Add beef broth, tomato puree and seasonings; cook and stir for 20-25 minutes or until sauce is desired consistency. Add turkey; heat through. Remove the bay leaf. Serve over pasta if desired. **Yield:** 6 servings.

Sour Cream 'n' Dill Chicken

Rebekah Brown, Three Hills, Alberta

This recipe is an updated version of a dish my mother would often make for Sunday dinner when I was a girl. Now it's become a real favorite on our table on Sundays.

8 boneless skinless chicken breast halves (2 pounds)
Pepper to taste
1 can (10-3/4 ounces) low-fat condensed cream of mushroom soup, undiluted
1 envelope dry onion soup mix

1 cup (8 ounces) light sour cream
1 tablespoon lemon juice
1 tablespoon chopped fresh dill *or* 1 teaspoon dill weed
1 can (4 ounces) sliced mushrooms, drained
Paprika

Place chicken in a single layer in a 13-in. x 9-in. x 2-in. baking pan coated with nonstick cooking spray. Sprinkle with pepper. Combine soup, soup mix, sour cream, lemon juice, dill and mushrooms; pour over chicken. Sprinkle with paprika. Bake, uncovered, at 350° for 1 hour or until chicken is tender and juices run clear. **Yield:** 8 servings.

NUTRITIONAL INFORMATION

Serving Size: 1/8 recipe

Calories: 207
Total Fat: 6 gm
Calories from Fat: 29%
Saturated Fat: 3 gm
Cholesterol: 85 mg
Sodium: 369 mg
Carbohydrate: 6 gm
Protein: 30 gm

Chicken Aloha

Beth Corbin, Sarasota, Florida

When time gets tight around dinnertime, I often "wing it" in the kitchen—by turning out this chicken dish featuring a tangy tropical sauce. Before my family knows it, dinner is served!

8 boneless skinless chicken breast halves (2 pounds)
1 bottle (14 ounces) ketchup
1 can (10-3/4 ounces) low-fat condensed tomato soup, undiluted

1 large green pepper, chopped
1/4 cup packed brown sugar
1/3 cup vinegar
1 teaspoon ground mustard
1 can (8 ounces) unsweetened pineapple chunks, undrained

Place chicken in a 13-in. x 9-in. x 2-in. baking pan coated with nonstick cooking spray. Combine all remaining ingredients; pour over chicken. Bake, covered, at 375° for 1 hour. Uncover and bake 15 minutes more or until chicken is tender. **Yield:** 8 servings.

NUTRITIONAL INFORMATION

Serving Size: 1/8 recipe

Calories: 293
Total Fat: 4 gm
Calories from Fat: 12%
Saturated Fat: 1 gm
Cholesterol: 73 mg
Sodium: 804 mg
Carbohydrate: 37 gm
Protein: 28 gm

Quick Chicken Cacciatore

Marcia Hostetter, Canton, New York

My family raves over this recipe, saying it tastes better than any restaurant's. This colorful, flavorful dish is my favorite because it's fast to fix.

1 medium green pepper, cut into strips
1 medium onion, sliced into rings
1/2 pound fresh mushrooms, sliced
4 boneless skinless chicken breast halves (1 pound)
1 can (15 ounces) tomato sauce
1 can (4 ounces) chopped green chilies
1/4 to 1/2 teaspoon dried basil
1/4 to 1/2 teaspoon dried oregano
1/8 to 1/4 teaspoon garlic powder
Dash cayenne pepper

In a large skillet coated with nonstick cooking spray, saute green pepper, onion and mushrooms for 4-5 minutes or until crisp-tender. Place chicken over the vegetables. Combine tomato sauce, chilies and seasonings; pour over the chicken. Cover and simmer for 20 minutes or until chicken is no longer pink. **Yield:** 4 servings.

Sauerkraut 'n' Turkey Sausage

Edna Hoffman, Hebron, Indiana

I've fixed this satisfying stovetop supper for dozens of group gatherings, and everyone seems to enjoy the wonderful blend of flavors. Sweet and tart ingredients balance nicely, complemented with sausage and spices.

1 small onion, chopped
1 teaspoon margarine
1 jar (32 ounces) sauerkraut, rinsed and drained
1 pound fully cooked low-fat smoked turkey sausage, cut into 1/2-inch chunks
3-1/2 cups diced cooked peeled potatoes
1 medium unpeeled tart apple, diced
1 cup apple juice
2 tablespoons brown sugar
2 tablespoons all-purpose flour
1 tablespoon caraway seeds
2 bacon strips, cooked and crumbled

In a large saucepan, saute onion in margarine until tender. Add the sauerkraut, sausage, potatoes, apple and juice. In a small bowl, combine the brown sugar, flour and caraway; stir into saucepan. Simmer for 35 minutes, stirring occasionally. Sprinkle with bacon. **Yield:** 12 servings.

Grilled Citrus Chicken

Dana Fulton, Stone Mountain, Georgia

(Pictured above)

I've served this main dish numerous times for dinner guests and have received many compliments. In fact, every time I make it for my husband, he'll comment, "This is the best chicken I've ever had."

6 boneless skinless chicken
   breast halves (1-1/2
   pounds)
1/2 cup packed brown sugar
1/4 cup cider vinegar
3 tablespoons lemon juice

3 tablespoons lime juice
3 tablespoons Dijon
   mustard
3/4 teaspoon garlic powder
1/4 teaspoon pepper

Place chicken in a shallow glass dish. Combine remaining ingredients; pour over chicken. Cover and refrigerate 4 hours or overnight. Drain, discarding marinade. Grill chicken over medium-hot coals, turning once, until juices run clear, about 15-18 minutes. **Yield:** 6 servings.

NUTRITIONAL INFORMATION

Serving Size: 1/6 recipe

Calories: 172
Total Fat: 3 gm
Calories from Fat: 18%
Saturated Fat: 1 gm
Cholesterol: 73 mg
Sodium: 161 mg
Carbohydrate: 7 gm
Protein: 27 gm

Marinated Turkey Tenderloin

Rachel Wellborne, Jacksonville, North Carolina

(Pictured below)

For years, I've been exchanging recipes by correspondence with friends. What's best about this recipe is that you can enjoy wonderful turkey flavor without preparing a whole bird.

NUTRITIONAL INFORMATION

Serving Size: 1/4 recipe

Calories: 180
Total Fat: 1 gm
Calories from Fat: 5%
Saturated Fat: trace
Cholesterol: 54
Sodium: 88 mg
Carbohydrate: 14 gm
Protein: 27 gm

1 turkey breast tenderloin (1 pound), trimmed	1/8 teaspoon pepper
1-1/2 cups unsweetened pineapple juice	1/8 teaspoon ground ginger
1/3 cup sugar	Dash ground cloves
	Dash garlic powder

Place the turkey in a shallow glass dish. Combine remaining ingredients; mix well. Remove 1/3 cup; cover and refrigerate. Pour the remaining marinade over turkey. Cover and refrigerate 4 hours or overnight. Drain and discard marinade. Place turkey in an ungreased 11-in. x 7-in. x 2-in. baking dish. Pour reserved marinade over turkey. Cover and bake at 350° for 30 minutes. Uncover and bake 20-30 minutes longer or until no longer pink, basting twice. Slice and serve immediately. **Yield:** 4 servings.

Grilled Chicken Kabobs

Paul Miller, Green Bay, Wisconsin

I have fun trying new recipes and creating dishes of my own. I especially enjoy main entrees like this that are a little lighter and let the food's natural flavors come through.

2 teaspoons ground
  mustard
1 tablespoon
  Worcestershire sauce
1/2 cup water
1/2 cup light soy sauce
1 teaspoon vegetable oil
4 boneless skinless chicken
  breast halves (1 pound)

2 medium zucchini, cut
  into 1-1/2-inch slices
1 medium onion, cut into
  wedges
1 medium green pepper,
  cut into chunks
8 medium fresh mushrooms

In a resealable plastic bag, combine the mustard and Worcestershire sauce. Add water, soy sauce and oil; remove 1/3 cup and set aside for basting. Cut chicken into 1-1/2-in. chunks; add to bag. Seal and refrigerate for 1-1/2 to 2 hours. Drain, discarding marinade. Thread chicken and vegetables alternately on skewers. Baste with reserved marinade. Grill over hot coals for 10 minutes. Turn and baste. Cook 10 minutes more or until chicken juices run clear. **Yield:** 4 servings.

NUTRITIONAL INFORMATION

Serving Size: 1/4 recipe

Calories: 197
Total Fat: 5 gm
Calories from Fat: 22%
Saturated Fat: 1 gm
Cholesterol: 73 mg
Sodium: 593 mg
Carbohydrate: 8 gm
Protein: 30 gm

Chicken and Barley Boiled Dinner

Susan Greeley, Morrill, Maine

I was looking for a recipe that was nutritious and would adequately feed my two teenage sons and husband. I'm a busy teacher, and time is of the essence. This tasty recipe is easily prepared for an evening meal.

2 broiler-fryer chickens
  (3 pounds *each*), cut up
  and skinned
2 quarts low-sodium
  chicken broth
1 cup uncooked brown rice
1/2 cup pearl barley
1 medium onion, chopped
2 bay leaves

1/2 teaspoon dried basil
1/4 teaspoon pepper
8 carrots, cut into 1-inch
  slices
2-1/2 cups frozen cut green
  beans
2 celery ribs, cut into
  1-inch slices

In an 8-qt. kettle or Dutch oven coated with nonstick cooking spray, brown chicken. Remove chicken and set aside. Drain. In the same kettle, combine the broth, rice, barley, onion, bay leaves, basil and pepper; bring to a boil. Reduce heat. Return chicken to pan; cover and simmer for 45 minutes. Stir in the carrots, beans and celery. Cook over medium heat for 30 minutes or until the chicken and grains are tender. Remove bay leaves before serving. **Yield:** 10 servings.

NUTRITIONAL INFORMATION

Serving Size: 1/10 recipe

Calories: 383
Total Fat: 10 gm
Calories from Fat: 23%
Saturated Fat: 3 gm
Cholesterol: 107 mg
Sodium: 585 mg
Carbohydrate: 32 gm
Protein: 41 gm

Turkey with Country Ham Stuffing

Bobbie Love, Kapaa, Hawaii

As delicious as this is right out of the oven, the bird and stuffing both taste great as leftovers, too.

3 cups cubed crustless day-old white bread
3 cups cubed crustless day-old whole wheat bread
1-1/2 cups cubed fully cooked low-fat ham
3 cups chopped onion
2 cups chopped celery
1-1/2 teaspoons rubbed sage
1-1/2 teaspoons dried thyme
1/2 teaspoon pepper
1-1/2 cups low-sodium chicken broth
1 turkey (12 pounds)

Place bread cubes in a single layer in a 13-in. x 9-in. x 2-in. baking pan. Bake at 325° for 20-25 minutes or until golden, stirring occasionally. Place in a large bowl; set aside. In a large skillet coated with nonstick cooking spray, cook ham until edges are crisp. Remove with a slotted spoon and place over bread cubes. In the same skillet, saute the onion, celery, sage, thyme and pepper until vegetables are tender; toss with bread and ham. Stir in enough broth to moisten. Just before baking, stuff the turkey. Skewer openings; tie drumsticks together. Place on a rack in a roasting pan. Bake at 325° for 4 to 4-1/2 hours or until meat thermometer reads 185°. When the turkey begins to brown, cover lightly with a tent of aluminum foil. Remove all stuffing. **Yield:** 14 servings. **Editor's Note:** Stuffing may be baked in a 3-qt. covered baking dish coated with nonstick cooking spray at 325° for 70 minutes (uncover for the last 10 minutes). Stuffing yields 10 cups.

NUTRITIONAL INFORMATION

Serving Size: 3 ounces skinless turkey and 3/4 cup stuffing

Calories: 384
Total Fat: 11 gm
Calories from Fat: 28%
Saturated Fat: 4 gm
Cholesterol: 137 mg
Sodium: 426 mg
Carbohydrate: 11 gm
Protein: 57 gm

Hungarian Chicken

Crystal Garza, Shamrock, Texas

Ever since I made Hungarian Chicken for the first time (after coming across it in an old church cookbook), it's been a family favorite.

6 tablespoons all-purpose flour
Pepper to taste
1 broiler-fryer chicken (3 pounds), skinned and cut up
1 large onion, chopped
2/3 cup tomato juice
2/3 cup low-sodium chicken broth
1 tablespoon paprika
1 teaspoon sugar
1 bay leaf
2/3 cup light sour cream

Combine flour and pepper in a plastic bag. Add chicken, a few pieces at a time, and shake. In a large skillet coated with nonstick cooking spray, saute onion until tender. Remove from pan and set aside. In the same skillet, brown chicken on all sides. Combine tomato juice, broth, paprika, sugar, bay leaf and onion; pour over chicken. Cover and simmer for 45-60 minutes or until chicken is tender. Remove chicken to a platter and keep warm. Reduce heat to low; remove bay leaf and stir in sour cream. Heat through for 2-3 minutes (do not boil). Pour over chicken and serve immediately. **Yield:** 6 servings.

NUTRITIONAL INFORMATION

Serving Size: 1/6 recipe

Calories: 278
Total Fat: 10 gm
Calories from Fat: 34%
Saturated Fat: 4 gm
Cholesterol: 99 mg
Sodium: 216 mg
Carbohydrate: 12 gm
Protein: 33 gm

Apricot Chicken

Bonnie Baumgardner, Sylva, North Carolina

(Pictured below)

This is one of my original recipes, but I've made it so long that it's an old standby for my family! The combination of ingredients is quite unusual but so tasty.

4 boneless skinless chicken breast halves (1 pound)	2 cups low-sodium chicken broth
1 medium onion, chopped	1 cup (8 ounces) light sour cream
1/2 cup chopped green pepper	1/4 teaspoon grated lemon peel
1 tablespoon all-purpose flour	1/2 cup finely chopped dried apricots
1 tablespoon paprika	Hot cooked egg noodles, optional
1/4 teaspoon white pepper	

In a skillet coated with nonstick cooking spray, cook chicken until browned. Remove chicken. Add onion and green pepper to skillet; saute until soft. Add flour, paprika and pepper; stir until well blended. Gradually add broth, stirring until smooth and thickened. Remove from the heat; stir in sour cream, lemon peel and apricots. Arrange chicken in an 11-in. x 7-in. x 2-in. baking dish coated with nonstick cooking spray. Pour sauce over chicken. Bake, uncovered, at 350° for 20-30 minutes or until chicken is tender. If desired, place hot noodles in a serving dish. Arrange chicken over noodles. Top with sauce. **Yield:** 4 servings.

NUTRITIONAL INFORMATION

Serving Size: 1/4 recipe
(calculated without noodles)

Calories: 292
Total Fat: 9 gm
Calories from Fat: 28%
Saturated Fat: 5 gm
Cholesterol: 94 mg
Sodium: 158 mg
Carbohydrate: 20 gm
Protein: 33 gm

Poultry Pointers

When purchasing fresh chicken, check the "Sell by" date on the package. This date allows for 2 to 3 additional days of refrigerated storage at home before cooking. Chicken should have no detectable odor. The flesh should feel firm and the surface should not feel slick.

Before wrapping chicken for the freezer, spray sheets of aluminum foil with nonstick cooking spray. When you unwrap it later, the foil comes right off without sticking or tearing.

When a recipe requires you to cut raw chicken or turkey, partially freeze it beforehand. You'll find it's easier and faster to slice.

Sour Cream Apple Chicken

Carolyn Popwell, Lacey, Washington

I've found that apples and chicken go well together because they both have subtle flavors. I developed this recipe myself, and family and friends were delighted with the results. I think it's not only a great-tasting main course, it also looks nice on the table. Why not try it today?

4 boneless skinless chicken breast halves (1 pound)	1 teaspoon dried basil
2 medium tart apples, peeled and thinly sliced	1 cup (8 ounces) light sour cream
1/2 cup apple juice	1 tablespoon all-purpose flour
1/3 cup chopped onion	Paprika

In a large skillet coated with nonstick cooking spray, cook chicken over medium heat until browned and juices run clear, about 6-8 minutes per side. Remove to a serving platter and keep warm. Add apples, juice, onion and basil to the skillet; bring to a boil. Reduce heat; cover and simmer until apples are tender. Combine sour cream and flour; add to skillet. Cook and stir until sauce is warm (do not boil). Spoon over chicken. Sprinkle with paprika. **Yield:** 4 servings.

Orange Chicken

Betty Sexton, Blairsville, Georgia

I found this recipe several years ago while looking for a new way to prepare chicken. My husband, daughter and I live on a small farm in the mountains of north Georgia. This has become our favorite evening meal after we complete our chores.

1 egg	1 tablespoon grated orange peel
1/3 cup orange juice	8 boneless skinless chicken breast halves (2 pounds)
1 cup herb-seasoned stuffing mix, crushed	2 tablespoons margarine, melted
1-1/2 teaspoons paprika	

In a shallow bowl, beat egg; add orange juice. In another bowl, combine stuffing mix, paprika and orange peel. Dip chicken into the egg mixture, then into crumbs, turning to coat well. Place in a 13-in. x 9-in. x 2-in. baking dish coated with nonstick cooking spray. Drizzle with margarine. Bake, uncovered, at 375° for 45 minutes or until the chicken is tender and juices run clear. **Yield:** 8 servings.

Turkey Tetrazzini

Gladys Waldrop, Calvert City, Kentucky

(Pictured above)

This recipe comes from a cookbook our church compiled. It's convenient because it can be made ahead and frozen. After the holidays, we use leftover turkey to prepare a meal for university students. They clean their plates!

1 package (7 ounces)
  spaghetti, broken into
  2-inch pieces
2 cups cubed cooked
  turkey breast
1 cup (4 ounces) shredded
  reduced-fat cheddar
  cheese
1 can (10-3/4 ounces) low-
  fat condensed cream of
  mushroom soup,
  undiluted

1 medium onion, chopped
2 cans (4 ounces *each*)
  sliced mushrooms,
  drained
1/3 cup skim milk
1/4 cup chopped green pepper
1 jar (2 ounces) diced
  pimientos, drained
1/8 teaspoon pepper
Additional shredded reduced-
  fat cheddar cheese, optional

NUTRITIONAL INFORMATION

Serving Size: 1/8 recipe
(calculated without
additional cheese)

Calories: 223
Total Fat: 6 gm
Calories from Fat: 25%
Saturated Fat: 3 gm
Cholesterol: 28 mg
Sodium: 288 mg
Carbohydrate: 26 gm
Protein: 16 gm

Cook spaghetti according to package directions; drain. Transfer to a large bowl; add the next nine ingredients and mix well. Spoon into a 2-1/2-qt. casserole coated with nonstick cooking spray; sprinkle with cheese if desired. Bake, uncovered, at 375° for 40-45 minutes or until heated through. **Yield:** 8 servings.

Picante-Dijon Grilled Chicken

Karen Page, St. Louis, Missouri

(Pictured above)

We love to barbecue so much that we do it all year long. This recipe is one of my most dependable because it has few ingredients and, since it doesn't need marinating, can be prepared for the grill in just minutes.

NUTRITIONAL INFORMATION

Serving Size: 1/8 recipe

Calories: 183
Total Fat: 4 gm
Calories from Fat: 19%
Saturated Fat: 1 gm
Cholesterol: 73 mg
Sodium: 400 mg
Carbohydrate: 9 gm
Protein: 27 gm

8 boneless skinless chicken breast halves (2 pounds)
1-1/2 cups picante sauce

2 tablespoons Dijon mustard
1/4 cup packed brown sugar

Flatten chicken breasts to about 1/2-in. thickness. Combine picante sauce, mustard and brown sugar; mix well. Grill chicken over medium-hot coals for 2 minutes. Turn and brush generously with some of the picante sauce mixture. Grill 10-12 minutes longer or until chicken is tender and juices run clear, turning and brushing occasionally with remaining picante sauce mixture. **Yield:** 8 servings.

Creole Skillet Dinner

Bonnie Brann, Pasco, Washington

While living in Canada, I sampled this colorful dish at a neighbor's. The following Christmas, I served it instead of my traditional turkey, and I received numerous compliments on it.

4 cups low-sodium chicken broth
2-1/2 cups uncooked long grain rice
1 cup chopped red onion
3 garlic cloves, minced, *divided*
1-1/4 teaspoons chili powder
1/2 teaspoon ground turmeric
1/4 teaspoon pepper
1 bay leaf
1 large sweet red pepper, julienned
1 large green pepper, julienned
2 green onions, sliced
1 teaspoon chopped fresh parsley
1/2 teaspoon dried basil
1/2 teaspoon dried thyme
1/4 teaspoon hot pepper sauce
1 cup sliced fresh mushrooms
1 medium tomato, chopped
1 cup frozen peas, thawed
1 pound boneless skinless chicken breasts, thinly sliced
2 tablespoons lemon juice

In a saucepan, combine broth, rice, red onion, 1 teaspoon garlic, chili powder, turmeric, pepper and bay leaf; bring to a boil. Reduce heat; cover and simmer for 20 minutes or until rice is tender. Discard bay leaf. In a skillet coated with nonstick cooking spray, combine the next seven ingredients and remaining garlic; saute for 2 minutes over medium-high heat. Add mushrooms; cook until peppers are crisp-tender. Add tomato and peas; heat through. Remove from the heat. Add rice; keep warm. Over medium-high heat, cook and stir chicken in lemon juice until chicken juices run clear. Add to rice mixture; toss. **Yield:** 8 servings.

Stuffed Chicken Breast

Alvena Franklin, Coldwater, Michigan

As a widow, I've learned to scale down recipes for dishes that I served when our four kids were still at home. I make this often for myself.

1 skinless bone-in chicken breast half
1/8 teaspoon pepper
1 tablespoon chopped onion
1 tablespoon chopped celery
2 slices day-old white bread, cubed
1/8 teaspoon *each* dried thyme, basil and parsley flakes
3 tablespoons low-sodium chicken broth

Place chicken with cavity side up on a piece of heavy-duty foil large enough to fold over the chicken. Sprinkle with pepper; set aside. In a skillet coated with nonstick cooking spray, saute onion and celery until soft; stir in bread cubes, seasonings and broth. Place in cavity of chicken; fold foil over top and seal. Place in a small baking pan. Bake at 375° for 45 minutes. Open foil and bake 5 minutes more or until chicken is tender, juices run clear and stuffing is lightly browned. **Yield:** 1 serving.

Sesame Ginger Chicken

Nancy Johnson, Connersville, Indiana

(Pictured below)

Why grill plain chicken breasts when a simple ginger-honey basting sauce can make them extra special? This tempting chicken is a wonderful summer main dish since it's quick and light. My family loves it.

2 tablespoons light soy
  sauce
2 tablespoons honey
1 tablespoon sesame seeds,
  toasted

1/2 teaspoon ground ginger
4 boneless skinless chicken
  breast halves (1 pound)
2 green onions with tops,
  cut into thin strips

In a small bowl, combine the first four ingredients; set aside. Flatten the chicken breasts to 1/4-in. thickness. Grill over medium-hot coals, turning and basting frequently with soy sauce mixture, for 8 minutes or until juices run clear. Garnish with onions. **Yield:** 4 servings.

NUTRITIONAL INFORMATION

Serving Size: 1/4 recipe

Calories: 199
Total Fat: 4 gm
Calories from Fat: 18%
Saturated Fat: 1 gm
Cholesterol: 73
Sodium: 317 mg
Carbohydrate: 11 gm
Protein: 28 gm

Asparagus, Chicken and Wild Rice Casserole

Mary Drache, Roseville, Minnesota

I found this recipe several years ago while looking for something unusual but simple I could prepare for company. It's a dish that I've served many times since then—with a salad and rolls, it makes a complete meal.

1 cup uncooked wild rice, rinsed
2 cups low-sodium chicken broth
1 can (4 ounces) sliced mushrooms, undrained
6 boneless skinless chicken breast halves (1-1/2 pounds)

2 tablespoons dry onion soup mix
1 can (10-3/4 ounces) low-fat cream of mushroom soup, undiluted
1-1/2 pounds fresh asparagus, trimmed
1 tablespoon margarine, melted
Paprika

Spread rice in an 11-in. x 7-in. x 2-in. baking dish. Add broth and mushrooms. Place chicken in the center of the dish; sprinkle with onion soup mix. Spoon mushroom soup over all. Bake, uncovered, at 350° for 1 hour. Arrange asparagus around outer edges of baking dish; brush with melted margarine and sprinkle with paprika. Bake 15-20 minutes more or until asparagus is tender. **Yield:** 6 servings.

Barbecued Raspberry Chicken

Lorraine Cloutier, Legal, Alberta

Whenever I serve this chicken at backyard barbecues, folks always comment on the wonderful flavor of the raspberry marinade and sauce.

1/2 cup raspberry vinegar
2 tablespoons vegetable oil
1 tablespoon chopped fresh tarragon *or* 1 teaspoon dried tarragon

4 boneless skinless chicken breast halves (1 pound)
1 cup undiluted frozen raspberry juice
1 tablespoon cornstarch
Pepper to taste

In a small bowl, combine vinegar, oil and tarragon; mix well. Set aside 1/4 cup for basting; cover and refrigerate. Place chicken in a re-sealable plastic bag or bowl; pour remaining marinade over chicken. Seal or cover and refrigerate for 30 minutes. Lightly coat cold grill rack with nonstick cooking spray. Drain chicken, discarding marinade. Grill, uncovered, 4 in. from hot coals, basting frequently with reserved marinade, for 15-18 minutes or until juices run clear. Meanwhile, whisk together juice, cornstarch and pepper in a saucepan. Cook over medium-low heat, stirring constantly, for 5-7 minutes or until thickened and smooth. Serve with chicken. **Yield:** 4 servings.

Honey-Mustard Chicken Kabobs

Marilyn Dick, Centralia, Missouri

My husband and I have two boys who really keep me hopping. But I feel lucky to have three hungry men to feed—they don't turn down a thing I serve! People who try these kabobs say they love the combination of tangy and sweet tastes. And the best part is you can make them in less than 30 minutes.

1 pound boneless skinless
  chicken breasts
4 small zucchini
4 small yellow squash
2 medium sweet red peppers
4 ounces small fresh
  mushrooms

GLAZE:
  1/4 cup prepared mustard
  3 tablespoons honey
  2 tablespoons water
  1 tablespoon light soy sauce
  1 tablespoon cornstarch
1-1/2 teaspoons cider vinegar

Cut chicken, squash and peppers into 1-in. pieces; thread alternately with mushrooms onto skewers. In a saucepan, whisk glaze ingredients together; bring to a boil. Boil for 1 minute or until thickened. Grill the kabobs over hot coals for 10 minutes, turning often. Brush with glaze; grill 5 minutes more or until the chicken is no longer pink and vegetables are tender. **Yield:** 4 servings.

NUTRITIONAL INFORMATION

Serving Size: 1/4 recipe

Calories: 343
Total Fat: 4 gm
Calories from Fat: 11%
Saturated Fat: 1 gm
Cholesterol: 73 mg
Sodium: 391 mg
Carbohydrate: 50 gm
Protein: 30 gm

Apricot Chicken Stir-Fry

Jo Martin, Patterson, California

My husband and I have been growing apricots for more than 25 years. In this chicken dish, dried apricots add color and just the right amount of sweetness.

1/2 cup dried apricot halves,
  cut in half
1/4 cup hot water
  1 tablespoon all-purpose
  flour
  1 tablespoon chopped
  fresh cilantro, optional
1/8 teaspoon pepper
3/4 pound boneless skinless
  chicken breasts, cut into
  1/2-inch chunks

4 teaspoons cooking oil,
  divided
1 medium onion, halved
  and sliced
1 cup chopped celery
1/2 cup halved snow peas
1/2 teaspoon ground ginger
1 garlic clove, minced
1 tablespoon lemon juice

In a small bowl, soak apricots in water; set aside (do not drain). Combine flour, cilantro if desired and pepper; sprinkle over the chicken and set aside. Heat 2 teaspoons oil in a large skillet or wok over medium heat; stir-fry onion and celery for 2-3 minutes or until tender. Add peas, ginger, garlic and apricots; stir-fry for 2 minutes. Remove and keep warm. Add remaining oil to skillet; stir-fry chicken for 6-7 minutes or until no longer pink. Sprinkle with lemon juice. Return apricot mixture to skillet and heat through. **Yield:** 4 servings.

NUTRITIONAL INFORMATION

Serving Size: 1/4 recipe

Calories: 203
Total Fat: 7 gm
Calories from Fat: 30%
Saturated Fat: 1 gm
Cholesterol: 47 mg
Sodium: 70 mg
Carbohydrate: 17 gm
Protein: 19 gm

Chicken Cannelloni

Barbara Nowakowski, North Tonawanda, New York

(Pictured above)

I entered this recipe in a contest sponsored by a local radio station years ago, and it won Grand Prize! It's a unique takeoff on cannelloni—stuffing chicken breasts instead of the usual pasta tubes. I reach for this recipe often.

1 small onion, sliced
1 garlic clove, minced
3/4 cup thinly sliced carrots
1/2 cup thinly sliced celery
1/2 cup sliced fresh
  mushrooms
1 can (6 ounces) tomato
  paste
1 can (8 ounces) tomatoes,
  diced and undrained
1-1/2 teaspoons Italian
  seasoning, *divided*

1 teaspoon sugar
6 boneless skinless chicken
  breast halves (1-1/2
  pounds)
1/2 cup light ricotta cheese
1/4 cup sliced green onions
2 tablespoons grated
  Parmesan cheese
Dash pepper
1/2 cup part-skim mozzarella
  cheese
Hot cooked pasta, optional

In a large saucepan coated with nonstick cooking spray, saute onion, garlic, carrots, celery and mushrooms until onion is tender. Add tomato paste, tomatoes, 1 teaspoon Italian seasoning and sugar; bring to a boil. Reduce heat and simmer, uncovered, for 10 minutes. Meanwhile, flatten chicken breasts to 1/4-in. thickness. Combine ricotta, green onions, Parmesan, pepper and remaining Italian seasoning; spoon onto chicken breasts. Roll up; place seam side down in an 8-in. square baking dish. Pour sauce over chicken. Bake, uncovered, at 375° for 25-30 minutes or until the chicken is tender. Sprinkle with mozzarella cheese; let stand until melted. Serve over pasta if desired. **Yield:** 6 servings.

MEATY MEALS. Top to bottom: *Vegetable Beef Casserole, Dan's Peppery London Broil* (both recipes on page 175) and *Teriyaki Shish Kabobs* (recipe on page 176).

Beef & Ground Beef

Vegetable Beef Casserole

Evangeline Rew, Manassas, Virginia

(Pictured at left)

This easy one-dish recipe was handed down to me 35 years ago from my husband's aunt, and I've passed it on to many people. I always keep the ingredients on hand. A simple salad goes nicely with this dish.

3 medium unpeeled
  potatoes, sliced
3 carrots, sliced
3 celery ribs, sliced
2 cups fresh *or* frozen green
  beans
1 medium onion, chopped
1 pound ground round

1 teaspoon dried thyme
1 teaspoon pepper
4 medium tomatoes, peeled,
  seeded and chopped
1 cup (4 ounces) shredded
  reduced-fat cheddar
  cheese

In a 3-qt. casserole, layer half of the potatoes, carrots, celery, green beans and onion. Crumble half of the uncooked beef over vegetables. Sprinkle with 1/2 teaspoon each of thyme and pepper. Repeat layers. Top with tomatoes. Cover and bake at 400° for 15 minutes. Reduce heat to 350°; bake about 1 hour longer or until vegetables are tender and meat is done. Sprinkle with cheese; cover and let stand until cheese is melted. **Yield:** 8 servings.

Dan's Peppery London Broil

Dan Wright, San Jose, California

(Pictured at left)

I was bored making the usual London broil, so I got a little creative and sparked up the flavor with garlic, crushed red pepper and Worcestershire sauce.

1 flank steak (about
  1 pound)
1 garlic clove, minced
1/2 teaspoon salt-free
  seasoning blend

1/8 teaspoon crushed red
  pepper flakes
1/4 cup Worcestershire
  sauce

With a meat fork, pierce holes in both sides of meat. Make a paste with garlic, seasoning blend and red pepper; rub over both sides of meat. Place the steak in a resealable gallon-size plastic bag. Add Worcestershire sauce and close bag. Refrigerate for at least 4 hours, turning once. Remove meat; discard marinade. Broil or grill over hot coals until meat reaches desired doneness, 4-5 minutes per side. To serve, slice thinly across the grain. **Yield:** 4 servings.

Teriyaki Shish Kabobs

Suzanne Pelegrin, Ocala, Florida

(Pictured on page 174)

My father worked for an airline in the 1960's, when I was a teenager, and my family lived on the island of Guam in the South Pacific. A friend of Mother's there gave her this wonderful recipe. We ate this delicious warm-weather dish often, and now I prepare it for my family.

1/2 cup ketchup	2 small zucchini, cut into
1/2 cup sugar	1-inch chunks
1/2 cup light soy sauce	1/2 pound whole fresh
1 teaspoon garlic powder	mushrooms (medium size
1 teaspoon ground ginger	work best)
2 pounds boneless sirloin	1/2 pound pearl onions,
steak (1-1/2 inches thick),	peeled
trimmed and cut into	1 large green *or* sweet red
1-1/2-inch cubes	pepper, cut into 1-inch
1/2 fresh pineapple, trimmed	pieces
and cut into 1-inch	
chunks	

Combine the first five ingredients in a bowl or resealable plastic bag; toss with beef. Cover or close bag and refrigerate overnight. Drain beef, reserving marinade. Thread beef, pineapple and vegetables alternately on eight long skewers. Grill over hot coals for 15-20 minutes, turning often, or until meat reaches desired doneness and vegetables are tender. Meanwhile, in a small saucepan over low heat, bring marinade to a boil; cook for 5 minutes. Remove meat and vegetables from skewers; serve with marinade. **Yield:** 8 servings.

Mom's Roast Beef

Linda Gaido, New Brighton, Pennsylvania

(Pictured on the front cover)

Everyone loves slices of this fork-tender roast beef and its savory gravy. People are always surprised to hear the secret ingredient in the gravy is coffee!

1 eye of round beef roast	1 low-sodium beef bouillon
(2-1/2 pounds)	cube
1 medium onion, chopped	2 teaspoons dried basil
1 cup brewed coffee	1 teaspoon dried rosemary,
3/4 cup water	crushed
1 garlic clove, minced	1/2 teaspoon pepper

In a Dutch oven coated with nonstick cooking spray, brown roast on all sides. Add onion and cook until transparent. Add coffee, water, garlic, bouillon, basil, rosemary and pepper. Cover and simmer for 2-1/2 hours or until meat is tender. Thicken pan juices to make gravy if desired. **Yield:** 10 servings.

Porcupine Meatballs

Darlis Wilfer, Phelps, Wisconsin

(Pictured above)

These well-seasoned meatballs in a rich tomato sauce are one of my mom's best main dishes. I used to love this meal when I was growing up. I made it for our children, and now my daughters make it for their families.

1/2 cup uncooked long grain
   rice
1/2 cup water
1/3 cup chopped onion
1/2 teaspoon celery salt
1/8 teaspoon pepper
1/8 teaspoon garlic powder

1 pound ground round
1 can (15 ounces) tomato
   sauce
1 cup water
2 tablespoons brown sugar
2 teaspoons Worcestershire
   sauce

In a bowl, combine the first six ingredients. Add beef and mix well. Shape into 1-1/2-in. balls. In a large skillet coated with nonstick cooking spray, brown meatballs; drain. Combine tomato sauce, water, brown sugar and Worcestershire sauce; pour over meatballs. Reduce heat; cover and simmer for 1 hour. **Yield:** 6 servings.

NUTRITIONAL INFORMATION

Serving Size: 1/6 recipe

Calories: 222
Total Fat: 7 gm
Calories from Fat: 29%
Saturated Fat: 3 gm
Cholesterol: 28 mg
Sodium: 558 mg
Carbohydrate: 22 gm
Protein: 18 gm

Daddy's Sunday Roast

Mary Lewis, Memphis, Tennessee

(Pictured above)

Daddy was a friend of the local butcher, who always saved the preferred cut for his best customer! To please Daddy, that roast had to be big enough so he could count on leftovers for sandwiches the following week.

1 boneless rump roast
  (5 pounds), trimmed
1/2 cup cider vinegar
Pepper to taste
  1 cup water

GRAVY:
1/2 cup all-purpose flour
1 cup cold water
1 teaspoon browning sauce
Pepper to taste

Place roast in a deep roasting pan. Puncture meat with tenderizing tool or meat fork; pour vinegar over. Let stand for 15 minutes. Sprinkle with pepper. Add water to pan. Cover and bake at 400° for 3-1/2 hours or until meat is tender, adding additional water if needed. About 15 minutes before roast is done, uncover to brown the top. Remove roast from pan and keep warm; skim fat from pan juices. Measure the juices, adding water if needed to equal 3 cups. Mix flour and cold water until smooth; stir into pan juices. Cook and stir until thickened and bubbly. Cook and stir 1 minute more. Stir in browning sauce. Season with pepper. Serve gravy with roast. **Yield:** 20 servings.

Hungarian Goulash

Robert Fallon, Sayville, New York

When I retired, I took over cooking duties from my wife. This is one of my specialties that I like to serve guests.

1 pound round steak,
   trimmed and cut into
   1-inch pieces
1/2 cup sliced onion
1 garlic clove, minced
1/3 cup ketchup
2 tablespoons
   Worcestershire sauce

1/2 teaspoon vinegar
1/2 teaspoon brown sugar
1-1/4 teaspoons paprika
1/2 teaspoon ground mustard
Dash crushed red pepper flakes
1-2/3 cups water, *divided*
1 tablespoon all-purpose
   flour

In a Dutch oven coated with nonstick cooking spray, brown beef over medium-high heat. Add onion and garlic; cook until tender. Meanwhile, combine ketchup, Worcestershire sauce, vinegar, brown sugar, seasonings and 1-1/2 cups water. Stir into beef; reduce heat and simmer for 2 to 2-1/2 hours or until meat is tender. Just before serving, combine flour and remaining water; stir into meat mixture. Cook until thickened, about 10 minutes. **Yield:** 4 servings.

NUTRITIONAL INFORMATION

Serving Size: 1/4 recipe

Calories: 208
Total Fat: 6 gm
Calories from Fat: 26%
Saturated Fat: 2 gm
Cholesterol: 70 mg
Sodium: 357 mg
Carbohydrate: 11 gm
Protein: 26 gm

Colossal Cornburger

Lesley Colgan, London, Ontario

It's been such a long time since I added this recipe to my file that I don't even remember where it came from. Cooking is something I thoroughly enjoy, especially when the dishes turn out as delicious as this!

1 egg
1 cup frozen corn, thawed
1/2 cup coarsely crushed
   reduced-fat cheese
   crackers
1/4 cup sliced green onions

1/4 cup chopped fresh parsley
1 teaspoon Worcestershire
   sauce
2 pounds ground round
1/2 teaspoon pepper
1/2 teaspoon rubbed sage

In a medium bowl, combine egg, corn, crackers, onions, parsley and Worcestershire sauce; set aside. In a large bowl, combine meat and seasonings. On sheets of waxed paper, pat half of the meat mixture at a time into an 8-1/2-in. circle. Spoon corn mixture to within 1 in. of the edge of one circle of meat. Top with second circle of meat; remove top sheet of waxed paper and seal edges. Invert onto a wire grill basket coated with nonstick cooking spray; peel off waxed paper. Grill over medium coals, turning once, for 25-30 minutes or until meat is no longer pink. Cut into wedges to serve. **Oven Method:** Place burger on a baking pan coated with nonstick cooking spray. Bake at 350° for 40-45 minutes or until meat is no longer pink. **Yield:** 8 servings.

NUTRITIONAL INFORMATION

Serving Size: 1/8 recipe

Calories: 203
Total Fat: 6 gm
Calories from Fat: 28%
Saturated Fat: 2 gm
Cholesterol: 87 mg
Sodium: 124 mg
Carbohydrate: 8 gm
Protein: 27 gm

Barbecued Brisket

Page Alexander, Baldwin City, Kansas

(Pictured above)

For a mouth-watering main dish, this brisket can't be beat. Baked slowly, the meat gets nice and tender and picks up the sweet and tangy flavor of the barbecue sauce.

1 beef brisket (3 pounds)*	2 tablespoons brown sugar
1-1/4 cups water, *divided*	1 tablespoon
1/2 cup chopped onion	Worcestershire sauce
3 garlic cloves, minced	2 teaspoons cornstarch
1 cup ketchup	1 teaspoon paprika
3 tablespoons red wine	1 teaspoon chili powder
vinegar	1/4 teaspoon pepper
2 tablespoons lemon juice	1/4 teaspoon liquid smoke

Place brisket in a large Dutch oven. Add 1/2 cup water. Cover and bake at 325° for 1-1/2 hours. Meanwhile, in a medium saucepan coated with nonstick cooking spray, saute onion and garlic until tender. Add ketchup, vinegar, lemon juice, brown sugar, Worcestershire sauce, cornstarch, paprika, chili powder, pepper and remaining water. Simmer, uncovered, for 1 hour, stirring occasionally. Add liquid smoke; mix well. Drain drippings from Dutch oven. Pour sauce over meat. Cover and bake 1-2 hours longer or until meat is tender. **Yield:** 12 servings. *Editor's Note: This is a fresh beef brisket, not corned beef.

Hearty Hash

Kathy Winzer, Coulee Dam, Washington

Potatoes are an economical way to fill up a hungry family. This lighter version of hash calls for lean roast beef and makes a flavorful meal.

4 cups diced cooked lean roast beef	1-1/2 cups low-sodium beef broth
6 cups diced peeled potatoes	1/4 teaspoon pepper
3/4 cup chopped onion	

In an electric skillet, combine beef, potatoes, onion, broth and pepper. Cover and simmer, stirring occasionally, until potatoes are tender, about 25 minutes. Thicken if desired. **Yield:** 8 servings.

Inside-Out Brussels Sprouts

Shirley Max, Cape Girardeau, Missouri

(Pictured below)

I usually make this easy dish for large gatherings. It's a must for people who enjoy beef. I've been fixing it for years.

2 pounds ground round
1-1/2 cups uncooked instant
   rice
1 medium onion, chopped
2 eggs
1/4 teaspoon garlic powder
1/2 teaspoon pepper

1 package (10 ounces)
   frozen brussels sprouts
2 cans (15 ounces *each*)
   tomato sauce
1 cup water
1 teaspoon dried thyme

In a large bowl, combine the first six ingredients and mix well. Shape a scant 1/4 cupful around each frozen brussels sprout to form a meatball. Place in an ungreased 15-in. x 10-in. x 1-in. baking dish. Combine tomato sauce, water and thyme; pour over meatballs. Cover and bake at 350° for 1 hour and 15 minutes or until no pink remains. **Yield:** 10 servings.

NUTRITIONAL INFORMATION

Serving Size: 1/10 recipe

Calories: 226
Total Fat: 7 gm
Calories from Fat: 28%
Saturated Fat: 3 gm
Cholesterol: 100 mg
Sodium: 621 mg
Carbohydrate: 22 gm
Protein: 21 gm

Swiss Steak

Dianne Esposite, New Middletown, Ohio

(Pictured below)

Mom was always glad to prepare this tender, flavorful dish when anyone requested it for their birthday dinner. The celery, onion and mushrooms make it extra special. Now my family enjoys this meal.

1/4 cup all-purpose flour
1/4 teaspoon pepper
1-1/2 pounds round steak, trimmed
1 tablespoon cooking oil
1 cup chopped celery

1 cup chopped onion
1/2 pound fresh mushrooms, sliced
1 cup water
1 garlic clove, minced
1 tablespoon steak sauce

Combine flour and pepper. Cut steak into serving-size pieces; dredge in flour mixture. In a skillet, brown steak in oil. Drain and place in a 2-1/2-qt. casserole. Top with celery, onion and mushrooms. Combine water, garlic and steak sauce; pour over vegetables. Cover and bake at 350° for 1-1/2 hours or until the meat is tender. **Yield:** 6 servings.

NUTRITIONAL INFORMATION

Serving Size: 1/6 recipe

Calories: 258
Total Fat: 11 gm
Calories from Fat: 38%
Saturated Fat: 3 gm
Cholesterol: 82 mg
Sodium: 313 mg
Carbohydrate: 9 gm
Protein: 30 gm

For Your Birthday

Southwestern Beef Burritos

Jacqueline Hergert, Payson, Arizona

We became acquainted with Mexican food after moving here from the Midwest. I got this recipe from my brother-in-law, who ran a Mexican restaurant.

2 pounds round steak, trimmed and cut into 1-inch cubes
2 large onions, chopped
2 garlic cloves, minced
1 can (15 ounces) enchilada sauce
1 can (14-1/2 ounces) diced tomatoes, undrained
1 can (4 ounces) chopped green chilies
1/4 teaspoon pepper
2 tablespoons all-purpose flour
1/4 cup cold water
8 fat-free flour tortillas
Optional garnishes: diced tomatoes, sliced ripe olives, shredded fat-free cheddar cheese, nonfat sour cream, chopped green onions *and/or* shredded lettuce

In a large skillet coated with nonstick cooking spray, brown meat over medium heat; drain. Add onions and garlic; cook and stir for 2 minutes. Add the enchilada sauce, tomatoes, chilies and pepper; bring to a boil. Reduce heat; cover and simmer for 2 hours or until meat is tender. Combine flour and water; add to beef mixture, stirring constantly. Bring to a boil; cook and stir for 1 minute or until thickened. Warm tortillas; spoon 1/2 cup filling, off center, on each one. Fold sides and bottom of tortilla over filling, then roll up. Spoon additional filling over top of burritos. Serve immediately. Garnish with tomatoes, olives, cheese, sour cream, onions and lettuce if desired. **Yield:** 8 servings.

NUTRITIONAL INFORMATION

Serving Size: 1 burrito
(calculated without garnishes)

Calories: 314
Total Fat: 7 gm
Calories from Fat: 20%
Saturated Fat: 2 gm
Cholesterol: 70 mg
Sodium: 686 mg
Carbohydrate: 33 gm
Protein: 28 gm

Barbecued Pot Roast

Emma Nye, New Oxford, Pennsylvania

Through the years, this was always one of my family's favorite meals. Now I still often fix it for just my husband and myself. Whenever I do, we get to enjoy the bonus of leftovers!

1 boneless chuck roast (3 pounds), trimmed
1/4 teaspoon pepper
1 can (8 ounces) tomato sauce
1 cup water
3 medium onions, sliced
2 garlic cloves, minced
1/4 cup lemon juice
1/4 cup ketchup
2 tablespoons brown sugar
1 tablespoon Worcestershire sauce
1/2 teaspoon ground mustard

Sprinkle roast with pepper. In a Dutch oven coated with nonstick cooking spray, brown roast on all sides. Add the tomato sauce, water, onions and garlic. Cover and simmer for 30 minutes. Combine remaining ingredients; pour over meat. Cover and simmer for 3-4 hours or until the meat is tender. **Yield:** 12 servings.

NUTRITIONAL INFORMATION

Serving Size: 1/12 recipe

Calories: 198
Total Fat: 7 gm
Calories from Fat: 31%
Saturated Fat: 2 gm
Cholesterol: 78 mg
Sodium: 241 mg
Carbohydrate: 8 gm
Protein: 26 gm

Kodiak Casserole

Kathy Crow, Cordova, Alaska

(Pictured above)

Because it packs a little kick and has an interesting and tasty mix of ingredients, this is the perfect potluck dish. One of my husband's favorites, it's an Alaskan recipe I found in the early 1950's.

NUTRITIONAL INFORMATION

Serving Size: 1 cup

Calories: 168
Total Fat: 6 gm
Calories from Fat: 30%
Saturated Fat: 2 gm
Cholesterol: 37 mg
Sodium: 725 mg
Carbohydrate: 18 gm
Protein: 13 gm

2 pounds ground round
4 cups diced onions
2 garlic cloves, minced
3 medium green peppers, diced
4 cups diced celery
3 cups medium egg noodles, cooked and drained
1 bottle (18 ounces) barbecue sauce
1 can (10-3/4 ounces) low-fat condensed tomato soup, undiluted

1 jar (8 ounces) picante sauce
1 jar (5-3/4 ounces) stuffed olives, undrained
1 can (4 ounces) mushroom stems and pieces, undrained
2 tablespoons Worcestershire sauce
1 cup (4 ounces) shredded reduced-fat cheddar cheese

In a Dutch oven, brown beef with onions and garlic; drain. Add remaining ingredients except cheese; mix well. Cover and bake at 350° for 1 hour or until hot and bubbly. Sprinkle with the cheese just before serving. **Yield:** 20 servings.

Homemade Pizza

Marianne Edwards, Lake Stevens, Washington

Whenever I plan a pizza party for family and friends, this homemade version is the star. With everyone pitching in on the preparation, it's fun to make.

1 package (1/4 ounce)
  active dry yeast
1 teaspoon sugar
1-1/4 cups warm water
  (110° to 115°)
1/4 cup vegetable oil
1 teaspoon salt
3-1/2 cups all-purpose flour
1/2 pound ground round
1 small onion, chopped

1 can (15 ounces) tomato
  sauce
1 tablespoon dried oregano
1 teaspoon dried basil
1 medium green pepper,
  diced
2 cups (8 ounces)
  shredded part-skim
  mozzarella cheese

In a large bowl, dissolve yeast and sugar in water; let stand for 5 minutes. Add oil and salt. Stir in flour, a cup at a time, to form a soft dough. Turn onto a floured surface; knead until smooth and elastic, about 2-3 minutes. Place in a bowl coated with nonstick cooking spray, turning once to grease top. Cover and let rise in a warm place until doubled, about 45 minutes. Meanwhile, brown beef and onion; drain. Punch dough down; divide in half. Press each into a 12-in. pizza pan coated with nonstick cooking spray. Combine the tomato sauce, oregano and basil; spread over each crust. Top with beef mixture, green pepper and cheese. Bake at 400° for 25-30 minutes or until crust is lightly browned. **Yield:** 2 pizzas (6 servings each).

NUTRITIONAL INFORMATION

Serving Size: 1/12 recipe

Calories: 263
Total Fat: 9 gm
Calories from Fat: 31%
Saturated Fat: 3 gm
Cholesterol: 19 mg
Sodium: 534 mg
Carbohydrate: 32 gm
Protein: 13 gm

Deviled Baked Steak

Betty Shaw, Weirton, West Virginia

When we were growing up, this was one of my brother's favorite dishes. We girls often thought Mother made this just for him, but she knew we enjoyed it, too. Since I'm the oldest, my brothers and sisters often "come home" to my house, and I make baked steak for them.

2 pounds round steak
  (1 inch thick), trimmed
3/4 cup all-purpose flour
1 teaspoon ground mustard
1/2 teaspoon pepper
4 teaspoons cooking oil
1 medium onion, sliced

1 can (14-1/2 ounces)
  diced tomatoes, undrained
1 carrot, diced
1 teaspoon brown sugar
2 teaspoons Worcestershire
  sauce

Cut steak into serving-size pieces. Combine flour, mustard and pepper; pound into steak. In a skillet, brown steak, half at a time, in oil. Place meat in a large baking dish; top with onion. Combine tomatoes, carrot, brown sugar and Worcestershire sauce; pour over meat. Cover and bake at 325° for 1-1/2 to 2 hours or until meat is tender. Remove meat to a serving platter and keep warm. Simmer tomato-onion mixture until it is reduced to a thick gravy; pour over meat. **Yield:** 8 servings.

NUTRITIONAL INFORMATION

Serving Size: 1/8 recipe

Calories: 282
Total Fat: 11 gm
Calories from Fat: 35%
Saturated Fat: 3 gm
Cholesterol: 82 mg
Sodium: 357 mg
Carbohydrate: 14 gm
Protein: 30 gm

Stuffed Zucchini

Marjorie Roberts, West Chazy, New York

An abundance of squash from my garden inspired me to make up this recipe. It's a flavorful variation of stuffed green peppers. Even folks not fond of zucchini will enjoy this meal.

1-1/2 pounds ground round
1 large onion, chopped
1 large green pepper, chopped
1 jalapeno pepper, minced
1-1/4 cups soft bread crumbs
1 egg
1 tablespoon dried parsley flakes
1 teaspoon dried basil
1 teaspoon Italian seasoning
1/8 teaspoon pepper
2 cans (8 ounces *each*) tomato sauce, *divided*
2 medium tomatoes, coarsely chopped
5 medium zucchini
2 cups (8 ounces) shredded part-skim mozzarella cheese

In a large bowl, combine the first 10 ingredients and one can of tomato sauce; mix well. Stir in tomatoes. Halve zucchini lengthwise; scoop out seeds. Fill with meat mixture; place in two 13-in. x 9-in. x 2-in. baking dishes. Spoon remaining tomato sauce over each. Bake, uncovered, at 375° for 45 minutes or until the zucchini is tender. Sprinkle with cheese during the last few minutes of baking. **Yield:** 10 servings.

Favorite Meat Loaf

Jim Hopkins, Whittier, California

My all-time favorite dish to make is meat loaf. In fact, a few years ago, my aunt and I put together a meat loaf cookbook that includes over 50 variations of that old-fashioned main course. This version has a traditional mix of ingredients, but shredded carrot gives it added flair.

2 eggs
1/4 cup skim milk
1 tablespoon Worcestershire sauce
1 teaspoon salt-free seasoning blend
1 teaspoon onion powder
1 cup quick-cooking oats
1 carrot, shredded
2 tablespoons chopped fresh parsley
1-1/2 pounds ground round
1 pound ground turkey breast
1/2 cup ketchup

In a large bowl, beat eggs. Add milk, Worcestershire sauce, seasoning blend and onion powder; mix well. Stir in oats, carrot and parsley. Combine beef and turkey; add to egg mixture and mix well. Press into a 9-in. x 5-in. x 3-in. loaf pan. Top with ketchup. Bake at 350° for 1-1/2 hours or until no pink remains. Drain. **Yield:** 10 servings.

Pot Roast with Spaghetti

Ellen Cote, Sealy, Texas

(Pictured above)

My mother gave me this recipe some time ago. It's a winner in our family—kids especially seem to like the spaghetti. It's a different way to serve pot roast…and it sure makes the house smell good when it's simmering! Everyone I've shared the recipe with has said how much they've enjoyed it.

1 boneless chuck roast
  (2 pounds), trimmed
1 garlic clove, minced
1 small onion, chopped
2 teaspoons dried oregano
1 teaspoon dried thyme
1/2 teaspoon dried basil
1/2 teaspoon pepper
1/8 teaspoon ground
  cinnamon
3 cups hot water
3 cans (6 ounces *each*)
  tomato paste
1 pound spaghetti, cooked
  and drained

In a Dutch oven coated with nonstick cooking spray, brown roast evenly on all sides. Remove and set aside. Add garlic, onion and seasonings. Cook slowly for about 5 minutes, stirring constantly. Stir in water and tomato paste; blend well. Return roast to Dutch oven and spoon sauce over it. Cover and simmer for 2-1/2 to 3 hours or until the meat is tender. Remove roast; cut into slices. Serve with spaghetti and sauce. **Yield:** 8 servings.

Nutritional Information

Serving Size: 1/8 recipe

Calories: 473
Total Fat: 8 gm
Calories from Fat: 15%
Saturated Fat: 3 gm
Cholesterol: 96 mg
Sodium: 560 mg
Carbohydrate: 58 gm
Protein: 41 gm

Beef and Sauerkraut Dinner

Marilyn Dietz, White, South Dakota

(Pictured below)

I've been making this one-dish meal for more than 30 years. The original recipe called for less sauerkraut—but there wasn't enough for us! I also enjoy preparing this for church potlucks.

NUTRITIONAL INFORMATION

Serving Size: 1/8 recipe

Calories: 253
Total Fat: 7 gm
Calories from Fat: 25%
Saturated Fat: 2 gm
Cholesterol: 82 mg
Sodium: 823 mg
Carbohydrate: 27 gm
Protein: 21 gm

1-1/2 pounds ground round
1 egg
1-1/2 cups soft rye bread crumbs
1/3 cup skim milk
1/4 cup chopped onion
1 tablespoon cider vinegar
1-1/2 teaspoons caraway seeds
2 cans (15 ounces *each*) sliced potatoes, drained
2-1/2 cups sauerkraut, undrained
2 tablespoons minced fresh parsley

In a bowl, combine beef, egg, crumbs, milk, onion, vinegar and caraway; mix well. Shape into 1-1/2-in. balls. In a Dutch oven coated with nonstick cooking spray, brown meatballs over medium heat. Add the potatoes and sauerkraut; mix well. Bring to a boil. Reduce heat; cover and simmer for 15-20 minutes or until heated through. Sprinkle with parsley. **Yield:** 8 servings.

Mardi Gras Beef

Lucy Meyring, Walden, Colorado

The beef for this main dish can be prepared on the grill, so it's juicy and flavorful. Plus, it makes cleanup extra speedy. The seasonings and vegetables give the beef a wonderful summertime twist.

1 medium onion, chopped
1 small green pepper, cut into strips
1 teaspoon dried thyme
2 teaspoons garlic powder, *divided*

1 pound sirloin steak (1 inch thick), trimmed
1 can (14-1/2 ounces) stewed tomatoes
2 teaspoons cornstarch
Pepper to taste

In a skillet coated with nonstick cooking spray, saute onion, green pepper, thyme and 1/2 teaspoon garlic powder until vegetables are crisp-tender. Meanwhile, sprinkle steak with remaining garlic powder; grill or broil 5 in. from the heat for 6-8 minutes (for medium-rare), turning once, or until desired doneness is reached. Drain tomatoes, reserving juice; add tomatoes to skillet. Combine juice with cornstarch; add to vegetable mixture. Cook and stir until thickened. Add pepper. Thinly slice meat; top with vegetables. **Yield:** 4 servings.

NUTRITIONAL INFORMATION

Serving Size: 1/4 recipe

Calories: 217
Total Fat: 6 gm
Calories from Fat: 26%
Saturated Fat: 2 gm
Cholesterol: 75 mg
Sodium: 319 mg
Carbohydrate: 13 gm
Protein: 27 gm

Plantation Stuffed Peppers

Sherry Morgan, Mansfield, Louisiana

We always have a lot of extra peppers in the garden. So I prepare a bunch of these stuffed peppers, then freeze them for baking later. That way, we can enjoy them year-round. They're always a treat, no matter how often I serve them!

8 medium green peppers, tops and seeds removed
1 pound ground round
1 cup chopped onion
1 garlic clove, minced
2 teaspoons chili powder
1/2 teaspoon pepper

2 cans (10-3/4 ounces *each*) condensed low-fat tomato soup, undiluted
1-1/2 cups (6 ounces) shredded reduced-fat cheddar cheese
1-1/2 cups cooked rice

In boiling water, cook peppers for 3-5 minutes. Remove and set aside. In a skillet, cook beef, onion and garlic until meat is browned and onion is tender. Drain. Add seasonings and soup; simmer, uncovered, for 10 minutes. Stir in cheese and rice. Stuff peppers; place in a shallow baking dish. Bake at 350° for 20 minutes. **Yield:** 8 servings.

NUTRITIONAL INFORMATION

Serving Size: 1/8 recipe

Calories: 226
Total Fat: 8 gm
Calories from Fat: 32%
Saturated Fat: 4 gm
Cholesterol: 44 mg
Sodium: 349 mg
Carbohydrate: 22 gm
Protein: 19 gm

Busy-Day Dinner

Mrs. Cort Smith, Corydon, Indiana

(Pictured above)

I use this recipe a lot because it is delicious and so easy to make. You can mix it up in an electric skillet or on your stovetop. Kids love the tomato flavor and the crunch of the celery.

1 pound ground round, browned and drained
1 package (7 ounces) elbow macaroni, cooked and drained
1 cup finely chopped celery
1 cup chopped green pepper
1 cup finely chopped onion

2 cups thinly sliced carrots
1 can (28 ounces) diced tomatoes, undrained
1 can (8 ounces) tomato sauce
1 teaspoon chili powder
1/4 teaspoon pepper

Combine all ingredients in a saucepan; bring to a boil over medium heat. Reduce heat; cover and simmer for 30 minutes. Add water to thin if desired. **Yield:** 6 servings.

NUTRITIONAL INFORMATION

Serving Size: 1/6 recipe

Calories: 307
Total Fat: 6 gm
Calories from Fat: 18%
Saturated Fat: 2 gm
Cholesterol: 48 mg
Sodium: 595 mg
Carbohydrate: 44 gm
Protein: 21 gm

Mom's Best Meat Loaf

Linda Nilsen, Anoka, Minnesota

This is no ordinary meat loaf—the recipe is so good and has been passed down in our family for generations. The zesty seasoning gives the flavor a spark. I remember Mom loved to serve this meat loaf.

1-1/2 pounds ground round
1 cup skim milk
1 egg
3/4 cup soft bread crumbs
1 medium onion, chopped
1 tablespoon chopped green pepper

1 tablespoon ketchup
1 teaspoon prepared horseradish
1 teaspoon sugar
1 teaspoon ground allspice
1 teaspoon dill weed

In a large bowl, combine all ingredients; mix well. Press into an ungreased 8-in. x 4-in. x 2-in. loaf pan. Bake at 350° for 1 hour and 15 minutes or until no pink remains. Drain. **Yield:** 6 servings.

NUTRITIONAL INFORMATION

Serving Size: 1/6 recipe

Calories: 248
Total Fat: 11 gm
Calories from Fat: 42%
Saturated Fat: 4 gm
Cholesterol: 78 mg
Sodium: 174 mg
Carbohydrate: 8 gm
Protein: 27 gm

Grilled Steak Pinwheels

Mary Hills, Scottsdale, Arizona

(Pictured below)

I've been serving this dish to family and friends for 20 years and very seldom do I have any leftovers. Herbs in this recipe lend a delicious aroma.

2 flank steaks (1 pound *each*), trimmed
1/4 pound sliced turkey bacon, cooked and crumbled
1 cup finely chopped fresh mushrooms

1 cup finely chopped green onions
1/4 cup finely chopped fresh basil *or* 4 teaspoons dried basil
2 tablespoons minced fresh chives

Pound flank steaks on each side. Combine bacon, mushrooms, onions, basil and chives; spread evenly over steaks. Roll up the meat and secure with skewers or wooden picks. Cut each roll into 1/2- to 3/4-in. slices and secure with a wooden pick or skewer. Grill over hot coals for 4-6 minutes per side or until meat reaches desired doneness. Remove picks before serving. **Yield:** 8 servings.

NUTRITIONAL INFORMATION

Serving Size: 1/8 recipe

Calories: 224
Total Fat: 12 gm
Calories from Fat: 48%
Saturated Fat: 5 gm
Cholesterol: 71 mg
Sodium: 261 mg
Carbohydrate: 2 gm
Protein: 26 gm

Chili Skillet

Katherine Brown, Fredericktown, Ohio

Like most farmers, my husband loves chili. And with all of the vegetables, cheese and meat in it, this quick dish makes a real meal-in-one. I serve it frequently in fall and winter.

1 pound ground round
1 cup chopped onion
1/2 cup chopped green pepper
1 garlic clove, minced
1 cup tomato juice
1 can (8 ounces) kidney beans, undrained
4 teaspoons chili powder

1 teaspoon dried oregano
1/2 cup uncooked long grain rice
1 cup frozen corn, thawed
1/2 cup sliced ripe olives
1 cup (4 ounces) shredded reduced-fat cheddar cheese

In a large skillet over medium heat, cook beef, onion, green pepper and garlic until meat is browned and vegetables are tender. Drain. Add tomato juice, kidney beans, chili powder, oregano and rice; cover and simmer for 25 minutes or until rice is tender. Stir in corn and olives; cover and cook 5 minutes more. Sprinkle with cheese; cover and let stand until cheese melts. **Yield:** 6 servings.

NUTRITIONAL INFORMATION

Serving Size: 1/6 recipe

Calories: 310
Total Fat: 10 gm
Calories from Fat: 29%
Saturated Fat: 4 gm
Cholesterol: 55 mg
Sodium: 577 mg
Carbohydrate: 34 gm
Protein: 25 gm

Caraway Beef Roast

Beverly Swanson, Red Oak, Iowa

It seems there aren't many beef roasts that are both extra special and extra easy. This one is, though. Over the years, many men have requested that I copy the recipe for their wives.

1 boneless chuck roast (3 pounds), trimmed
1 cup hot water
1-1/2 teaspoons instant low-sodium beef bouillon granules
1/4 cup ketchup

1 tablespoon Worcestershire sauce
1 tablespoon instant minced onion
1/2 teaspoon pepper
2 teaspoons caraway seeds
2 bay leaves

In a Dutch oven coated with nonstick cooking spray, brown roast on all sides over medium-high heat. Drain. Combine water, bouillon, ketchup, Worcestershire sauce, onion, pepper and caraway. Pour over roast. Add bay leaves. Cover and bake at 325° for 3 hours or until tender. Remove roast to a serving platter and keep warm. Remove bay leaves. Thicken cooking liquid for gravy if desired. **Yield:** 12 servings.

NUTRITIONAL INFORMATION

Serving Size: 3 ounces

Calories: 119
Total Fat: 4 gm
Calories from Fat: 30%
Saturated Fat: 2 gm
Cholesterol: 51 mg
Sodium: 113 mg
Carbohydrate: 2 gm
Protein: 17 gm

Shepherd's Pie

Diane Gillingham, Carman, Manitoba

(Pictured above)

As the second oldest in a big family, I had plenty of opportunity to practice cooking while I was growing up. For "country eaters", this hearty pie is perfect!

1 pound ground round	1/2 cup diced green pepper
3/4 cup chopped onion	1/2 cup diced sweet red
2 garlic cloves, minced	pepper
1 cup chopped fresh	8 medium potatoes, peeled
mushrooms	and cubed
1 tablespoon tomato paste	1/3 cup hot skim milk
1/2 cup low-sodium beef broth	1 cup (4 ounces) shredded
2 teaspoons prepared	reduced-fat cheddar
horseradish	cheese
1 teaspoon ground mustard	2 egg whites
1/4 teaspoon pepper	

In a large skillet coated with nonstick cooking spray, brown beef, onion and garlic. Add the mushrooms. Cook and stir for 3 minutes; drain. Place the tomato paste in a bowl; gradually whisk in broth until smooth. Stir in horseradish, mustard and pepper. Add to meat mixture. Pour into an 11-in. x 7-in. x 2-in. baking pan coated with nonstick cooking spray; set aside. In the same skillet, saute the peppers until tender, about 3 minutes. Drain and spoon over meat mixture. Cook potatoes in boiling water until tender; drain. Mash with milk and cheese. Beat egg whites until stiff peaks form; gently fold into potatoes. Spoon over pepper layer. Bake, uncovered, at 425° for 15 minutes. Reduce heat to 350°; bake 20 minutes longer or until meat layer is bubbly. **Yield:** 6 servings.

NUTRITIONAL INFORMATION

Serving Size: 1/6 recipe

Calories: 334
Total Fat: 8 gm
Calories from Fat: 21%
Saturated Fat: 4 gm
Cholesterol: 55 mg
Sodium: 288 mg
Carbohydrate: 42 gm
Protein: 26 gm

Instant Mashing Potatoes

Do your potatoes sprout before you use them? Peel, slice and boil them until partially cooked. Drain and freeze in small quantities. When you want mashed potatoes, remove as many as needed, pop them into boiling water to finish cooking, drain and mash!

Reuben Baked Potatoes

Erika Antolic, Vancouver, Washington

(Pictured below)

During the Depression, my mother frequently served these to the family as the main course. Now I prepare them for busy weeknight meals or as a side dish to pork.

4 large baking potatoes
2 cups finely diced cooked reduced-fat corned beef
1 can (14 ounces) sauerkraut, rinsed, well drained and finely chopped
1/2 cup shredded reduced-fat Swiss cheese
1 garlic clove, minced
3 tablespoons sliced green onions
1 tablespoon prepared horseradish
1 teaspoon caraway seeds
3 ounces light cream cheese, softened
3 tablespoons grated Parmesan cheese
Paprika

Bake the potatoes at 425° for 45 minutes or until tender. Cool. In a bowl, combine the corned beef, sauerkraut, Swiss cheese, garlic, onions, horseradish and caraway. Cut potatoes in half lengthwise. Carefully scoop out pulp, leaving shells intact. Mash pulp with cream cheese; stir into the corned beef mixture. Mound potato mixture into the shells. Sprinkle with Parmesan cheese and paprika. Return to the oven for 25 minutes or until heated through. **Yield:** 8 servings.

Harvest Ground Beef Casserole

Grace Hagen, Roggen, Colorado

During harvesttime, I take this dish out to the field for my family's lunch. It sure makes things easy when you have your meat and vegetables all in one dish. And, as many times as I've carried a full casserole out to the field, I have never brought anything back to the house but the empty dish.

1 pound ground round
1 cup chopped onion
1 can (28 ounces) diced
  tomatoes, undrained
1 tablespoon Worcestershire
  sauce
2 cups sliced peeled
  potatoes
1/3 cup all-purpose flour

1 package (10 ounces)
  frozen corn, thawed
1 package (10 ounces)
  frozen lima beans, thawed
1 green pepper, cut into
  strips
1-1/2 cups (6 ounces) shredded
  reduced-fat cheddar
  cheese

In a skillet, brown beef; drain. Add onion, tomatoes and Worcestershire sauce. Spoon into a 3-qt. casserole coated with nonstick cooking spray. Layer with potatoes, flour, corn, lima beans and green pepper. Cover and bake at 375° for 1-1/4 hours. Sprinkle with cheese; cover and let stand until melted. **Yield:** 8 servings.

Cranberry Meatballs

Helen Wiegmink, Tucson, Arizona

Although this recipe is perfect for the holidays, plan to use it all year-round. And, if you're looking for an appetizer idea, shape the meatballs smaller and serve with party picks.

1 pound ground round
1 egg
1/2 cup crushed saltines
1/2 small onion, diced
1/2 teaspoon pepper

1 can (16 ounces) whole-
  berry cranberry sauce
1 can (10-3/4 ounces)
  low-fat condensed
  tomato soup, undiluted
Cooked rice *or* noodles,
  optional

In a bowl, combine the first five ingredients. Shape into 1-1/2-in. balls. Place on a rack in a baking pan. Bake at 400° for 20 minutes. Meanwhile, in a large saucepan, combine cranberry sauce and soup; heat through. Add meatballs and simmer for 10 minutes. Serve over rice or noodles if desired. **Yield:** 6 servings.

SUCCULENT SPREAD. *Clockwise from top: Ham with Peach Chutney, Sweet-and-Sour Pork (both recipes on page 197) and Autumn Pork Chop Dinner (recipe on page 198).*

Plentiful Pork

Ham with Peach Chutney

Margarette Bennett, Westfield, Wisconsin

(Pictured at left)

Whether served for a special-occasion supper or weekday dinner, this fruity ham is sure to please.

1 boneless fully cooked
  low-fat ham (4 pounds)
1 can (16 ounces) sliced
  peaches in natural juices,
  drained and coarsely
  chopped
1/2 cup cider vinegar

1/2 cup packed brown sugar
1/4 cup minced onion
1 apple, peeled and
  coarsely chopped
2 tablespoons lemon juice
1 teaspoon mixed pickling
  spices

Place ham in a shallow pan. Bake at 325° for 1-1/2 hours or until a meat thermometer reads 140°. Meanwhile, combine remaining ingredients in a saucepan; bring to a boil. Reduce heat and simmer for 25-30 minutes or until thickened. Cool. Slice ham; serve with chutney. **Yield:** 16 servings.

NUTRITIONAL INFORMATION

Serving Size: 3 ounces of ham and 2 tablespoons of chutney

Calories: 186
Total Fat: 6 gm
Calories from Fat: 28%
Saturated Fat: 2 gm
Cholesterol: 53 mg
Sodium: 1,623 mg
Carbohydrate: 11 gm
Protein: 22 gm

Sweet-and-Sour Pork

Sally Pelszynski, Princeton, Illinois

(Pictured at left)

My kids call this "Mom's Secret Recipe" because I often substitute good-for-you broccoli and cauliflower for some of the other ingredients. This is the best way I've found to get them to eat their vegetables!

2 teaspoons cooking oil
1 pound boneless lean pork,
  cut into 1-inch cubes
1 teaspoon paprika
1/3 cup water
3 tablespoons brown sugar
2 tablespoons cornstarch
1 can (20 ounces)
  unsweetened pineapple
  chunks, juice drained and
  reserved

1/3 cup vinegar
1 tablespoon soy sauce
1 teaspoon Worcestershire
  sauce
1 green pepper, sliced
1 small onion, sliced
1 can (8 ounces) sliced
  water chestnuts, drained
Hot cooked rice, optional

In a wok or skillet, heat oil over medium-high heat. Add pork; sprinkle with paprika. Brown pork on all sides. Reduce heat. Add water; cover and simmer for 20-25 minutes or until meat is tender. Meanwhile, in a medium bowl, combine brown sugar and cornstarch. Gradually add pineapple juice, vinegar, soy sauce and Worcestershire sauce; stir until smooth. Add to pork; increase heat to medium and cook, stirring constantly, until thick and bubbly. Cook and stir 2 minutes longer. Stir in pineapple, green pepper, onion and water chestnuts; cover and simmer for 5 minutes or until vegetables are crisp-tender. Serve over rice if desired. **Yield:** 6 servings.

NUTRITIONAL INFORMATION

Serving Size: 1/6 recipe
(calculated without rice)

Calories: 289
Total Fat: 7 gm
Calories from Fat: 22%
Saturated Fat: 2 gm
Cholesterol: 46 mg
Sodium: 280 mg
Carbohydrate: 39 gm
Protein: 17 gm

Autumn Pork Chop Dinner

Cecelia Wilson, Rockville, Connecticut

(Pictured on page 196)

This one-dish meal may be small in size, but it's big on taste thanks to a great combination of pork chops, tasty green beans and tangy cabbage. I like to cook for two and make just the right amount so I don't have leftovers.

2 loin pork chops (1 inch thick), trimmed
2 cups shredded cabbage
2 tablespoons brown sugar
1 tablespoon chopped fresh parsley
2 medium potatoes, peeled and sliced 1/4 inch thick
1 cup fresh *or* frozen green beans
1 teaspoon salt-free lemon-pepper seasoning
3/4 cup apple juice
1/4 cup seasoned bread crumbs
1 teaspoon margarine, melted

In a large skillet coated with nonstick cooking spray, brown chops on both sides over medium-high heat; remove and set aside. Toss cabbage with brown sugar and parsley; place in an 11-in. x 7-in. x 2-in. baking dish. Top with potatoes and beans. Arrange chops over vegetables. Sprinkle with lemon pepper. Pour apple juice over all. Cover and bake at 350° for 45 minutes or until the meat and vegetables are tender. Combine the bread crumbs and margarine; sprinkle on top. Return to the oven for 15 minutes. **Yield:** 2 servings.

Baked Ham and Apples

Marjorie Schmidt, St. Marys, Ohio

My mother often made magic in the kitchen when I was a child, and this recipe of hers is one of my most treasured. When my mother prepared ham this way, the flavor was especially sweet and appealing, and the apples were delicious.

1 fully cooked low-fat ham slice (1 inch thick and 2 pounds), trimmed
2 teaspoons ground mustard
1/2 cup packed brown sugar
3 medium baking apples
1 tablespoon margarine
Pepper to taste

Place ham in an ungreased 13-in. x 9-in. x 2-in. baking dish. Rub with mustard and sprinkle with brown sugar. Core apples and cut into 3/4-in. slices; arrange in a single layer over ham. Dot with margarine and sprinkle with pepper. Cover and bake at 400° for 15 minutes. Uncover and bake 15 minutes longer or until apples are tender. **Yield:** 8 servings.

Porkettes

Christy Jefferson, Reno, Nevada

(Pictured below)

My grandmother won an award with her version of this recipe in 1948, and it's just as delicious today as it was when the judges picked it years ago.

1 pound ground fully cooked
  low-fat ham
1 egg
1/4 cup sweet pickle relish
1 teaspoon prepared
  mustard
2 cups mashed cooked sweet
  potatoes

1 teaspoon grated orange
  peel
1/8 teaspoon pepper
8 turkey bacon strips,
  halved lengthwise
1 can (20 ounces) pineapple
  slices, drained and halved
  horizontally

NUTRITIONAL
INFORMATION

Serving Size: 1/8 recipe

Calories: 224
Total Fat: 7 gm
Calories from Fat: 26%
Saturated Fat: 3 gm
Cholesterol: 73 mg
Sodium: 1,072 mg
Carbohydrate: 27 gm
Protein: 15 gm

In a bowl, combine the ham, egg, relish and mustard. Shape into eight patties the same diameter as the pineapple rings. Combine the sweet potatoes, orange peel and pepper. Shape into eight patties the same diameter as pineapple rings. On a 15-in. x 10-in. x 1-in. baking sheet coated with nonstick cooking spray, assemble in the following order: Cross 2 strips of bacon, 1 pineapple slice, 1 ham patty, 1 sweet potato patty and 1 pineapple slice. Fold bacon ends up and over top; secure with a toothpick. Bake at 350° for 50-55 minutes or until bacon is crisp. Remove toothpicks; serve immediately. **Yield:** 8 servings.

Ham Loaf

Esther Mishler, Hollsopple, Pennsylvania

(Pictured above)

I copied this recipe from my grandma's worn cookbook. The difference today is I can't get home-smoked ham like those Grandpa used to cure in his old-fashioned smokehouse. But it's still a winner every time!

NUTRITIONAL INFORMATION

Serving Size: 1/8 recipe

Calories: 267
Total Fat: 7 gm
Calories from Fat: 23%
Saturated Fat: 2 gm
Cholesterol: 102 mg
Sodium: 1,381 mg
Carbohydrate: 24 gm
Protein: 27 gm

2 eggs
1 cup skim milk
1 cup dry bread crumbs
1/4 teaspoon pepper
1-1/2 pounds ground fully
    cooked low-fat ham

1/2 pound ground turkey
    breast
GLAZE:
    1/3 cup packed brown sugar
    1/4 cup vinegar
    2 tablespoons water
    1/2 teaspoon ground mustard

In a large bowl, beat the eggs; add milk, bread crumbs and pepper. Add ham and turkey; mix well. In a shallow baking pan, shape meat mixture into a loaf, about 8 in. x 4 in. x 2-1/2 in. Bake at 350° for 30 minutes. Meanwhile, combine glaze ingredients. Spoon over loaf. Continue baking about 40 minutes longer or until a meat thermometer reads 165°-170°, basting occasionally with glaze. **Yield:** 8 servings.

Orange-Glazed Pork Tenderloin

Janice MacLeod, Roanoke, Virginia

This recipe is yet another mouth-watering version of a classic combination—oranges and pork. It's a dish that can satisfy a man-sized appetite, but it's suitable for calorie-conscious folks, too. And it can be ready to serve in just 30 minutes!

1 pork tenderloin (1 pound), trimmed and cut into 1/4-inch slices	1/4 cup orange juice concentrate
Pepper to taste	2 tablespoons Worcestershire sauce
1/4 teaspoon garlic powder	4 green onions, sliced

In a large heavy skillet coated with nonstick cooking spray, brown tenderloin on both sides; sprinkle with pepper and garlic powder. Combine orange juice concentrate and Worcestershire sauce; pour over the tenderloin. Add onions; simmer until meat juices run clear and the sauce is thickened. **Yield:** 4 servings.

NUTRITIONAL INFORMATION

Serving Size: 1/4 recipe

Calories: 249
Total Fat: 7 gm
Calories from Fat: 27%
Saturated Fat: 3 gm
Cholesterol: 107 mg
Sodium: 159 mg
Carbohydrate: 9 gm
Protein: 35 gm

Chalupa Grande

Cindy Bertrand, Floydada, Texas

Mother made this dish for field lunches during cotton harvest. She's a great cook, and I give her lots of credit for my kitchen know-how. I plan to pass this recipe on to my daughter.

1 pound dry pinto beans	1 teaspoon dried oregano
1 bone-in lean pork roast (3 pounds)	1 can (4 ounces) chopped green chilies
7 cups water	Baked tortilla chips
1/2 cup chopped onion	Optional toppings: shredded fat-free cheddar cheese, diced tomatoes, chopped green onions *and/or* salsa
2 garlic cloves, minced	
2 tablespoons chili powder	
2 teaspoons ground cumin	

Place the first nine ingredients in a large kettle. (Beans do not need to be soaked.) Bring to a boil. Reduce heat; cover and simmer for 3 hours or until beans and roast are tender. Remove roast; cool slightly. Remove meat from bones; shred with a fork. Skim fat from sauce in kettle; return meat to kettle. Cook, uncovered, until thick, about 30 minutes. Serve over tortilla chips. Top with cheese, tomatoes, onions and/or salsa. **Yield:** 12 servings.

NUTRITIONAL INFORMATION

Serving Size: 1/12 recipe (without tortilla chips and toppings)

Calories: 260
Total Fat: 7 gm
Calories from Fat: 23%
Saturated Fat: 2 gm
Cholesterol: 50 mg
Sodium: 85 mg
Carbohydrate: 25 gm
Protein: 25 gm

Rhubarb Pork Chop Casserole

Jeanie Castor, Decatur, Illinois

(Pictured above)

This is an unusual use of rhubarb. I like rhubarb, but I'm not a dessert person, so I always thought there should be more to it than pies and cobblers.

4 loin pork chops (3/4 inch thick), trimmed
Pepper to taste
2-1/2 cups soft bread crumbs
1/2 cup packed brown sugar

1/4 cup all-purpose flour
1 teaspoon ground cinnamon
3 cups sliced fresh *or* frozen rhubarb (1-inch pieces)

In a large skillet coated with nonstick cooking spray, brown pork chops; season with pepper. Remove and keep warm. Combine 1/4 cup pan drippings (add water if necessary) with bread crumbs. Reserve 1/2 cup; sprinkle remaining crumbs into a 13-in. x 9-in. x 2-in. baking dish coated with nonstick cooking spray. Combine brown sugar, flour, cinnamon and rhubarb; spoon half over the crumbs. Arrange pork chops on top. Spoon remaining rhubarb mixture over chops. Cover and bake at 350° for 30-45 minutes. Uncover; sprinkle with reserved crumbs. Bake 10-15 minutes longer or until meat juices run clear. **Yield:** 4 servings.

NUTRITIONAL INFORMATION

Serving Size: 1/4 recipe

Calories: 323
Total Fat: 7 gm
Calories from Fat: 19%
Saturated Fat: 2 gm
Cholesterol: 55 mg
Sodium: 200 mg
Carbohydrate: 42 gm
Protein: 24 gm

Country Ham and Potatoes

Helen Bridges, Washington, Virginia

The browned potatoes give this dish a special touch. They pick up the flavor of the ham and make this entree very attractive.

1 fully cooked low-fat ham slice (3/4 inch thick and 1-1/2 pounds), trimmed

1-1/2 pounds potatoes, peeled, quartered and cooked
Snipped fresh parsley

In a large heavy skillet coated with nonstick cooking spray, cook ham over medium-high heat until browned on both sides and heated through. Move ham to one side of the skillet; brown potatoes in drippings. Sprinkle potatoes with parsley. **Yield:** 6 servings.

NUTRITIONAL INFORMATION

Serving Size: 1/6 recipe

Calories: 244
Total Fat: 6 gm
Calories from Fat: 21%
Saturated Fat: 2 gm
Cholesterol: 53 mg
Sodium: 1,619 mg
Carbohydrate: 21 gm
Protein: 24 gm

Citrus-Topped Pork Chops

Brenda Wood, Egbert, Ontario

(Pictured below)

This is a different way to prepare pork, and my family really enjoys it. The recipe originally had only oranges, but I added the lemons for tartness and color.

6 loin pork chops (1 inch
    thick), trimmed
Pepper to taste
1/4 teaspoon paprika
1/2 cup apple jelly
1 cup orange juice
1/2 teaspoon lemon juice
1 teaspoon ground mustard
Dash ground ginger
6 orange slices
6 lemon slices

In a large skillet coated with nonstick cooking spray, brown chops on both sides over medium-high heat. Season with pepper and paprika. Combine jelly, juices, mustard and ginger; pour over chops. Cover and simmer for 15 minutes. Turn chops; cover and simmer for 15 minutes. Top each chop with an orange and lemon slice. Cover and cook 6-8 minutes longer or until meat juices run clear. **Yield:** 6 servings.

NUTRITIONAL INFORMATION

Serving Size: 1/6 recipe

Calories: 243
Total Fat: 6 gm
Calories from Fat: 21%
Saturated Fat: 2 gm
Cholesterol: 54 mg
Sodium: 61 mg
Carbohydrate: 26 gm
Protein: 20 gm

Pork Hot Dish

Marie Leadens, Maple Grove, Minnesota

(Pictured above)

This recipe is truly a winner for our family of 10. It's a great meal in itself and a perennial favorite at get-togethers.

1 pound boneless lean pork, cut into 1-inch cubes
1/2 cup chopped celery
1/4 cup chopped sweet red *or* green pepper
1/4 cup chopped onion
1 package (10 ounces) medium egg noodles, cooked and drained
1 can (10-3/4 ounces) low-fat condensed cream of chicken soup, undiluted
1 can (10-3/4 ounces) low-fat condensed cream of mushroom soup, undiluted
1 can (16-1/2 ounces) cream-style corn
1/2 cup skim milk
1/4 teaspoon pepper
1 cup crushed saltines
1 tablespoon margarine, melted

In a large skillet coated with nonstick cooking spray, saute pork, celery, pepper and onion until the meat is browned and vegetables are tender. Combine pork mixture with noodles, soups, corn, milk and pepper; mix well. Spoon into an ungreased 13-in. x 9-in. x 2-in. baking dish. Combine cracker crumbs and margarine; sprinkle on top. Bake, uncovered, at 350° for 45 minutes or until heated through. **Yield:** 10 servings.

Cranberry Sweet-and-Sour Pork

Gert Snyder, West Montrose, Ontario

You'll create quite a stir at dinnertime when you present this swift sweet-and-sour stir-fry. Cranberry sauce provides a tasty touch.

1 can (8-3/4 ounces) unsweetened pineapple tidbits
1 tablespoon cornstarch
1/2 cup barbecue sauce
1 cup whole-berry cranberry sauce
1-1/2 pounds boneless lean pork, cut into 1/2-inch cubes
1/4 teaspoon pepper
1 medium green pepper, cut into strips

Drain pineapple, reserving juice; set pineapple aside. Combine juice with cornstarch. Stir in barbecue sauce and cranberry sauce; set aside. In a large skillet coated with nonstick cooking spray, stir-fry pork and pepper over medium-high heat for 3 minutes or until meat is no longer pink. Add green pepper and pineapple; stir-fry 2 minutes more. Stir cornstarch mixture and add to skillet. Cook, stirring constantly, over medium-high heat, until thickened. **Yield:** 6 servings.

Pork and Green Chili Casserole

Dianne Esposite, New Middletown, Ohio

This zippy casserole was brought to a picnic at my house. People raved over it.

1-1/2 pounds boneless lean pork, cut into 1/2-inch cubes
1 can (15 ounces) black beans, rinsed and drained
1 can (10-3/4 ounces) low-fat condensed cream of chicken soup, undiluted
1 can (14-1/2 ounces) diced tomatoes, undrained
2 cans (4 ounces *each*) chopped green chilies
1 cup quick-cooking brown rice
1/4 cup water
2 tablespoons salsa
1 teaspoon ground cumin
1/2 cup shredded fat-free cheddar cheese

In a large skillet coated with nonstick cooking spray, saute pork until no longer pink; drain. Add the beans, soup, tomatoes, chilies, rice, water, salsa and cumin; cook and stir until bubbly. Pour into an ungreased 2-qt. baking dish. Bake, uncovered, at 350° for 30 minutes or until bubbly. Sprinkle with cheese; let stand until melted. **Yield:** 6 servings.

Apple-Topped Chops

Susan Vinson, Granite Falls, North Carolina

(Pictured below)

The apple slices and juice keep these chops moist and tender, while the raisins, brown sugar and other spices give it wonderful flavor. This dish is a palate-pleaser every time!

NUTRITIONAL INFORMATION

Serving Size: 1/6 recipe

Calories: 240
Total Fat: 6 gm
Calories from Fat: 21%
Saturated Fat: 2 gm
Cholesterol: 54 mg
Sodium: 51 mg
Carbohydrate: 28 gm
Protein: 20 gm

6 loin pork chops (3/4 inch thick), trimmed
1 medium onion, thinly sliced into rings
1/2 cup raisins, *divided*
3 medium apples, cut into 1/2-inch slices
1 cup apple juice
1 tablespoon brown sugar
1/2 teaspoon dried basil
1/4 teaspoon ground nutmeg
1/8 teaspoon ground cloves

In a large skillet coated with nonstick cooking spray, brown pork chops over medium heat. Place in an ungreased 3-qt. baking dish. Place onion rings over the chops. Sprinkle with two-thirds of the raisins. Arrange the apple slices on top and sprinkle with remaining raisins. Combine apple juice, brown sugar, basil, nutmeg and cloves; pour over all. Cover and bake at 350° for 1 hour. Uncover and bake 30 minutes longer or until meat is tender. **Yield:** 6 servings.

Pork Piperade

Hyacinth Rizzo, Buffalo, New York

I like to spice up my meat dishes with peppers, and this Spanish recipe I adapted is a family favorite. The bright red and green peppers really complement the pork.

1 pound boneless lean pork
1/4 cup all-purpose flour
1 envelope taco seasoning
  mix, *divided*
2 teaspoons vegetable oil
PIPERADE:
  1 thinly sliced Spanish
    onion

2 sweet red peppers,
  julienned
2 green peppers, julienned
2 cups canned plum
  tomatoes, juice drained
  and reserved

Cut pork into 1-1/2-in. x 1-in. x 1/8-in. strips. In a small resealable plastic bag, combine flour and half of the taco seasoning mix. Add a few pork strips at a time and shake well to coat. Heat oil in a heavy 10-in. skillet; stir-fry pork until golden brown and tender. Meanwhile, in another skillet coated with nonstick cooking spray, stir-fry onion and peppers until crisp-tender. Chop tomatoes; add to skillet. In a small bowl, combine remaining taco seasoning and reserved tomato juice. Stir until blended; add to skillet. Cook and stir until thickened. Add pork to skillet; heat through. **Yield:** 8 servings.

NUTRITIONAL INFORMATION

Serving Size: 1/8 recipe

Calories: 138
Total Fat: 3 gm
Calories from Fat: 23%
Saturated Fat: 1 gm
Cholesterol: 34 mg
Sodium: 529 mg
Carbohydrate: 13 gm
Protein: 14 gm

Deluxe Potato Ham Bake

Diane Wilson Wing, Salt Lake City, Utah

When I take this creamy country-style casserole to potlucks, I always come home with an empty plate...and lots of recipe requests! I like the fact this dish gets a head start with canned soups and frozen hash browns.

2 cans (10-3/4 ounces
  each) low-fat condensed
  cream of chicken soup,
  undiluted
1 cup (8 ounces) light sour
  cream
1-1/2 cups (6 ounces) shredded
  reduced-fat cheddar
  cheese
1 medium onion, chopped

2 cups cubed fully cooked
  low-fat ham
1 package (32 ounces)
  frozen Southern-style
  hash brown potatoes,
  thawed
3/4 cup crushed cornflakes
1 tablespoon margarine,
  melted

In a large bowl, combine the first four ingredients; mix well. Stir in ham and potatoes. Spread into a 13-in. x 9-in. x 2-in. baking dish coated with nonstick cooking spray. Combine cornflakes and margarine; sprinkle over casserole. Bake, uncovered, at 350° for 1 hour or until potatoes are tender. **Yield:** 12 servings.

NUTRITIONAL INFORMATION

Serving Size: 1/12 recipe

Calories: 228
Total Fat: 8 gm
Calories from Fat: 30%
Saturated Fat: 4 gm
Cholesterol: 32 mg
Sodium: 628 mg
Carbohydrate: 26 gm
Protein: 14 gm

Pork Tenderloin with Raspberry Sauce Supreme

Bernice Janowski, Stevens Point, Wisconsin

Cooking is one of my favorite pastimes, especially when I get to try innovative recipes like this that combine unusual ingredients. This tenderloin is a simple way to impress dinner guests.

1 pork tenderloin (1 pound), trimmed and cut into 8 pieces
1/8 teaspoon cayenne pepper
6 tablespoons red raspberry preserves
2 tablespoons red wine vinegar
1 tablespoon ketchup
1/2 teaspoon prepared horseradish
1/2 teaspoon soy sauce
1 garlic clove, minced
2 kiwifruit, peeled and thinly sliced
Fresh raspberries

Flatten each tenderloin slice to 1-in. thickness; lightly sprinkle both sides with cayenne pepper. In a large heavy skillet coated with nonstick cooking spray, cook tenderloin over medium-high heat for 3-4 minutes on each side. Meanwhile, in a small saucepan, combine preserves, vinegar, ketchup, horseradish, soy sauce and garlic; simmer for 3 minutes, stirring occasionally. Keep warm. Place tenderloin on a warm serving plate; top with sauce. Garnish with kiwi and raspberries. **Yield:** 4 servings.

Hearty Ham Kabobs

Gloria Houghton, Winter Park, Florida

To me, there's nothing better than grilling out in the backyard and enjoying good times and great food with family and friends. We often rely on these quick and easy kabobs when entertaining.

1 large green pepper, cut into chunks
1 medium onion, cut into wedges
2 cups cubed fully cooked low-fat ham (1-1/2-inch pieces)
12 cherry tomatoes
1 can (20 ounces) unsweetened pineapple chunks, drained
1 cup low-fat Italian salad dressing
1 teaspoon Worcestershire sauce

Blanch the green pepper and onion if desired. Thread alternately with ham, tomatoes and pineapple onto six metal skewers. Combine salad dressing and Worcestershire sauce; brush over kabobs. Broil or grill, basting occasionally, until all ingredients are heated through, about 6-8 minutes. **Yield:** 6 servings.

Apricot Baked Ham

Marge Clark, West Lebanon, Indiana

(Pictured above)

Ham is a super choice for a holiday meal because once you put it in the oven, it practically takes care of itself until dinnertime. The coating in this recipe makes the ham beautiful to serve.

1 bone-in fully cooked
   ham (5 pounds), trimmed
20 whole cloves
1/2 cup apricot preserves

3 tablespoons ground
   mustard
1/2 cup packed light brown
   sugar

Score the surface of the ham with shallow diamond-shaped cuts. Insert cloves in cuts. Combine preserves and mustard; spread over ham. Pat brown sugar over apricot mixture. Place ham on a rack in a roasting pan. Bake at 325° for 1-1/2 hours or until ham is heated through and a meat thermometer reads 140°. **Yield:** 10 servings.

NUTRITIONAL
INFORMATION

Serving Size: 1/10 recipe

Calories: 253
Total Fat: 7 gm
Calories from Fat: 26%
Saturated Fat: 2 gm
Cholesterol: 57 mg
Sodium: 1,388 mg
Carbohydrate: 18 gm
Protein: 27 gm

Ham with Pineapple Sauce

Patty Bryant, Cedar Knolls, New Jersey

The sauce for my ham dish is one I adapted from a recipe on the back of a can of pineapple. While its origin may be nothing fancy, you'd never guess it from its inviting appearance. It's delicious, and a great time-saver, too!

1 fully cooked low-fat ham slice (1/2 inch thick and 1 pound), trimmed
1 can (8 ounces) unsweetened crushed pineapple, undrained

1/2 cup raisins
1/4 cup packed brown sugar
2 tablespoons prepared mustard
Dash ground cloves

In a skillet coated with nonstick cooking spray, heat ham slice until warmed. Meanwhile, in a saucepan, combine the remaining ingredients; simmer for 3 minutes. Serve over ham. **Yield:** 4 servings.

Zesty Grilled Chops

Blanche Babinski, Minot, North Dakota

(Pictured below)

These pork chops make a quick company dish. Our family enjoys them on the grill, as the summer weather in our part of the country is hot and muggy. In the wintertime, they're wonderful prepared in the broiler.

3/4 cup soy sauce
1/4 cup lemon juice
1 tablespoon chili sauce
1 tablespoon brown sugar

1 garlic clove, minced
6 loin pork chops (1 inch thick), trimmed

Combine the first five ingredients. Place chops in a glass baking dish and add 2/3 cup marinade. Refrigerate remaining marinade. Cover chops and refrigerate 3-6 hours or overnight. Drain chops, discarding marinade. Grill or broil 4 in. from the heat until juices run clear. Brush occasionally with the reserved marinade. **Yield:** 6 servings.

Pork Chops Olé

Laura Turner, Channelview, Texas

(Pictured above)

This recipe is a fun and simple way to give pork chops south-of-the-border flair. The flavorful seasoning, rice and cheese make this dish a crowd-pleaser. A dear friend shared this recipe with me several years ago.

6 loin pork chops
(1/2 inch thick), trimmed
Salt-free herb seasoning blend
and pepper to taste
3/4 cup uncooked long grain
rice
1-1/2 cups water

1 can (8 ounces) tomato
sauce
2 tablespoons taco
seasoning mix
1 medium green pepper,
chopped
1/2 cup shredded reduced-fat
cheddar cheese

NUTRITIONAL INFORMATION

Serving Size: 1/6 recipe

Calories: 268
Total Fat: 7 gm
Calories from Fat: 25%
Saturated Fat: 3 gm
Cholesterol: 61 mg
Sodium: 487 mg
Carbohydrate: 24 gm
Protein: 25 gm

In a large skillet coated with nonstick cooking spray, brown pork chops; sprinkle with seasoning blend and pepper. Meanwhile, in a 13-in. x 9-in. x 2-in. baking dish coated with nonstick cooking spray, combine rice, water, tomato sauce and taco seasoning; mix well. Arrange chops on top; sprinkle with green pepper. Cover and bake at 350° for 1-1/2 hours. Uncover and sprinkle with cheese; return to the oven until cheese is melted. **Yield:** 6 servings.

Baked Ham with Cumberland Sauce

Eunice Stoen, Decorah, Iowa

(Pictured below)

The centerpiece of a beautiful family dinner, this golden ham with tangy jewel-toned sauce is impressive to serve.

1 bone-in fully cooked
  ham (4 pounds), trimmed
1/2 cup packed brown sugar
  1 teaspoon ground mustard
Whole cloves

CUMBERLAND SAUCE:
  1 cup apple *or* red currant
  jelly
1/4 cup orange juice
1/4 cup lemon juice
1/4 cup apple juice
2 tablespoons honey
1 tablespoon cornstarch

Score the surface of ham with shallow diagonal cuts, making diamond shapes. Mix brown sugar and mustard; rub into ham. Insert a whole clove in each diamond. Place ham on a baking rack in a large roaster. Bake, uncovered, at 325° for 1-1/2 hours or until ham is heated through and a meat thermometer reads 140°. Combine sauce ingredients in a medium saucepan; cook over medium heat until thickened, stirring often. Serve over sliced ham. **Yield:** 8 servings (1-3/4 cups sauce).

Oven-Barbecued Pork Chops

Teresa King, Whittier, California

(Pictured above)

My mother has made this recipe for years and now I prepare it for my family. The chops are delicious with a green salad.

6 loin pork chops (3/4
  inch thick), trimmed
3/4 cup ketchup
1/3 cup hot water
2 tablespoons vinegar

1 tablespoon
  Worcestershire sauce
2 teaspoons brown sugar
1/2 teaspoon pepper
1/2 teaspoon chili powder
1/2 teaspoon paprika

Place chops in a heavy cast-iron skillet. Combine all remaining ingredients; pour over chops. Bake, uncovered, at 375° for 1 hour or until meat is tender. **Yield:** 6 servings.

NUTRITIONAL INFORMATION

Serving Size: 1/6 recipe

Calories: 164
Total Fat: 5 gm
Calories from Fat: 28%
Saturated Fat: 2 gm
Cholesterol: 38 mg
Sodium: 419 mg
Carbohydrate: 14 gm
Protein: 16 gm

Honey-Garlic Pork Chops

Helen Carpenter, Marble Falls, Texas

"Mmm, mmm good" is what people say when I serve these juicy chops. I like them for another reason—they're easy to prepare ahead of time!

4 boneless loin pork chops
  (1 inch thick), trimmed
1/4 cup lemon juice

1/4 cup honey
2 tablespoons soy sauce
2 garlic cloves, minced

Place pork chops in a shallow dish or resealable plastic bag. Combine remaining ingredients; pour over chops. Cover and refrigerate for 4-8 hours. Drain, discarding marinade. Grill chops, covered, over medium coals for about 15 minutes or until juices run clear. **Yield:** 4 servings.

NUTRITIONAL INFORMATION

Serving Size: 1/4 recipe

Calories: 182
Total Fat: 6 gm
Calories from Fat: 29%
Saturated Fat: 2 gm
Cholesterol: 59 mg
Sodium: 372 mg
Carbohydrate: 10 gm
Protein: 22 gm

CATCH OF THE DAY. *Top to bottom:*
Tuna Mushroom Casserole, Catfish Cakes
(both recipes on page 215) and Fish Fillets
with Stuffing (recipe on page 216).

From the Sea

Tuna Mushroom Casserole

Jone Furlong, Santa Rosa, California

(Pictured at left)

Green beans add nice texture, color and flavor to dressed-up tuna casserole.

1/2 cup water
1 teaspoon low-sodium chicken bouillon granules
1 package (10 ounces) frozen cut green beans
1 cup chopped onion
1 cup sliced fresh mushrooms
1/4 cup chopped celery
1 garlic clove, minced
1/2 teaspoon dill weed
1/8 teaspoon pepper

4 teaspoons cornstarch
1-1/2 cups skim milk
1/2 cup shredded reduced-fat Swiss cheese
1/4 cup light mayonnaise
2-1/2 cups medium noodles, cooked and drained
1 can (12-1/4 ounces) light tuna in water, drained and flaked
1/3 cup dry bread crumbs
1 teaspoon margarine

In a large saucepan, bring water and bouillon to a boil, stirring to dissolve. Add the next seven ingredients; bring to a boil. Reduce heat; cover and simmer for 5 minutes or until vegetables are tender. Dissolve cornstarch in milk; add to vegetable mixture, stirring constantly. Bring to a boil; boil for 2 minutes or until thickened. Remove from the heat; stir in cheese and mayonnaise until cheese is melted. Fold in noodles and tuna. Pour into a 2-1/2-qt. baking dish coated with nonstick cooking spray. Brown bread crumbs in margarine; sprinkle over casserole. Bake, uncovered, at 350° for 25-30 minutes or until heated through. **Yield:** 6 servings.

NUTRITIONAL INFORMATION

Serving Size: 1/6 recipe

Calories: 291
Total Fat: 7 gm
Calories from Fat: 22%
Saturated Fat: 2 gm
Cholesterol: 44 mg
Sodium: 400 mg
Carbohydrate: 32 gm
Protein: 25 gm

Catfish Cakes

Jan Campbell, Purvis, Mississippi

(Pictured at left)

These cakes are crispy on the outside and moist and flavorful on the inside!

1-1/2 pounds catfish fillets
Egg substitute equivalent to 2 eggs
1 large potato, peeled, cooked and mashed
1 large onion, finely chopped
1 tablespoon chopped fresh parsley

2 drops hot pepper sauce
1 garlic clove, minced
1/2 teaspoon pepper
1/2 teaspoon dried basil
2 cups finely crushed reduced-fat butter-flavored crackers
2 tablespoons cooking oil

Poach or bake catfish fillets. Drain and refrigerate. Flake cooled fish into a large bowl. Add egg substitute, potato, onion, parsley, hot pepper sauce, garlic, pepper and basil; mix well. Shape into eight patties; coat with cracker crumbs. Heat oil in a large skillet. Cook patties, a few at a time, until browned on both sides and heated through. **Yield:** 8 servings.

NUTRITIONAL INFORMATION

Serving Size: 1/8 recipe

Calories: 229
Total Fat: 8 gm
Calories from Fat: 30%
Saturated Fat: 2 gm
Cholesterol: 50 mg
Sodium: 272 mg
Carbohydrate: 21 gm
Protein: 18 gm

Fish Fillets with Stuffing

Donna Smith, Victor, New York

(Pictured on page 214)

This fish is moist and the stuffing adds crunch. It's a great microwave recipe.

1 tablespoon margarine, melted
1/3 cup chicken broth
1/2 cup finely chopped onion
1/2 cup finely grated carrots
1/2 cup chopped fresh mushrooms
1/4 cup minced fresh parsley

1/2 cup dry bread crumbs
1 egg
1 tablespoon lemon juice
1/8 teaspoon pepper
2-1/2 pounds cod, haddock *or* whitefish fillets
Paprika

In a large bowl, combine the first 10 ingredients; mix well. In a 13-in. x 9-in. x 2-in. microwave-safe dish coated with nonstick cooking spray, arrange the fillets with stuffing between them. Moisten microwave-safe paper towels with water; place over fish. Cook on high for 15-16 minutes or until fish flakes easily with a fork, rotating dish occasionally. Sprinkle with paprika. **Yield:** 8 servings.

NUTRITIONAL INFORMATION

Serving Size: 1/8 recipe
(calculated with cod)

Calories: 174
Total Fat: 3 gm
Calories from Fat: 19%
Saturated Fat: 1 gm
Cholesterol: 88 mg
Sodium: 187 mg
Carbohydrate: 7 gm
Protein: 27 gm

Hot Kippered Salmon

Barbara Njaa, Nikiski, Alaska

I developed this recipe as one of the many ways to enjoy our catch from the inlet in front of our home. It's healthy and delicious.

2 salmon fillets (2 pounds each)
2 teaspoons salt
Pepper to taste

2 tablespoons plus 2 teaspoons brown sugar
2 tablespoons liquid smoke

Place fillets skin side down, side by side, in a shallow baking pan coated with nonstick cooking spray. Sprinkle with salt, pepper and brown sugar; drizzle with liquid smoke. Cover and refrigerate 4-8 hours. Drain any liquid. Bake at 350° for 30-45 minutes or until fish flakes easily with a fork. **Yield:** 8 servings.

NUTRITIONAL INFORMATION

Serving Size: 1/8 recipe

Calories: 274
Total Fat: 8 gm
Calories from Fat: 27%
Saturated Fat: 1 gm
Cholesterol: 118 mg
Sodium: 686 mg
Carbohydrate: 3 gm
Protein: 45 gm

Stuffed Trout

Shirley Coleman, Monkton, Vermont

Since it's so quick and easy to prepare, fish is perfect for a busy cook like me. I look for recipes like this that enhance trout's naturally pleasant taste.

2 turkey bacon strips, cooked and crumbled
1/2 cup fresh coarse bread crumbs
1/4 cup chopped onion

2 tablespoons chopped fresh parsley
1/8 teaspoon pepper
4 dressed trout (1/2 pound each)

In a medium bowl, combine the first five ingredients; mix well. Stuff 1/4 cup into cavity of each trout. Place on a rack coated wtih nonstick cooking spray in a shallow roasting pan. Bake at 350° for 35-40 minutes or until fish flakes easily with a fork. **Yield:** 8 servings.

NUTRITIONAL INFORMATION

Serving Size: 1/8 recipe

Calories: 306
Total Fat: 10 gm
Calories from Fat: 29%
Saturated Fat: 2 gm
Cholesterol: 192 mg
Sodium: 332 mg
Carbohydrate: 10 gm
Protein: 40 gm

Catfish Parmesan

Mrs. W.D. Baker, Starkville, Mississippi

(Pictured above)

Mississippi is the nation's largest producer of farm-raised catfish. My family loves this dish and asks for it often. One reason I like it is it's so simple to prepare. I hope you enjoy it, too.

3/4 cup dry bread crumbs	1/8 teaspoon *each* pepper,
3 tablespoons grated	dried oregano and basil
Parmesan cheese	6 fresh *or* frozen catfish
2 tablespoons chopped	fillets (4 ounces *each*)
fresh parsley	3 egg whites, beaten
1/4 teaspoon paprika	

In a shallow bowl, combine the bread crumbs, Parmesan cheese, parsley and seasonings. Dip catfish in egg whites, then in crumb mixture. Arrange in a 13-in. x 9-in. x 2-in. baking dish coated with nonstick cooking spray. Lightly spray fillets with nonstick cooking spray. Bake, uncovered, at 375° for 20-25 minutes or until fish flakes easily with a fork. **Yield:** 6 servings.

NUTRITIONAL INFORMATION

Serving Size: 1/6 recipe

Calories: 181
Total Fat: 5 gm
Calories from Fat: 25%
Saturated Fat: 2 gm
Cholesterol: 68 mg
Sodium: 243 mg
Carbohydrate: 10 gm
Protein: 23 gm

Crab-Stuffed Potatoes

Ruby Williams, Bogalusa, Louisiana

(Pictured below)

Crabmeat is a favorite in this part of the country. It gives twice-baked potatoes great flavor—potato lovers rave about them.

4 medium baking potatoes
1 tablespoon margarine
1/3 cup skim milk
1/4 teaspoon pepper
1 cup (4 ounces) shredded reduced-fat cheddar cheese
1/4 cup finely chopped green onions *or* chives
1 can (6 ounces) crabmeat, drained, flaked and cartilage removed *or* 1 package (8 ounces) imitation crabmeat, chopped
Paprika

Bake potatoes at 425° for 45-55 minutes or until tender. When cool enough to handle, halve potatoes lengthwise. Carefully scoop out pulp into a bowl, leaving a thin shell. Set shells aside. Beat or mash potato pulp with margarine, milk and pepper until smooth. Using a fork, stir in cheese and onions. Gently mix in crab. Stuff shells. Sprinkle with paprika. Return to the oven for 15 minutes or until heated through. **Yield:** 8 servings.

NUTRITIONAL INFORMATION

Serving Size: 1/8 recipe
(calculated with canned crab)

Calories: 152
Total Fat: 5 gm
Calories from Fat: 26%
Saturated Fat: 2 gm
Cholesterol: 29 mg
Sodium: 205 mg
Carbohydrate: 17 gm
Protein: 11 gm

Lemon Garlic Fish Fillets

Denise Blackman, Port Cartier, Quebec

Not only does this dish go from start to finish in a flash, it features seafood that's a mealtime mainstay in our home. It's so easy, even my husband can make it!

2 tablespoons margarine
2 small garlic cloves, minced
4 cod *or* whitefish fillets (6 ounces *each*)

1/4 cup thinly sliced green onions
Lemon wedges

In a skillet, melt margarine over medium heat. Saute garlic for 1 minute. Add fish fillets; cover and cook over low heat 3 minutes. Carefully turn fish; sprinkle with onions. Cover and continue to cook until fish flakes easily with a fork, about 2-3 minutes. Squeeze lemon over fish. Serve immediately. **Yield:** 4 servings.

NUTRITIONAL INFORMATION

Serving Size: 1 fillet (calculated with cod)

Calories: 169
Total Fat: 4 gm
Calories from Fat: 22%
Saturated Fat: 1 gm
Cholesterol: 73 mg
Sodium: 117 mg
Carbohydrate: 1 gm
Protein: 31 gm

Bayou Country Seafood Casserole

Ethel Miller, Eunice, Louisiana

Seafood is popular in our area. Since crab and shrimp are so plentiful in our bayous and rivers, we use them in a variety of recipes.

2 teaspoons margarine
1 medium onion, chopped
1 medium green pepper, chopped
1 celery rib, chopped
1 garlic clove, minced
1 can (10-3/4 ounces) low-fat condensed cream of mushroom soup, undiluted
1 pound uncooked shrimp, peeled and deveined
1-1/2 cups cooked rice
4 slices day-old bread, cubed

2 cans (6 ounces *each*) crabmeat, drained, flaked and cartilage removed *or* 1-1/2 pounds fresh crabmeat, cooked
3/4 cup skim milk
1/4 cup chopped green onions with tops
1/4 teaspoon pepper
Dash cayenne pepper
TOPPING:
2 teaspoons margarine, melted
1/3 cup dry bread crumbs
2 tablespoons snipped fresh parsley

In a skillet, melt margarine over medium heat. Saute onion, green pepper, celery and garlic until tender. Add soup and shrimp; cook and stir over medium heat for 10 minutes or until shrimp turn pink. Stir in rice, bread cubes, crab, milk, onions and seasonings. Spoon into a 2-qt. baking dish coated with nonstick cooking spray. Combine topping ingredients; sprinkle over casserole. Bake at 375° for 30 minutes or until heated through. **Yield:** 8 servings.

NUTRITIONAL INFORMATION

Serving Size: 1/8 recipe (calculated with canned crab)

Calories: 241
Total Fat: 5 gm
Calories from Fat: 19%
Saturated Fat: 1 gm
Cholesterol: 109 mg
Sodium: 527 mg
Carbohydrate: 28 gm
Protein: 21 gm

Lemony Salmon Patties

Lorice Britt, Severn, North Carolina

With the tasty salmon and zippy sauce, my family finds these patties delicious. They're also a mouth-watering economical meal I often prepare when I want to impress dinner guests.

1 can (14-3/4 ounces) pink salmon, drained, skin and bones removed
3/4 cup skim milk
1 cup soft bread crumbs
1 egg, beaten
1 tablespoon chopped fresh parsley
1 teaspoon minced onion
1/2 teaspoon Worcestershire sauce
1/8 teaspoon pepper
LEMON SAUCE:
3/4 cup skim milk
4 teaspoons all-purpose flour
2 tablespoons lemon juice
1/4 teaspoon cayenne pepper

Combine the first eight ingredients; mix well. Spoon into eight muffin cups coated with nonstick cooking spray, using 1/4 cup in each. Bake at 350° for 45 minutes or until browned. In a saucepan, gradually stir milk into flour; bring to a boil over medium heat, stirring constantly. Cook for 2 minutes or until thickened. Remove from the heat; stir in lemon juice and cayenne. Serve over patties. **Yield:** 4 servings.

NUTRITIONAL INFORMATION

Serving Size: 1/4 recipe

Calories: 239
Total Fat: 8 gm
Calories from Fat: 30%
Saturated Fat: 2 gm
Cholesterol: 113 mg
Sodium: 206 mg
Carbohydrate: 13 gm
Protein: 27 gm

Seafood in Tomato Sauce

Jeffrey MacCord, New Castle, Delaware

We live near the Chesapeake Bay and reap its bountiful seafood harvest. I serve this to company often and receive rave reviews every time. I hope you'll enjoy it as much as my family does!

1/4 pound fresh mushrooms, sliced
1 garlic clove, minced
1 can (14-1/2 ounces) diced tomatoes, undrained
1-1/2 teaspoons dried oregano
1 teaspoon dried thyme
1 teaspoon sugar
Pepper to taste
1/2 pound uncooked bay scallops
1/2 pound uncooked small shrimp, peeled and deveined
1 cup cooked rice
1/2 pound fresh crabmeat, cooked *or* imitation crabmeat chunks
1/4 cup grated Parmesan cheese

In a large saucepan coated with nonstick cooking spray, saute mushrooms and garlic for 3-4 minutes. Add tomatoes, oregano, thyme, sugar and pepper; bring to a boil. Reduce heat; cover and simmer for 30 minutes. Uncover and cook 10 minutes longer. Meanwhile, heat skillet coated with nonstick cooking spray over medium heat. Cook scallops and shrimp until shrimp turn pink, about 3-4 minutes. Place 1/4 cup rice each in four individual ovenproof casseroles; top with shrimp and scallops. Stir crabmeat into tomato mixture and spoon over scallops. Sprinkle with Parmesan cheese. Broil until the cheese melts. Serve immediately. **Yield:** 4 servings.

NUTRITIONAL INFORMATION

Serving Size: 1/4 recipe
(calculated with fresh crab)

Calories: 281
Total Fat: 4 gm
Calories from Fat: 14%
Saturated Fat: 2 gm
Cholesterol: 161 mg
Sodium: 645 mg
Carbohydrate: 24 gm
Protein: 35 gm

New England Fish Bake

Norma DesRoches, Warwick, Rhode Island

(Pictured above)

I've lived in Rhode Island for over 30 years and love the fresh seafood dishes served here. This is a favorite. My mother-in-law gave me the recipe.

4 medium potatoes, peeled
1 teaspoon all-purpose
   flour
1 small onion, sliced into
   rings
1/4 teaspoon pepper
3/4 cup skim milk, *divided*

1-1/2 pounds whitefish or cod
   fillets
1 tablespoon grated
   Parmesan cheese
2 tablespoons minced fresh
   parsley *or* 2 teaspoons
   dried parsley flakes
1/4 teaspoon paprika

Place potatoes in a saucepan and cover with water; bring to a boil. Cook until almost tender; drain. Slice 1/8 in. thick; place in a shallow 2-qt. baking dish coated with nonstick cooking spray. Sprinkle with flour. Top with onion; sprinkle with pepper. Pour half of the milk over potatoes. Place fish on top; pour remaining milk over fish. Sprinkle with Parmesan cheese. Cover and bake at 375° for 20-30 minutes or until fish flakes easily with a fork. Sprinkle with parsley and paprika. **Yield:** 4 servings.

NUTRITIONAL INFORMATION

Serving Size: 1/4 recipe
(calculated with whitefish)

Calories: 277
Total Fat: 8 gm
Calories from Fat: 25%
Saturated Fat: 1 gm
Cholesterol: 72 mg
Sodium: 120 mg
Carbohydrate: 24 gm
Protein: 27 gm

THE BEST OF THE HARVEST. *Clockwise from top: Pasta with Tomatoes, Asparagus-Stuffed Potatoes (both recipes on page 223) and Basil Green Beans (recipe on page 224).*

Side Dishes

Pasta with Tomatoes

Earlene Ertelt, Woodburn, Oregon

(Pictured at left)

I found this delicious recipe in the newspaper a few years ago and have used it frequently ever since. With my busy life-style, it's important to have quick-and-easy dishes like this.

2 large tomatoes, chopped
2 tablespoons snipped
   fresh basil *or* 2 teaspoons
   dried basil
1 garlic clove, minced

1/4 teaspoon pepper
4 ounces bow tie *or* other
   pasta, cooked and drained
Additional fresh basil, optional

Combine the tomatoes, basil, garlic and pepper. Set aside at room temperature for several hours. Serve over hot pasta. Garnish with basil if desired. **Yield:** 2 servings.

Asparagus-Stuffed Potatoes

Helen Druse, Addieville, Illinois

(Pictured at left)

You can make this side dish anytime and for any occasion, although I have to say it tastes best when I use fresh asparagus grown in my backyard.

4 medium baking potatoes
1 tablespoon skim milk
1/2 cup light sour cream
1/4 teaspoon onion powder
1/8 teaspoon pepper

1 pound fresh asparagus,
   cut into 1-inch pieces
   and cooked
2 turkey bacon strips,
   cooked and crumbled
3/4 cup shredded reduced-fat
   cheddar cheese

Bake potatoes at 400° for about 1 hour or until done. Cut a thin slice off the top of each potato and discard. Carefully scoop out pulp while leaving shell intact. In a mixing bowl, mash pulp with milk, sour cream, onion powder and pepper until smooth. Fold in asparagus. Stuff shells; place in an ungreased shallow baking dish. Sprinkle with bacon. Bake at 400° for 20-25 minutes or until heated through. Top with cheese; return to the oven for 5 minutes or until cheese begins to melt. **Yield:** 4 servings.

Basil Green Beans

Laura Porter, Sheridan, Oregon

(Pictured on page 222)

This small-portioned fresh-tasting side dish goes great with any meat entree.

2 cups fresh green beans,
 cut into 2-inch pieces
2 tablespoons chopped
 onion
2 tablespoons chopped
 celery
1/4 cup water

1 tablespoon reduced-fat
 margarine
1-1/2 teaspoons minced fresh
 basil *or* 1/2 teaspoon
 dried basil
Pepper to taste

In a saucepan, combine beans, onion, celery and water. Cover and cook for 5 minutes or until beans are tender. Drain. Add the margarine, basil and pepper; stir to coat. Serve immediately. **Yield:** 2 servings.

Citrus Broccoli Toss

Lois McCutchan, Monticello, Missouri

(Pictured on the front cover)

In this recipe, orange and lemon give broccoli a wonderfully tangy flavor.

1 tablespoon margarine
4 cups fresh broccoli
 florets *or* 1 package
 (10 ounces) frozen cut
 broccoli, thawed

1-1/2 teaspoons grated orange
 peel
1-1/2 teaspoons grated lemon
 peel
Pepper to taste

In a skillet, melt margarine over medium heat. Saute broccoli until crisp-tender. Sprinkle with orange peel, lemon peel and pepper; toss to coat. Heat through. **Yield:** 4 servings.

Oven-Roasted Potatoes

Margie Wampler, Butler, Pennsylvania

(Pictured on the front cover)

This dish is simple to prepare yet elegant in color and flavor. Rosemary gives the potatoes a distinctive, subtle taste.

2 pounds small unpeeled
 red potatoes, cut into
 wedges
2 garlic cloves, minced

1 tablespoon minced fresh
 rosemary *or* 1 teaspoon
 dried rosemary, crushed
1/4 teaspoon pepper

Place potatoes in a 13-in. x 9-in. x 2-in. baking pan coated with nonstick cooking spray. Mist potatoes with nonstick cooking spray. Sprinkle with garlic, rosemary and pepper; toss gently to coat. Bake, uncovered, at 450° for 20-30 minutes or until potatoes are golden brown and tender when pierced with a fork. **Yield:** 8 servings.

Skillet Vegetable Side Dish

Ada Gendell, Claremont, New Hampshire

(Pictured above)

Since I'm an avid gardener, I always have an abundance of fresh vegetables on hand. This is a wonderful way to serve most any kind of vegetable.

3 carrots, thinly sliced
1 large onion, chopped
1/2 medium head cabbage, chopped
1/2 medium green pepper, chopped
1 tablespoon chopped celery

2 garlic cloves, minced
2 tablespoons Worcestershire sauce
1 tablespoon minced fresh parsley
1 teaspoon caraway seeds
1 teaspoon Italian seasoning

In a large skillet coated with nonstick cooking spray, stir-fry carrots, onion, cabbage, green pepper and celery over medium-high heat for 5 minutes. Add remaining ingredients; stir-fry 5 minutes longer or until the vegetables are cooked to desired doneness. **Yield:** 8 servings.

NUTRITIONAL INFORMATION

Serving Size: 1/8 recipe

Calories: 28
Total Fat: trace
Calories from Fat: 6%
Saturated Fat: trace
Cholesterol: 0
Sodium: 51 mg
Carbohydrate: 6 gm
Protein: 1 gm

Merry Christmas Rice

Karen Hoylo, Duluth, Minnesota

(Pictured below)

Instant rice makes this dish an instant success! It's a recipe I added to my collection "by children's demand", and we've found it to be a delicious and very colorful addition to our table throughout the year.

NUTRITIONAL INFORMATION

Serving Size: 1/6 recipe

Calories: 275
Total Fat: trace
Calories from Fat: 1%
Saturated Fat: trace
Cholesterol: 0
Sodium: 3 mg
Carbohydrate: 68 gm
Protein: 2 gm

2 cups water, *divided*
1-1/3 cups sugar, *divided*
2 cups (1/2 pound) fresh *or* frozen cranberries
1-1/3 cups uncooked instant rice
1/4 teaspoon ground cinnamon
1 apple, peeled and sliced

In a saucepan, combine 1/2 cup water and 1 cup sugar; bring to a boil. Add the cranberries; return to a boil. Reduce heat; simmer for 10 minutes or until most of the berries pop, stirring occasionally. Add rice, remaining water, remaining sugar and cinnamon. Bring to a boil. Reduce heat; cover and simmer for 10 minutes. Remove from the heat and stir in apple. Cover and let stand for 10 minutes. **Yield:** 6 servings.

Zesty Carrots

James McMonagle, Bethel Park, Pennsylvania

These are so great-tasting they might even make carrot lovers out of people who aren't fans of them now.

1-1/2 pounds carrots, sliced
    1/4 inch thick
1/2 cup light mayonnaise
1/4 cup shredded reduced-fat
    cheddar cheese
2 tablespoons grated onion

1 tablespoon prepared
    horseradish
1/4 teaspoon pepper
1/2 cup fresh bread crumbs
1 tablespoon margarine,
    melted
1/2 teaspoon paprika

In a saucepan, cook carrots in water for 5 minutes. Drain, reserving 1/4 cup cooking liquid. To the liquid, add mayonnaise, cheese, onion, horseradish and pepper. Stir in carrots; spoon into a 2-qt. casserole coated with nonstick cooking spray. Combine remaining ingredients; sprinkle on top. Bake, uncovered, at 350° for 20 minutes. **Yield:** 8 servings.

NUTRITIONAL INFORMATION

Serving Size: 1/8 recipe

Calories: 113
Total Fat: 7 gm
Calories from Fat: 56%
Saturated Fat: 1 gm
Cholesterol: 7 mg
Sodium: 177 mg
Carbohydrate: 11 gm
Protein: 2 gm

Summer Squash and Potato Saute

Denise Blackman, Port Cartier, Quebec

This speedy side dish takes advantage of plentiful seasonal squash.

1 tablespoon margarine
2 medium summer squash,
    sliced

2 small unpeeled red
    potatoes, thinly sliced
Minced fresh parsley
Pepper to taste

In a skillet, melt margarine over medium heat. Saute squash and potatoes until tender. Sprinkle with parsley and pepper. **Yield:** 4 servings.

NUTRITIONAL INFORMATION

Serving Size: 1/4 recipe

Calories: 101
Total Fat: 3 gm
Calories from Fat: 27%
Saturated Fat: 1 gm
Cholesterol: 0
Sodium: 39 mg
Carbohydrate: 17 gm
Protein: 4 gm

Easy Vegetable Linguine

Marie Herr, Berea, Ohio

Sometimes I'll substitute cauliflower for broccoli in this tasty pasta dish.

1 cup fresh broccoli florets
1 cup sliced fresh
    mushrooms
1/4 cup chopped onion
3 ounces linguine, cooked
    and drained

1/2 cup cherry tomato halves
4 turkey bacon strips,
    diced and cooked
1/4 cup grated Parmesan
    cheese

In a skillet coated with nonstick cooking spray, saute broccoli, mushrooms and onion for 3-4 minutes or until crisp-tender. Add linguine, tomatoes and bacon; mix lightly. Sprinkle with cheese. Serve immediately. **Yield:** 2 servings.

NUTRITIONAL INFORMATION

Serving Size: 1/2 recipe

Calories: 269
Total Fat: 6 gm
Calories from Fat: 20%
Saturated Fat: 2 gm
Cholesterol: 18 mg
Sodium: 403 mg
Carbohydrate: 43 gm
Protein: 14 gm

Ratatouille

Donna Rushing, Belk, Alabama

This simple-to-prepare side dish is chock-full of some of my family's favorite vegetables. Because it cooks up in no time on the stovetop, it's perfect during the hurried, hectic days of summer.

1 tablespoon olive *or* vegetable oil
3 medium zucchini, cut into 1/2-inch slices
2 large tomatoes, peeled and chopped
1 large onion, chopped
1/4 cup minced fresh parsley
1 green pepper, cut into strips
1 tablespoon minced fresh basil *or* 1 teaspoon dried basil
1/4 teaspoon pepper

In a large Dutch oven, heat oil over medium-high heat. Saute all ingredients for 5 minutes. Cover and simmer, stirring occasionally, for 15 minutes or until vegetables are tender. **Yield:** 8 servings.

Potato Onion Supreme

Claire Stryker, Bloomington, Illinois

I'm a pastor's wife and often find myself cooking for large groups. I first put together this dish for a wedding shower at church. Afterward, I had three requests for the recipe. It's fast and easy and adds a festive touch to a Sunday dinner. But it's equally at home at potlucks or socials.

8 medium potatoes (2-1/2 pounds), peeled
2 large sweet onions, sliced
1/4 cup water
2 tablespoons low-sodium chicken bouillon granules
2 cups (16 ounces) light sour cream
2 cups (8 ounces) shredded reduced-fat cheddar cheese
Paprika
Additional onion rings and chopped fresh parsley, optional

Cook potatoes; slice 1/4 in. thick. Set aside. In a saucepan, combine onions, water and bouillon; bring to a boil. Reduce heat; simmer for 5-7 minutes or until onions are tender. Drain and set aside. Combine sour cream and cheese. In a 2-1/2-qt. baking dish coated with nonstick cooking spray, layer half the potatoes, onions and cheese mixture. Repeat layers. Sprinkle with paprika. Bake, uncovered, at 350° for 20 minutes or until heated through. Garnish with onion rings and parsley if desired. **Yield:** 8 servings.

Sweet-and-Sour Red Cabbage

Barbara White, Cross Plains, Wisconsin

(Pictured below)

I used to help Mother shred the cabbage and cut up the apples for this recipe when I was younger. The touch of tartness is wonderful. I've found this is even tastier when made ahead. Plus, it keeps well in the freezer.

1 cup water
1/4 cup packed brown sugar
3 tablespoons vinegar
1 tablespoon vegetable oil

Dash pepper
4 cups shredded red cabbage
2 tart apples, peeled and
  sliced

In a large skillet, combine water, brown sugar, vinegar, oil and pepper. Cook for 2-3 minutes or until hot, stirring occasionally. Add cabbage; cover and cook for 10 minutes over medium-low heat, stirring occasionally. Add apples; cook, uncovered, for about 10 minutes more or until tender, stirring occasionally. **Yield:** 8 servings.

NUTRITIONAL INFORMATION

Serving Size: 1/8 recipe

Calories: 69
Total Fat: 2 gm
Calories from Fat: 26%
Saturated Fat: trace
Cholesterol: 0
Sodium: 6 mg
Carbohydrate: 14 gm
Protein: 1 gm

Southwestern Hominy

Clifford Wilson, Raytown, Missouri

(Pictured below)

This recipe has been in our family for a long time, but I'm not sure where it originated. Though it has a Southwestern flair, we love it here in Missouri.

1/2 cup chopped onion
1/2 cup chopped green pepper
1 tablespoon margarine
2 teaspoons chili powder
1/2 teaspoon paprika

2 cans (15-1/2 ounces *each*) golden hominy, rinsed and drained
1/8 teaspoon pepper

In a saucepan, saute onion and green pepper in margarine until tender. Add the remaining ingredients. Cook, uncovered, over medium-low heat for 5-10 minutes or until heated through, stirring occasionally. **Yield:** 6 servings.

Zucchini Corn Medley

Norma Erne, Albuquerque, New Mexico

With its creamy cheese sauce and zippy taste, this dish turns abundant garden vegetables into a comforting side dish.

5 medium zucchini, cut into 1/2-inch chunks
1/2 cup water
1 package (10 ounces) frozen corn
1 can (4 ounces) chopped green chilies
1 tablespoon margarine
2 tablespoons all-purpose flour
1/4 teaspoon ground mustard
1/4 teaspoon pepper
1 cup skim milk
1/2 cup shredded reduced-fat cheddar cheese

In a saucepan over medium heat, cook zucchini in water until just tender, about 6 minutes. Add corn; cook for 1 minute. Drain. Stir in chilies; pour into a 1-1/2-qt. shallow baking dish coated with nonstick cooking spray. Melt margarine in a saucepan; stir in flour, mustard and pepper until smooth. Gradually stir in milk; bring to a boil, stirring constantly. Boil for 2 minutes or until thickened. Pour over vegetables. Bake, uncovered, at 350° for 20 minutes or until bubbly. Top with cheese; return to the oven for 5 minutes or until cheese begins to melt. **Yield:** 6 servings.

NUTRITIONAL INFORMATION

Serving Size: 1/6 recipe

Calories: 163
Total Fat: 5 gm
Calories from Fat: 28%
Saturated Fat: 2 gm
Cholesterol: 4 mg
Sodium: 140 mg
Carbohydrate: 26 gm
Protein: 8 gm

Baked Stuffed Tomatoes

Bertille Cooper, St. Inigoes, Maryland

My family loves these tasty garden "containers" filled with rice and beef. I like to serve them with soup, but they're also a great meal by themselves.

6 medium fresh tomatoes
1/2 pound ground round
1 teaspoon chili powder
1 teaspoon sugar
1/2 teaspoon pepper
1/4 teaspoon dried oregano
2 cups uncooked instant rice
1/2 cup dry bread crumbs
2 teaspoons margarine, melted
2 tablespoons water

Cut a thin slice off the top of each tomato. Leaving a 1/2-in.-thick shell, scoop out and reserve pulp. Invert tomatoes onto paper towels to drain. Meanwhile, in a skillet, brown beef; drain. Add tomato pulp, chili powder, sugar, pepper and oregano; bring to a boil. Reduce heat; simmer for 45-50 minutes or until slightly thickened, stirring occasionally. Add rice; mix well. Simmer 5-6 minutes longer or until rice is tender. Stuff tomatoes and place in a 13-in. x 9-in. x 2-in. baking dish coated with nonstick cooking spray. Combine bread crumbs and margarine; sprinkle over tomatoes. Add water to baking dish. Bake, uncovered, at 375° for 20-25 minutes or until crumbs are lightly browned. **Yield:** 6 servings.

NUTRITIONAL INFORMATION

Serving Size: 1/6 recipe

Calories: 236
Total Fat: 4 gm
Calories from Fat: 15%
Saturated Fat: 1 gm
Cholesterol: 24 mg
Sodium: 117 mg
Carbohydrate: 38 gm
Protein: 12 gm

Baked Winter Vegetables Supreme

Pearl Wright, Waterdown, Ontario

Here's a delicious way that you can enjoy fresh vegetables all year-round.

2 pounds turnips
1 pound carrots
1 pound parsnips
2 medium kohlrabi
(1 pound)
3 tablespoons minced
fresh parsley
1/8 teaspoon pepper

2 tablespoons chopped
fresh tarragon *or* 2
teaspoons dried tarragon
3/4 cup low-sodium chicken
broth
2 medium onions, sliced
1/4 inch thick
2 garlic cloves, minced

Peel and slice turnips, carrots, parsnips and kohlrabi into 1/4-in. julienne strips. Place in a 13-in. x 9-in. x 2-in. baking pan coated with nonstick cooking spray. Sprinkle with parsley, pepper and tarragon. Pour broth over all. Top with onions and garlic. Cover and bake at 350° for 1 hour or until vegetables are crisp-tender. Uncover; bake 10-15 minutes longer or until vegetables reach desired tenderness. **Yield:** 14 servings.

NUTRITIONAL INFORMATION

Serving Size: 1 cup

Calories: 69
Total Fat: trace
Calories from Fat: 3%
Saturated Fat: trace
Cholesterol: 0
Sodium: 94 mg
Carbohydrate: 17 gm
Protein: 2 gm

Ginger-Orange Squash

Vonna Wendt, Ephrata, Washington

You can prepare this dish in a snap in the microwave. It has a festive flavor.

1 butternut squash
(2 pounds)
2 tablespoons frozen
orange juice concentrate

2 tablespoons brown sugar
2 teaspoons margarine
1/4 teaspoon ground ginger

Pierce squash several times with a knife or fork; place on a microwave-safe plate. Cook on high for 5 minutes. Cut into quarters; remove seeds. Return to plate, cut side down, and cover with waxed paper; microwave on high for 7 minutes. Turn over; microwave on high for 6-8 minutes or until soft. Scoop out pulp and place in a bowl; add remaining ingredients and mix well. **Yield:** 4 servings. **Editor's Note:** This recipe was tested in a 700-watt microwave oven.

NUTRITIONAL INFORMATION

Serving Size: 1/4 recipe

Calories: 97
Total Fat: 2 gm
Calories from Fat: 19%
Saturated Fat: trace
Cholesterol: 0
Sodium: 28 mg
Carbohydrate: 21 gm
Protein: 1 gm

Rice and Green Pea Side Dish

Kathie Landmann, Lexington Park, Maryland

I keep the ingredients on hand so I can quicky whip up this recipe anytime.

1 cup uncooked long grain
rice
2 cups water
2 cups frozen peas, thawed
1 carrot, shredded
1 medium onion, chopped

1 teaspoon low-sodium
chicken bouillon
granules
1 teaspoon salt-free
herb seasoning blend
Pepper to taste

Place all ingredients in a 3-qt. saucepan; cover and bring to a boil. Reduce heat; simmer for 15 minutes or until rice is tender. **Yield:** 6 servings.

NUTRITIONAL INFORMATION

Serving Size: 1/6 recipe

Calories: 163
Total Fat: trace
Calories from Fat: 1%
Saturated Fat: trace
Cholesterol: 0
Sodium: 51 mg
Carbohydrate: 34 gm
Protein: 5 gm

Sweet-and-Sour Green Beans

Oma Rollison, El Cajon, California

(Pictured above)

Green beans are the perfect accompaniment to many main dishes I make. The different flavors blend well.

4 turkey bacon strips
2 teaspoons margarine
1/2 cup chopped onion
2 tablespoons all-purpose flour

3/4 cup water
1/3 cup cider vinegar
2 tablespoons sugar
6 cups green beans, cooked and drained

In a skillet, cook bacon until crisp; drain. Crumble the bacon and set aside. Melt margarine in the same skillet; add onion and saute until tender. Stir in flour until thoroughly combined. Add water, vinegar and sugar. Cook and stir until thickened and bubbly; cook and stir 2 minutes longer. Gently stir in beans and heat through. Sprinkle with bacon. Serve immediately. **Yield:** 8 servings.

NUTRITIONAL INFORMATION

Serving Size: 1/8 recipe

Calories: 74
Total Fat: 2 gm
Calories from Fat: 24%
Saturated Fat: trace
Cholesterol: 3 mg
Sodium: 64 mg
Carbohydrate: 15 gm
Protein: 3 gm

Dilly Mashed Potatoes

Annie Tompkins, Deltona, Florida

My family loves the flavor of dill and mashed potatoes, so they were thrilled when I presented them with this dish.

6 medium potatoes
1/2 cup skim milk
1 cup (8 ounces) light sour cream
1 tablespoon dried minced onion

2 tablespoons minced fresh dill *or* 2 teaspoons dill weed
3/4 teaspoon salt-free herb seasoning blend

Peel and cube potatoes; place in a saucepan. Cover with water; cook until very tender. Drain; mash with milk. Stir in remaining ingredients. **Yield:** 8 servings.

Yellow Squash Casserole

Mae Kruis, Gallup, New Mexico

Green chilies add a little "zip" and turn a simple squash recipe into something splendid. Plus, this is a great way to get kids to eat vegetables.

3 yellow summer squash, sliced
1 medium onion, chopped
1 can (4 ounces) chopped green chilies

8 fat-free saltines, crushed
Pepper to taste
1-1/2 cups (6 ounces) shredded reduced-fat cheddar cheese

In a skillet coated with nonstick cooking spray, saute squash and onion over medium-high heat until crisp-tender. Remove from the heat; stir in chilies, crackers and pepper. Spoon into a 1-1/2-qt. casserole coated with nonstick cooking spray. Bake at 350° for 20 minutes. Sprinkle with cheese; let stand 5 minutes before serving. **Yield:** 6 servings.

Sweet Corn and Tomato Saute

Kim L'Hote, Neillsville, Wisconsin

This recipe combines two summer greats—fresh corn and tomato! Folks are surprised to hear the hint of sweetness comes from the brown sugar.

1 tablespoon margarine
2 cups corn
2 tablespoons brown sugar
1/4 cup chopped onion

1/4 cup chopped green pepper
2 tablespoons water
1 large tomato, diced

In a saucepan, melt margarine. Add corn, brown sugar, onion, green pepper and water; cover and simmer for 10 minutes. Stir in the tomato; simmer 5 minutes longer. **Yield:** 4 servings.

Calico Rice

Deborah Hill, Coffeyville, Kansas

(Pictured below)

Looking for an accompaniment to Mexican food or barbecued chicken? This spicy rice fits the bill. When I'm cooking, I head for my spice cupboard often—we like our food zesty!

1 medium green pepper, diced
1 medium sweet yellow pepper, diced
1 medium sweet red pepper, diced
1 medium onion, diced

1-1/2 cups uncooked long grain rice
1 envelope dry onion soup mix
2 tablespoons picante sauce
1 tablespoon ground cumin
4 garlic cloves, minced
3 cups water

In a skillet or saucepan coated with nonstick cooking spray, saute peppers and onion for 3 minutes. Stir in rice, soup mix, picante sauce, cumin, garlic and water; bring to a boil. Reduce heat; cover and simmer for 20-25 minutes or until rice is tender. **Yield:** 8 servings.

NUTRITIONAL INFORMATION

Serving Size: 1/8 recipe

Calories: 141
Total Fat: trace
Calories from Fat: 3%
Saturated Fat: trace
Cholesterol: 0
Sodium: 125 mg
Carbohydrate: 29 gm
Protein: 3 gm

Cider Baked Squash

Christine Gibson, Fontana, Wisconsin

(Pictured above)

I'm a free-lance writer who sometimes needs a break from a long session of working on a story. That's when I escape to the kitchen to whip up something that's good to eat, yet easy to prepare. This is one of my favorites!

2 medium acorn squash
1/2 cup apple cider
1/4 cup packed brown sugar

1/8 teaspoon ground cinnamon
1/8 teaspoon ground mace

Slice squash into 1-in.-thick rings and remove seeds. Place squash in a 15-in. x 10-in. x 1-in. baking pan. Pour cider over squash. Combine remaining ingredients and sprinkle on top. Cover with foil. Bake at 325° for 45 minutes or until squash is tender. **Yield:** 6 servings.

NUTRITIONAL INFORMATION

Serving Size: 1/6 recipe

Calories: 139
Total Fat: trace
Calories from Fat: 1%
Saturated Fat: trace
Cholesterol: 0
Sodium: 11 mg
Carbohydrate: 36 gm
Protein: 2 gm

Cardamom Sweet Potatoes

Sandy Waters, Mt. Lebanon, Pennsylvania

The delightful addition of cardamom to these potatoes is a taste sensation!

1 can (40 ounces) sweet
potatoes, drained *or* 1-1/2
pounds fresh sweet
potatoes, cooked
9 tablespoons brown sugar,
divided
1 tablespoon vanilla extract

1/2 teaspoon ground nutmeg
1/2 teaspoon ground
cardamom
2/3 cup skim milk
1 tablespoon margarine,
melted

In a mixing bowl, beat sweet potatoes, 6 tablespoons brown sugar, vanilla, nutmeg and cardamom. Add milk; mix well. Spoon into a 1-qt. casserole coated with nonstick cooking spray. Drizzle with margarine; sprinkle with remaining brown sugar. Bake, uncovered, at 350° for 40 minutes or until the top is lightly browned. **Yield:** 6 servings.

NUTRITIONAL INFORMATION

Serving Size: 1/6 recipe

Calories: 264
Total Fat: 2 gm
Calories from Fat: 7%
Saturated Fat: 1 gm
Cholesterol: 1 mg
Sodium: 134 mg
Carbohydrate: 58 gm
Protein: 4 gm

Secret Brussels Sprouts

Diane Hixon, Niceville, Florida

My husband and I love brussels sprouts, but our kids wouldn't touch them until I discovered this recipe. Now they can't get enough!

1 small onion, sliced
1 tablespoon margarine
1 cup tomato juice
2 tablespoons all-purpose
flour
1 teaspoon sugar
1/8 teaspoon pepper

2 packages (10 ounces
each) frozen brussels
sprouts *or* 1-1/4 pounds
fresh brussels sprouts,
cooked and drained
1/4 cup shredded reduced-fat
cheddar cheese

In a skillet, saute onion in margarine until tender. Remove onion and set aside. Combine tomato juice and flour; add to skillet. Cook and stir over low heat until thickened and smooth. Stir in sugar, pepper and onion. Arrange brussels sprouts in a 1-qt. baking dish coated with nonstick cooking spray; top with the tomato sauce. Bake, uncovered, at 350° for 15 minutes. Sprinkle with cheese; let stand 5 minutes before serving. **Yield:** 6 servings.

NUTRITIONAL INFORMATION

Serving Size: 1/6 recipe

Calories: 87
Total Fat: 3 gm
Calories from Fat: 31%
Saturated Fat: 1 gm
Cholesterol: 2 mg
Sodium: 228 mg
Carbohydrate: 10 gm
Protein: 5 gm

Lemon-Basil Carrots

Donna Smith, Palisade, Colorado

This is one of my favorite ways to prepare carrots—simple but flavorful.

4 medium carrots, cut into
1-1/2-inch pieces
1 tablespoon reduced-fat
margarine

1 teaspoon lemon juice
1/4 teaspoon dried basil
Dash garlic powder
Dash pepper

Place carrots in a small saucepan; add water to cover. Cook for 10 minutes or until tender; drain and return to pan. Add remaining ingredients; toss to coat. **Yield:** 2 servings.

NUTRITIONAL INFORMATION

Serving Size: 1/2 recipe

Calories: 98
Total Fat: 4 gm
Calories from Fat: 37%
Saturated Fat: 1 gm
Cholesterol: 0
Sodium: 110 mg
Carbohydrate: 15 gm
Protein: 2 gm

Stuffed Sweet Potatoes

DeAnn Alleva, Columbus, Ohio

I ran across this recipe when living in North Carolina. Pineapple is a sweet flavor accent for these twice-baked favorites.

6 medium sweet potatoes
1 can (8 ounces) crushed unsweetened pineapple, drained

1/2 cup orange juice
1 tablespoon margarine, melted

Pierce sweet potatoes with a fork. Bake at 400° for 55-65 minutes or until tender. Cool slightly. Cut a thin slice off the top of each potato and discard. Carefully scoop out pulp while leaving shell intact. In a bowl, mash pulp with pineapple, orange juice and margarine. Refill potato shells; place in a 13-in. x 9-in. x 2-in. baking dish coated with nonstick cooking spray. Bake at 400° for 20 minutes or until heated through. **Yield:** 6 servings.

Garden Casserole

Phyllis Hickey, Bedford, New Hampshire

This delicious cheesy casserole is made with the bounty from my garden. It's so nice to cook with those abundant crops.

2 pounds eggplant, peeled
2 teaspoons salt
2 medium onions, finely chopped
2 garlic cloves, minced
2 medium zucchini, sliced 1/2 inch thick
5 medium tomatoes, peeled and chopped
2 celery ribs, sliced
1/4 cup minced fresh parsley

1/4 cup minced fresh basil *or* 1 tablespoon dried basil
1/2 teaspoon pepper
1/3 cup grated Romano cheese
1/2 cup Italian-seasoned dry bread crumbs
1 tablespoon margarine, melted
1 cup (4 ounces) shredded part-skim mozzarella cheese

Cut eggplant into 1/2-in.-thick slices; sprinkle both sides with salt. Place in a deep dish; cover and let stand for 30 minutes. Rinse with cold water; drain and dry on paper towels. Cut into 1/2-in. cubes and saute in a skillet coated with nonstick cooking spray until lightly browned, about 5 minutes. Add onions, garlic and zucchini; cook 3 minutes. Add tomatoes, celery, parsley, basil and pepper; bring to a boil. Reduce heat; cover and simmer for 10 minutes. Remove from the heat; stir in Romano cheese. Pour into a 13-in. x 9-in. x 2-in. baking dish coated with nonstick cooking spray. Combine crumbs and margarine; sprinkle on top. Bake, uncovered, at 375° for 15 minutes. Sprinkle with mozzarella cheese. Return to the oven for 5 minutes or until cheese is melted. **Yield:** 12 servings.

Pineapple Beets

Bernice Morris, Marshfield, Missouri

(Pictured above)

This is a special way to dress up beets. Paired with pineapple, they have a fresh, tropical taste that even has people who don't usually like beets taking second helpings.

2 tablespoons brown sugar
1 tablespoon cornstarch
1 can (8 ounces)
   unsweetened pineapple
   tidbits, undrained

1 can (16 ounces) sliced
   beets, drained
1 tablespoon lemon juice
1 teaspoon margarine

In a saucepan, combine brown sugar and cornstarch; add pineapple and bring to a boil, stirring constantly until thick, about 2 minutes. Add the beets, lemon juice and margarine; cook over medium heat for 5 minutes, stirring occasionally. **Yield:** 4 servings.

Cranberry Wild Rice Pilaf

Pat Gardetta, Osage Beach, Missouri

This festive side dish is perfect for the holidays or anytime a meal requires a special touch. Dried cranberries, currants and almonds add color and texture. The ladies I work with all enjoy making this recipe.

3/4 cup uncooked wild rice
3 cups low-sodium
  chicken broth
1/2 cup pearl barley

1/4 cup dried cranberries
1/4 cup currants
1/4 cup sliced almonds,
  toasted

Rinse and drain rice; place in a saucepan. Add broth and bring to a boil. Reduce heat; cover and simmer for 10 minutes. Remove from the heat; stir in barley, cranberries and currants. Spoon into a 1-1/2-qt. baking dish coated with nonstick cooking spray. Cover and bake at 325° for 55 minutes or until liquid is absorbed and rice is tender. Add almonds and fluff with a fork. **Yield:** 8 servings.

Potato Dumplings

Karin Cousineau, Burlington, North Carolina

These moist dumplings are an extra-special way to serve potatoes. The bread centers add a comforting touch, and the potato taste really comes through. Their hearty, down-home appeal will warm the soul on cool days.

6 medium potatoes
5 tablespoons all-purpose
  flour
1 egg, beaten
1 teaspoon salt

1/4 teaspoon ground nutmeg
2 slices white bread, toasted
1/3 cup mashed potato
  flakes, optional

Cook potatoes in water just until tender; drain. Refrigerate for 2 hours or overnight. Peel and grate potatoes. In a bowl, combine the flour, egg, salt and nutmeg. Add potatoes and mix until a stiff batter is formed, adding additional flour if necessary. Slice toasted bread into 24 squares, 1/2 in. each; shape 2 tablespoons of the potato mixture around two bread squares, forming a 2-in. ball. In a large kettle, bring water to a boil; add the test dumpling. Reduce heat; cover and simmer for 15-20 minutes or until dumpling is no longer sticky in the center. If test dumpling falls apart during cooking, add the mashed potato flakes to the mixture. Let potato mixture sit for 5 minutes; form remaining dumplings. Add to boiling water; return to a boil and follow the same cooking procedure. Remove dumplings with a slotted spoon to a serving bowl. **Yield:** 8 servings.

Creamed Peas and Potatoes

Linda Nilsen, Anoka, Minnesota

(Pictured below)

Nothing beats this comforting side dish to go with your family's favorite entree. The peas and potatoes combined with a creamy white sauce make a satisfying dish that also adds appealing color to the meal.

4 medium red potatoes,
  cubed
1 package (10 ounces)
  frozen peas
1 teaspoon sugar
1 tablespoon margarine

2 tablespoons all-purpose
  flour
1/4 teaspoon white pepper
1-1/2 cups skim milk
2 tablespoons minced fresh
  dill

NUTRITIONAL INFORMATION

Serving Size: 1/8 recipe

Calories: 126
Total Fat: 2 gm
Calories from Fat: 14%
Saturated Fat: trace
Cholesterol: 1 mg
Sodium: 86 mg
Carbohydrate: 19 gm
Protein: 5 gm

Place potatoes in a saucepan; cover with water and cook until tender. Cook peas according to package directions, adding the sugar. Meanwhile, melt margarine in a saucepan; add flour and pepper to form a paste. Gradually stir in milk. Bring to a boil; boil for 1 minute. Add dill; cook until thickened and bubbly. Drain potatoes and peas; place in a serving bowl. Pour sauce over and stir to coat. Serve immediately. **Yield:** 8 servings.

Ken's Sweet Potatoes

Ken Churches, San Andreas, California

(Pictured below)

This simple recipe turns plain sweet potatoes into a wonderful side dish, which I like to serve around the holidays. The raisins add a nice touch, and the sweet syrup makes the potatoes taste extra-special.

8 medium sweet potatoes
1-1/4 cups packed brown sugar
1/2 cup apple juice

1/2 cup water
1/2 cup raisins
1 tablespoon margarine

Cook and peel potatoes; allow to cool. Slice and place in a 2-1/2-qt. baking dish coated with nonstick cooking spray. In a small saucepan, combine remaining ingredients; bring to a boil, stirring frequently. Pour over the potatoes. Bake, uncovered, at 350° for 45 minutes, basting occasionally. **Yield:** 10 servings.

NUTRITIONAL INFORMATION

Serving Size: 1/10 recipe

Calories: 294
Total Fat: 2 gm
Calories from Fat: 5%
Saturated Fat: trace
Cholesterol: 0
Sodium: 38 mg
Carbohydrate: 70 gm
Protein: 3 gm

Mom's Easy Bean Bake

Sue Gronholz, Columbus, Wisconsin

My mom's baked beans are the best I've ever tasted. Family and friends expect me to bring a big pot of these beans to gatherings…they've become my trademark.

2-1/2 cups dry great northern
    beans (1 pound)
12 turkey bacon strips,
    cooked and crumbled

1 cup packed brown sugar
3 tablespoons molasses
3 small onions, chopped

Place beans in a saucepan; add water to cover by 2 in. Bring to a boil; boil for 2 minutes. Remove from the heat; cover and let stand for 1 hour. Drain, discarding liquid, and return beans to pan. Cover with fresh water; bring to a boil. Reduce heat; cover and simmer for 1 hour or until beans are tender. Drain, reserving liquid. Combine beans, 1 cup liquid and the remaining ingredients in a 2-1/2-qt. baking dish coated with nonstick cooking spray. Cover and bake at 350° for 1-1/4 hours or until beans are tender, stirring occasionally (add additional reserved liquid as needed). **Yield:** 10 servings.

Homemade Noodles

Helen Heiland, Joliet, Illinois

Most folks agree there are few things that taste as good as homemade noodles. My family and friends enjoy these so much, I usually make several batches at a time and freeze the uncooked noodles in serving-size portions to enjoy months later. I just defrost the noodles and cook as directed.

2 to 2-1/2 cups all-purpose
    flour, *divided*
1/2 teaspoon salt

3 eggs
1 tablespoon cold water
1 teaspoon cooking oil

Place 2 cups flour and salt on a pastry board or in a deep mixing bowl. Make a well in the center of the flour; add eggs and water. Gradually mix with hands or a wooden spoon until well blended. Gather into a ball and knead on a floured surface until smooth, about 10 minutes. If necessary, add remaining flour to keep dough from sticking to surface or hands. Divide the dough into thirds. On a floured surface, roll each section into a paper-thin rectangle. Dust top of dough with flour to prevent sticking while rolling. Trim the edges and flour both sides of dough. Roll dough, jelly-roll style. Using a sharp knife, cut dough into 1/4-in. slices. Unroll noodles and allow to dry on paper towels before cooking. To cook, bring water to a rapid boil. Add 1 teaspoon oil to the water; drop noodles into water and cook until tender but not soft. **Yield:** 12 servings.

Pasta with Asparagus

Barbara Calhoun, Marquette Heights, Illinois

(Pictured above)

I make this dish often, using asparagus grown not far from our home. It's so easy to prepare—it takes only about half an hour from start to serving.

NUTRITIONAL INFORMATION

Serving Size: 1/8 recipe

Calories: 206
Total Fat: 9 gm
Calories from Fat: 39%
Saturated Fat: 3 gm
Cholesterol: 17 mg
Sodium: 262 mg
Carbohydrate: 24 gm
Protein: 10 gm

2 pounds fresh asparagus, sliced diagonally into 1-inch pieces
1 pound thin spaghetti
6 turkey bacon strips, cut into 1-inch pieces
1/2 cup sliced green onions
1/2 teaspoon pepper
3 tablespoons reduced-fat margarine
1/2 cup light sour cream
1/3 cup grated Parmesan cheese

Cook asparagus in boiling water for 3-4 minutes or until crisp-tender; drain and set aside. Cook spaghetti according to package directions. Meanwhile, in a skillet, cook bacon until crisp; drain and remove to a paper towel. In the same skillet, saute onions until soft. Add asparagus and pepper; heat through. Drain spaghetti; toss with asparagus mixture, bacon, margarine, sour cream and cheese. Serve immediately. **Yield:** 8 servings.

Apples, Berries and Yams

Dixy Moore, Avalon, California

When a little cooler weather comes our way, my family can find me whipping up this easy recipe. It's a refreshing, colorful side dish.

1 tablespoon margarine
3 apples, peeled and cut into chunks
1 can (23 ounces) yams, drained

1/2 teaspoon ground nutmeg
1 can (16 ounces) whole-berry cranberry sauce
1/2 cup orange marmalade

In a skillet, melt margarine over medium heat. Saute apples until crisp-tender. Place apples and yams in a 3-qt. casserole coated with nonstick cooking spray. Sprinkle with nutmeg. Combine cranberry sauce and marmalade; spoon over yams. Bake, uncovered, at 350° for 30 minutes. **Yield:** 10 servings.

NUTRITIONAL INFORMATION

Serving Size: 1/10 recipe

Calories: 200
Total Fat: 1 gm
Calories from Fat: 5%
Saturated Fat: trace
Cholesterol: 0
Sodium: 50 mg
Carbohydrate: 49 gm
Protein: 1 gm

Mashed Potatoes with Horseradish

Cynthia Gobeli, Norton, Ohio

The sharp taste of horseradish enlivens these ordinary, everyday mashed potatoes. What a taste treat!

6 medium potatoes, peeled and cubed
2 tablespoons margarine, melted
1/4 teaspoon salt

1/8 teaspoon pepper
1/2 cup light sour cream
2 tablespoons prepared horseradish

Cook the potatoes in boiling water until tender, about 8-10 minutes; drain. Add margarine, salt and pepper. Whip with an electric mixer on low speed or mash with a potato masher. Add sour cream and horseradish; mix well. Serve immediately. **Yield:** 6 servings.

NUTRITIONAL INFORMATION

Serving Size: 1/6 recipe

Calories: 168
Total Fat: 4 gm
Calories from Fat: 21%
Saturated Fat: 1 gm
Cholesterol: 0
Sodium: 170 mg
Carbohydrate: 29 gm
Protein: 5 gm

Quick Carrots

Florence Jacoby, Granite Falls, Minnesota

Carrots and green onions are a flavorful combination I'm sure your family will enjoy as much as mine does.

2 cups fresh *or* frozen sliced carrots
2 tablespoons sliced green onions

1 tablespoon water
2 teaspoons margarine
Chopped fresh parsley

In a saucepan, combine the first four ingredients; cover and simmer for 8-10 minutes or until the carrots are crisp-tender. Sprinkle with parsley. **Yield:** 4 servings.

NUTRITIONAL INFORMATION

Serving Size: 1/4 recipe

Calories: 47
Total Fat: 2 gm
Calories from Fat: 38%
Saturated Fat: trace
Cholesterol: 0
Sodium: 46 mg
Carbohydrate: 7 gm
Protein: 1 gm

Spinach Noodles

Bernice Smith, Sturgeon Lake, Minnesota

Imagine homemade noodles that are green! This easy recipe gives "from scratch" satisfaction even if you've never made noodles.

1 package (10 ounces) frozen chopped spinach, thawed and well drained	2 eggs 1/2 teaspoon salt 2 cups all-purpose flour

In a blender or food processor, combine the spinach, eggs and salt; process until smooth. Pour into a bowl. Gradually add enough flour to make a firm, but not sticky, dough. On a floured surface, knead about 20 times. Wrap in plastic wrap and let rest 30 minutes. Divide dough in half. On a floured surface, roll each half to 1/16-in. thickness. Roll up jelly-roll style and cut into 1/4-in. slices. Separate the slices and let rest on a clean towel for at least 1 hour. Cook noodles in boiling water until tender, about 15-20 minutes; drain. **Yield:** 6 servings.

Country Green Beans

Linda Gaido, New Brighton, Pennsylvania

This is a beautiful and tasty dish with real country appeal. The garlic, ham and onion blend so well with the beans.

1 pound fresh green beans, trimmed 1/4 cup chopped onion 1/4 cup chopped fully cooked low-fat ham	1/4 cup water 2 teaspoons margarine 1 garlic clove, minced 1/4 teaspoon pepper

In a saucepan, combine all ingredients. Cover and simmer for 15-20 minutes or until the beans are tender. **Yield:** 4 servings.

Potato-Spinach Casserole

Mary Allen, Orange, California

Spinach gives regular mashed potatoes added color and vitamins. And chives complement this casserole with their sweet oniony taste.

2 pounds potatoes, peeled and cubed 2/3 cup skim milk 2 tablespoons margarine, softened 1/4 teaspoon pepper	2 packages (10 ounces *each*) frozen chopped spinach, thawed and well drained 1/4 cup snipped chives 1 teaspoon dill weed

In a saucepan over medium heat, cook potatoes in boiling water until tender; drain. In a mixing bowl, mash potatoes until no lumps remain. Add the milk, margarine and pepper; beat until light and fluffy. Stir in spinach, chives and dill. Spread in a 2-1/2-qt. casserole coated with nonstick cooking spray. Cover and bake at 350° for 30-40 minutes or until heated through. **Yield:** 12 servings.

Hot Fruit Compote

Judy Kimball, Haverhill, Massachusetts

(Pictured above)

This simple-to-prepare compote is a tasty way to get fruit into your meal when fresh fruit is not plentiful. Perfect with ham, pork, chicken or turkey, this dish can also help stretch a meal when guests pop in.

1 can (12 ounces) frozen orange juice concentrate, thawed
2 tablespoons cornstarch
2 pounds apples, peeled and sliced
1 can (8 ounces) pineapple chunks, drained
1 can (16-1/2 ounces) pitted Bing cherries, drained
1-1/2 cups fresh *or* frozen cranberries
1 package (6 ounces) dried apricots, cooked and drained
1/4 cup apple juice

In a large bowl, combine orange juice concentrate and cornstarch; stir until smooth. Add fruit; stir to coat. Pour into a 3-qt. casserole coated with nonstick cooking spray. Pour apple juice over all. Cover and bake at 350° for 50-60 minutes or until hot and bubbly. **Yield:** 12 servings.

NUTRITIONAL INFORMATION

Serving Size: 1/2 cup

Calories: 179
Total Fat: trace
Calories from Fat: 2%
Saturated Fat: trace
Cholesterol: 0
Sodium: 6 mg
Carbohydrate: 45 gm
Protein: 1 gm

TEMPTING TOPPINGS. *Clockwise from top left: Herb Vinegar, Easy Apricot Jam and Microwave Salsa (all recipes on page 249).*

Country Condiments

Herb Vinegar

Sue Yaeger, Brookings, South Dakota

(Pictured at left)

I like to double this recipe to fill my favorite decorative bottle.

1 garlic clove
12 to 18 inches fresh oregano,
   tarragon *or* basil sprigs

1-1/4 cups white vinegar *or*
   white wine vinegar

Cut garlic in half and skewer with a toothpick. Place in a glass jar or bottle. Add herb sprigs; set aside. In a saucepan, bring vinegar to a simmer (do not boil). Carefully pour into container. Let cool to room temperature. Remove garlic after 24 hours. Cover and store in a cool dry place for up to a year. **Yield:** 1-1/4 cups.

NUTRITIONAL INFORMATION

Serving Size: 1 tablespoon
(calculated with white vinegar)

Calories: 2
Total Fat: 0
Calories from Fat: 0%
Saturated Fat: 0
Cholesterol: 0
Sodium: 0
Carbohydrate: 1 gm
Protein: 0

Easy Apricot Jam

Geri Davis, Prescott, Arizona

(Pictured at left)

With this recipe, making flavorful homemade jam couldn't be easier!

1 pound dried apricots
2-1/2 cups orange juice
3/4 cup sugar

1 tablespoon lemon juice
1/2 teaspoon ground cinnamon
1/4 teaspoon ground ginger

In a large kettle, combine apricots, orange juice and sugar. Cover and simmer for 30 minutes. Mix in lemon juice, cinnamon and ginger. Remove from the heat and cool to room temperature. Puree in a food processor or blender until smooth. Spoon into jars or freezer containers, leaving 1/2-in. headspace. Cover with lids. Refrigerate or freeze. **Yield:** 4 cups.

NUTRITIONAL INFORMATION

Serving Size: 1 tablespoon

Calories: 30
Total Fat: trace
Calories from Fat: 1%
Saturated Fat: 0
Cholesterol: 0
Sodium: 1 mg
Carbohydrate: 8 gm
Protein: trace

Microwave Salsa

Pamela Schroeder, Santee, California

(Pictured at left)

This salsa is so simple we can enjoy it anytime with Mexican food or baked tortilla chips.

3 medium tomatoes,
   chopped
1 green onion, sliced
1 to 2 garlic cloves, minced
3 tablespoons minced
   green pepper
1 tablespoon lemon juice

1-1/2 teaspoons minced fresh
   basil *or* 1/2 teaspoon
   dried basil
1/2 teaspoon chili powder
1/8 teaspoon pepper

In a microwave-safe bowl, combine the tomatoes, onion and garlic. Add green pepper, lemon juice and seasonings; mix well. Microwave on high for 45-60 seconds or until heated through. Serve immediately or store in the refrigerator for up to 3 days. **Yield:** 4 cups.

NUTRITIONAL INFORMATION

Serving Size: 2 tablespoons

Calories: 3
Total Fat: trace
Calories from Fat: 12%
Saturated Fat: trace
Cholesterol: 0
Sodium: 1 mg
Carbohydrate: 1 gm
Protein: trace

Pepper Jelly

Marion Kowalski, Wauwatosa, Wisconsin

This spicy-sweet jelly may be colored for Christmas…but it's flavored right for year-round use. I recommend spreading it on crackers with cream cheese for a snack or serving it as an accompaniment to pork roast.

1 jalapeno pepper, seeded and chopped
7 medium green peppers, cut into 1-inch pieces
1-1/2 cups vinegar
1-1/2 cups apple juice
1 package (1-3/4 ounces) powdered fruit pectin
1/2 teaspoon salt
5 cups sugar
About 8 drops green food coloring, optional

Place the jalapeno, half of the green peppers and half of the vinegar in a blender or food processor; puree. Pour into a large bowl. Puree remaining green peppers and vinegar; add to the bowl. Add apple juice; mix well. Cover and chill overnight. Strain through several layers of damp cheesecloth. Measure 4 cups juice into a large kettle (add water if needed to make 4 cups). Stir in pectin and salt; bring to a rolling boil over high heat, stirring constantly. Add sugar; return to a rolling boil. Boil for 1 minute, stirring constantly. Remove from the heat; skim off foam. Add food coloring if desired. Ladle hot liquid into hot jars, leaving 1/4-in. headspace. Adjust caps. Process for 5 minutes in a boiling-water bath. **Yield:** 6 half-pints.

Four-Berry Spread

Marie St. Thomas, Sterling, Massachusetts

For a big berry taste, you can't beat this tasty spread. With a flavorful foursome of strawberries, raspberries, blackberries and blueberries, this lovely jam brightens any breakfast.

1-1/2 cups fresh *or* frozen strawberries
1-1/2 cups fresh *or* frozen raspberries
1 cup fresh *or* frozen blackberries
1 cup fresh *or* frozen blueberries
1 package (1-3/4 ounces) powdered fruit pectin
7 cups sugar

Crush berries in a large kettle. Stir in pectin; bring to a rolling boil over high heat, stirring constantly. Stir in sugar; return to a rolling boil. Boil for 1 minute, stirring constantly. Remove from the heat; skim off any foam. Ladle hot mixture into hot jars, leaving 1/4-in. headspace. Adjust caps. Process for 10 minutes in a boiling-water bath. **Yield:** 7 half-pints.

Zucchini Relish

Claire Fitzgaireld, Willow, Alaska

(Pictured above)

Because zucchini is such a big producer in our garden, I'm always looking for ways to use it up. This relish won a blue ribbon for me at the Alaska State Fair a few years ago.

10 cups chopped unpeeled zucchini (7 medium)	3 tablespoons canning salt
4 cups chopped onion (4 large)	3-1/2 cups sugar
	3 cups vinegar
1 large sweet red pepper, chopped	4 teaspoons celery seed
1 can (4 ounces) chopped green chilies	1 tablespoon ground turmeric
	1 teaspoon pepper
	1/2 teaspoon ground nutmeg

In a large container, combine zucchini, onion, red pepper, chilies and canning salt; stir well. Chill overnight. Rinse thoroughly; drain. In a large kettle, combine remaining ingredients; bring to a boil. Add zucchini mixture; simmer for 10 minutes. Pour hot mixture into hot jars, leaving 1/4-in. headspace. Adjust lids. Process for 10 minutes in a boiling-water bath. **Yield:** 5 pints.

NUTRITIONAL INFORMATION

Serving Size: 2 tablespoons

Calories: 45
Total Fat: trace
Calories from Fat: 3%
Saturated Fat: trace
Cholesterol: 0
Sodium: 137 mg
Carbohydrate: 11 gm
Protein: 1 gm

Raspberry Peach Jam

Patricia Larsen, Leslieville, Alberta

(Pictured below)

While my jam won a first-place ribbon, that's not the highest compliment it's received. My friends tell me if they don't hide the jam from their families, they'll devour an entire jarful in no time!

NUTRITIONAL INFORMATION

Serving Size: 1 tablespoon

Calories: 33
Total Fat: trace
Calories from Fat: 1%
Saturated Fat: 0
Cholesterol: 0
Sodium: trace
Carbohydrate: 9 gm
Protein: trace

3 cups sugar
2-2/3 cups finely chopped
   peeled peaches

1-1/2 cups crushed fresh *or*
   frozen raspberries
1-1/2 teaspoons lemon juice

In a large kettle, combine all ingredients. Cook over low heat, stirring occasionally, until sugar is dissolved and mixture is bubbly, about 10 minutes. Bring to a rolling boil; boil for 15 minutes, stirring constantly. Remove from the heat; skim off foam. Pour hot jam into hot jars, leaving 1/4-in. headspace. Adjust caps. Process for 15 minutes in a boiling-water bath. **Yield:** 5 half-pints. **Editor's Note:** If you'd like to serve this jam with low-fat biscuits, see the Potato Biscuits on page 87 and Buttermilk Biscuits on page 95.

Cranberry Plus Relish

Marion Reeder, Medford, New Jersey

(Pictured on page 146)

I started out with a basic cranberry-orange relish and worked with it until I came up with this recipe. I've found that even those folks who don't care for cranberries seem to "relish" this condiment.

4 cups (1 pound) fresh *or* frozen cranberries	1 can (8-1/2 ounces) crushed pineapple, undrained
4 oranges, peeled, sectioned and seeded	1 unpeeled apple, sliced
2 cups sugar	1/2 teaspoon almond extract

Chop cranberries in a food processor; add oranges and chop. Add remaining ingredients; pulse for several seconds to blend. Chill several hours before serving. **Yield:** 6 cups.

NUTRITIONAL INFORMATION

Serving Size: 1/4 cup

Calories: 92
Total Fat: trace
Calories from Fat: 1%
Saturated Fat: trace
Cholesterol: 0
Sodium: 1 mg
Carbohydrate: 24 gm
Protein: trace

Homemade Horseradish

Jan Roat, Red Lodge, Montana

Once you've tried this horseradish, you'll never go back to store-bought!

1 cup cubed peeled horseradish root (1/2-inch pieces)	3/4 cup vinegar
	2 teaspoons sugar
	1/4 teaspoon salt

Combine all ingredients in a food processor or blender; process until pureed. Carefully remove cover of processor or blender, keeping face away from container. Cover and store in the refrigerator. **Yield:** 1-1/4 cups.

NUTRITIONAL INFORMATION

Serving Size: 1 teaspoon

Calories: 2
Total Fat: trace
Calories from Fat: 2%
Saturated Fat: 0
Cholesterol: 0
Sodium: 9 mg
Carbohydrate: 1 gm
Protein: trace

Spiced Rhubarb

Paula Pelis, Rocky Point, New York

This recipe's been in my family for years—it was handed down to me by my mother, who got it from her mother.

10 cups diced fresh *or* frozen rhubarb	1/2 to 1 teaspoon ground cloves
4-1/2 cups sugar	1/2 to 1 teaspoon ground allspice
1 cup cider vinegar	
2 teaspoons ground cinnamon	

In a large Dutch oven or kettle, combine all ingredients. Bring to a rapid boil; reduce heat and simmer for 60-70 minutes. Pour into pint jars and refrigerate. Use as a glaze for ham or spread on biscuits. **Yield:** 4 pints.

NUTRITIONAL INFORMATION

Serving Size: 1 tablespoon

Calories: 29
Total Fat: trace
Calories from Fat: 1%
Saturated Fat: trace
Cholesterol: 0
Sodium: trace
Carbohydrate: 8 gm
Protein: trace

Herbed Honey Lime Sauce

Chris Kallies, Windsor, California

This taste-tempting condiment highlights honey's delightful natural sweetness and beautiful golden color.

1/2 cup diced onion	1 teaspoon minced fresh
1 cup low-sodium chicken	rosemary *or* 1/4 teaspoon
broth	dried rosemary, crushed
1/4 cup honey	Dash pepper
1/4 cup lime juice	1 tablespoon cornstarch
2 teaspoons ground mustard	1 tablespoon water

In a saucepan coated with nonstick cooking spray, saute onion until tender. Stir in broth, honey, lime juice, mustard, rosemary and pepper; bring to a boil. Reduce heat. Combine cornstarch and water; stir into sauce. Cook and stir over medium heat until thickened. Serve over turkey, chicken, fish or pork. Cover and refrigerate leftovers. **Yield:** 1-1/2 cups.

Fruity Ham Glaze

Elizabeth Baltes, Greenfield, Wisconsin

This simple sauce gives your traditional ham a jewel-toned look and a taste your dinner crowd will savor. And with just two ingredients, it's easy to make at a moment's notice.

1/4 cup cranberry-orange	1/4 cup apricot *or* peach
sauce	preserves

Combine ingredients in a small bowl. About 30 minutes before ham is done, remove from the oven. Spoon glaze over ham. Return to the oven, basting occasionally. **Yield:** 1/2 cup.

Rhubarb Relish

Mina Dyck, Boissevain, Manitoba

Crisp, colorful rhubarb brings springtime sparkle to your table in this relish.

2-1/2 cups packed brown sugar	1/2 teaspoon ground
2 cups finely chopped	cinnamon
fresh *or* frozen rhubarb	1/4 teaspoon salt
2 cups finely chopped onion	1/4 teaspoon ground cloves
1 cup vinegar	1/4 teaspoon pepper
1/2 teaspoon ground allspice	

In a saucepan, combine all ingredients. Cook over medium heat for 30 minutes or until thickened, stirring occasionally. Cool; store in the refrigerator. Serve with poultry, pork or beef. **Yield:** 3-1/3 cups.

Spiced Pear Jam

Karen Bockelman, Portland, Oregon

(Pictured above)

I've canned plenty of pears through the years. Then a neighbor passed along this favorite recipe. I've given many jars of this jam as gifts.

8 cups chopped *or* coarsely ground peeled pears (5-1/2 pounds)	1 teaspoon ground cinnamon
4 cups sugar	1/4 teaspoon ground cloves

Combine all ingredients in a large kettle. Simmer, uncovered, for 1-1/2 to 2 hours or until thick, stirring occasionally. Stir more frequently as the mixture thickens. Remove from the heat; skim off foam. Pour hot jam into hot jars, leaving 1/4-in. headspace. Adjust caps. Process for 10 minutes in a boiling-water bath. **Yield:** 6 half-pints. **Editor's Note:** This recipe does not require pectin.

NUTRITIONAL INFORMATION

Serving Size: 1 tablespoon

Calories: 41
Total Fat: trace
Calories from Fat: 1%
Saturated Fat: trace
Cholesterol: 0
Sodium: trace
Carbohydrate: 10 gm
Protein: trace

Raspberry Vinegar

Debbie Jones, California, Maryland

For an extra-special gift to give guests at holidays or a shower, try this ruby-red vinegar. You can jot down the recipe to accompany the gift.

2 cups fresh *or* frozen unsweetened raspberries	1/3 cup honey
3/4 cup cider vinegar	1 cinnamon stick

In a saucepan, bring all ingredients to a boil. Reduce heat; cover and simmer for 20 minutes. Remove from the heat; cool. Strain through cheesecloth. Pour into a clean bottle or decanter. Cover and refrigerate until ready to use. **Yield:** 1-1/4 cups.

NUTRITIONAL INFORMATION

Serving Size: 1 tablespoon

Calories: 24
Total Fat: trace
Calories from Fat: 3%
Saturated Fat: 0
Cholesterol: 0
Sodium: trace
Carbohydrate: 7 gm
Protein: trace

Blackberry Apple Jelly

Liz Endacott, Matsqui, British Columbia

(Pictured above)

August is the busiest month of the year on our farm, but I always make time to put up this jelly. The combination of blackberries and apples is delicious...and the jelly's usually gone by January!

3 pounds blackberries
(2-1/2 quarts)
1-1/4 cups water
7 medium apples
Additional water *or* bottled
apple juice, optional

1/4 cup lemon juice
8 cups sugar
2 pouches (3 ounces *each*)
liquid fruit pectin

In a large kettle, combine the blackberries and water; simmer for 5 minutes. Strain through a jelly bag, reserving juice and discarding pulp. Remove and discard stems and blossom ends from apples (do not pare or core); cut into small pieces. Place in the kettle; add just enough water to cover. Simmer until apples are soft, about 20 minutes. Strain through a jelly bag, reserving juice and discarding pulp. Measure the reserved blackberry and apple juices; return to the kettle. If necessary, add water or bottled apple juice to equal 4 cups. Stir in lemon juice and sugar. Bring to a rolling boil, stirring constantly. Add pectin, stirring until mixture boils. Boil for 1 minute. Remove from the heat; skim off foam. Ladle hot liquid into hot jars, leaving 1/4-in. headspace. Adjust caps. Process for 15 minutes in a boiling-water bath. **Yield:** 9 half-pints.

Mint Jelly

Kandy Clarke, Columbia Falls, Montana

Hard work on our peppermint farm means hearty appetites. During harvest, I spend my afternoons preparing supper for our crew and then take the meal out to them in the field. The invigorating scent of mint keeps our taste buds tuned for treats like this.

2 cups water	1/2 teaspoon margarine
1 cup packed peppermint leaves	2 pouches (3 ounces *each*) liquid fruit pectin
6-1/2 cups sugar	3 to 4 drops green food coloring
1 cup vinegar	

In a Dutch oven, bring water and mint to a boil; boil for 1 minute. Remove from the heat and pour through a fine sieve, reserving mint liquid. Discard leaves. Return liquid to Dutch oven. Add sugar, vinegar and margarine; bring to a boil, stirring constantly. Quickly add pectin; bring to a rolling boil. Boil for 1 minute, stirring constantly. Remove from the heat; skim off any foam. Add food coloring. Ladle hot liquid into hot jars, leaving 1/4-in. headspace. Adjust caps. Refrigerate or process for 5 minutes in a boiling-water bath. **Yield:** 6 half-pints.

Barbecue Sauce with Mustard

Ruthie Knote, Cape Girardeau, Missouri

My husband, Charlie, and I turn a basic barbecue into a taste sensation with this marvelous sauce. The combination of herbs is tangy to the taste! This is a simple way to add flavor to grilled meat.

1/2 cup sugar	1/2 cup vinegar, *divided*
1/2 teaspoon cornstarch	1 cup molasses
1/2 teaspoon ground thyme	1 cup ketchup
1/2 teaspoon pepper	1 cup prepared mustard
1/4 teaspoon ground oregano	2 tablespoons vegetable oil
1/8 teaspoon cayenne pepper	

Combine the first six ingredients in a small saucepan. Stir in enough vinegar to make a paste. Combine molasses, ketchup, mustard, oil and remaining vinegar; add to herb paste. Bring to a boil, stirring constantly. Reduce heat and simmer for 10 minutes. Remove from the heat; cool completely. Pour into a glass jar; cover tightly. Refrigerate for up to 3 months. Baste over grilled chicken, turkey, ham or hot dogs. **Yield:** 4 cups.

Pineapple Sauce for Ham

Julie Leonard, Joao Pessoa, Brazil

As this recipe shows, the classic combination of pineapple and ham is unbeatable!

1 cup crushed pineapple
  with juice
1 cup packed brown sugar
1 tablespoon ketchup

1/2 cup water, *divided*
1 tablespoon soy sauce
1 teaspoon ground mustard
4-1/2 teaspoons cornstarch

Combine pineapple, brown sugar, ketchup, 1/4 cup water, soy sauce and mustard in a saucepan; bring to a boil. Reduce heat; simmer for 8 minutes. Stir cornstarch into remaining water until smooth; add to pineapple mixture. Cook and stir until thickened. Serve over ham. **Yield:** 2-2/3 cups.

Strawberry Marmalade

Mrs. Craig Presbrey, Pascoag, Rhode Island

This recipe makes ordinary orange marmalade into something really special. Sometimes I make it using strawberries that I've frozen without adding sugar or water. I just thaw them in the refrigerator overnight.

2 medium oranges
2 medium lemons
1/2 cup water
1/8 teaspoon baking soda

1 quart ripe strawberries,
  crushed
7 cups sugar
1 pouch (3 ounces) liquid
  fruit pectin

Peel outer layer of oranges and lemons; set aside. Cut between the membrane to remove each section. Set the fruit and juice aside; discard membrane. Chop peels; place in a large saucepan. Add water and baking soda; cover and bring to a boil. Reduce heat; simmer for 10 minutes. Add sectioned fruit and juice to saucepan; cover and simmer for 20 minutes. Add strawberries. Measure fruit; return 4 cups to the saucepan. (If more than 4 cups, discard any extra; if less, add water to equal 4 cups.) Add sugar and mix well. Boil, uncovered, for 5 minutes; add pectin, stirring until mixture boils. Boil for 1 minute. Remove from the heat; skim off foam. Pour hot mixture into hot half-pint jars or freezer containers, leaving 1/4-in. headspace. Adjust caps. Process for 10 minutes in a boiling-water bath or store in the freezer. **Yield:** 10 half-pints.

Paradise Cran-Applesauce

Sallie McQuay, Sayre, Pennsylvania

(Pictured below)

Appealing apple slices peek through a tangy ruby-red cranberry sauce in this simple but extraordinary side dish. Whether I use this recipe for a holiday dinner or to spark up a Sunday supper, it wouldn't be a feast without a bowl of this beautiful and delicious applesauce!

4 cups fresh *or* frozen cranberries	8 cups sliced peeled cooking apples
1/4 cup water	2 cups sugar

In a covered saucepan, simmer cranberries and water for 20-25 minutes or until tender. Press through a sieve or food mill; return to the saucepan. Add apples; cover and simmer for 35-40 minutes or until apples are tender but retain their shape. Add sugar. Simmer for 5 minutes, stirring occasionally. **Yield:** 10 servings.

NUTRITIONAL INFORMATION

Serving Size: 2/3 cup

Calories: 243
Total Fat: 1 gm
Calories from Fat: 4%
Saturated Fat: trace
Cholesterol: 0
Sodium: trace
Carbohydrate: 63 gm
Protein: trace

DELIGHTFUL DESSERTS. *Clockwise from top left: Apple Torte, Oatmeal Cookie Bites (both recipes on page 261), Pumpkin Chiffon Pie and Cranberry Sherbet (both recipes on page 262).*

Sweet Treats

Apple Torte

Iona Redemer, Calumet, Oklahoma

(Pictured at left)

Apples were plentiful in the area where I grew up, so they were the staple of many desserts served at our table. Today, this recipe reigns supreme in my own family as the choice dessert. Warm or cold, it's a treat every time!

3 tablespoons margarine,
   softened
1 cup sugar
Egg substitute equivalent
   to 1 egg
1 cup all-purpose flour
1 teaspoon baking soda
1/2 teaspoon ground
   cinnamon
1/2 teaspoon ground nutmeg
1/2 teaspoon salt
3 cups diced peeled apples
3 tablespoons chopped
   walnuts
1 teaspoon vanilla extract
Light whipped topping and
   apple wedges, optional

In a mixing bowl, cream margarine, sugar and egg substitute. Stir together dry ingredients; add to creamed mixture (batter will be very thick). Stir in the apples, nuts and vanilla. Spread into an 8-in. square baking pan coated with nonstick cooking spray. Bake at 350° for 35-40 minutes or until cake tests done. Serve warm or cold. Garnish with whipped topping and apple wedges if desired. **Yield:** 9 servings.

NUTRITIONAL INFORMATION

Serving Size: 1/9 recipe
(calculated without garnish)

Calories: 216
Total Fat: 6 gm
Calories from Fat: 25%
Saturated Fat: 1 gm
Cholesterol: 0
Sodium: 318 mg
Carbohydrate: 40 gm
Protein: 3 gm

Oatmeal Cookie Bites

Laura Letobar, Livonia, Michigan

(Pictured at left)

When we get the "munchies" around our house, I offer these little treats with a sweet chewy taste. Folks are surprised to hear they're low in fat.

3 cups quick-cooking oats
2/3 cup all-purpose flour
2/3 cup sugar
1/3 cup packed brown sugar
1 teaspoon baking powder
1/4 teaspoon salt
Egg substitute equivalent
   to 2 eggs
1/3 cup light corn syrup
1 teaspoon vanilla extract

In a mixing bowl, combine oats, flour, sugars, baking powder and salt. Add egg substitute, corn syrup and vanilla; mix well. Drop by rounded teaspoonfuls onto cookie sheets coated with nonstick cooking spray. Bake at 350° for 10-12 minutes. **Yield:** 2 dozen.

NUTRITIONAL INFORMATION

Serving Size: 2 cookies

Calories: 102
Total Fat: 1 gm
Calories from Fat: 9%
Saturated Fat: trace
Cholesterol: trace
Sodium: 54 mg
Carbohydrate: 22 gm
Protein: 3 gm

Pumpkin Chiffon Pie

Karen Grimes, Stephens City, Virginia

(Pictured on page 260)

This extra-speedy pie is a great standby in the kitchen. Simply stir the ingredients together and chill until you're ready to serve it!

3 ounces fat-free cream
  cheese, softened
1 tablespoon sugar
1-1/2 cups light whipped
  topping
1 reduced-fat graham
  cracker crust (8 inches)
1 cup cold skim milk

2 packages (3.4 ounces
  each) instant vanilla
  pudding mix
1 can (16 ounces) solid-
  pack pumpkin
1 teaspoon ground
  cinnamon
1/2 teaspoon ground ginger
1/4 teaspoon ground cloves

In a mixing bowl, beat cream cheese and sugar until smooth. Add whipped topping and mix well. Spread into crust. In another bowl, beat milk and pudding mixes on low speed until combined; beat on high for 2 minutes. Let stand for 3 minutes. Stir in pumpkin and spices; mix well. Spread over cream cheese layer. Chill. **Yield:** 8 servings.

NUTRITIONAL INFORMATION

Serving Size: 1/8 recipe

Calories: 258
Total Fat: 4 gm
Calories from Fat: 14%
Saturated Fat: 2 gm
Cholesterol: 3 mg
Sodium: 528 mg
Carbohydrate: 50 gm
Protein: 4 gm

Cranberry Sherbet

Heather Clement, Indian River, Ontario

(Pictured on page 260)

This recipe was published in my son's Sunday school paper quite a few years ago. First-time tasters comment on how light it is...and say they can't believe it's made with cranberries.

1 package (12 ounces) fresh
  or frozen cranberries
2-3/4 cups water, *divided*
  2 cups sugar

1 envelope unflavored
  gelatin
1/2 cup orange juice

In a saucepan, combine cranberries and 2-1/2 cups of water. Bring to a boil; cook gently until all the cranberries have popped, about 10 minutes. Remove from the heat; cool slightly. Press mixture through a sieve or food mill, reserving juice and discarding skins and seeds. In another saucepan, combine cranberry juice and sugar; cook over medium heat until the sugar dissolves. Remove from the heat and set aside. Combine gelatin and remaining water; stir until softened. Combine cranberry mixture, orange juice and gelatin; mix well. Pour into a 2-qt. container; freeze for 4-5 hours or until mixture is slushy. Remove from freezer; beat with an electric mixer until sherbet is a bright pink color. Freeze until firm. **Yield:** 6 cups.

NUTRITIONAL INFORMATION

Serving Size: 1/2 cup

Calories: 146
Total Fat: trace
Calories from Fat: 0%
Saturated Fat: trace
Cholesterol: 0
Sodium: trace
Carbohydrate: 37 gm
Protein: 1 gm

Berry Rhubarb Fool

Cheryl Miller, Fort Collins, Colorado

(Pictured above)

A "fool" is a British dessert that's usually made with whipping cream or custard. This is a modified, healthier version I created. My kids love it because it doesn't taste like rhubarb—so I guess it's well named!

3 cups sliced fresh *or* frozen rhubarb (1-inch pieces)
1/3 cup sugar
1/4 cup orange juice
2 cups light whipped topping
1 pint fresh strawberries, halved
Fresh mint, optional

In a saucepan, combine rhubarb, sugar and orange juice; bring to a boil. Reduce heat; cover and simmer for 6-8 minutes or until rhubarb is tender. Cool slightly. Pour into a blender container; cover and blend until smooth. Chill. Just before serving, fold rhubarb mixture into whipped topping until lightly streaked. In six chilled parfait glasses, alternate layers of cream mixture and strawberries. Top with strawberries and a sprig of mint if desired. **Yield:** 6 servings.

Miniature Christmas Fruitcakes

Libby Over, Phillipsburg, Ohio

(Pictured below)

Even people who normally won't eat fruitcake enjoy these, I've found.

1/2 cup light molasses
1/4 cup water
1 teaspoon vanilla extract
1 package (15 ounces) raisins
1 pound mixed candied fruit, chopped
1/2 cup margarine, softened
2/3 cup sugar
3 eggs

1 cup plus 2 tablespoons all-purpose flour
1 teaspoon ground cinnamon
1 teaspoon ground nutmeg
1/4 teaspoon baking soda
1/4 teaspoon ground allspice
1/4 teaspoon ground cloves
1/4 cup skim milk
1/2 cup chopped walnuts

In a saucepan, combine molasses, water and vanilla; add raisins and bring to a boil. Reduce heat and simmer for 5 minutes. Remove from the heat and stir in fruit; cool. Meanwhile, in a mixing bowl, cream margarine and sugar. Add eggs, one at a time, beating well after each addition. Stir together dry ingredients; add to creamed mixture alternately with milk. Stir in fruit mixture; mix well. Fold in nuts. Spoon into paper-lined miniature muffin cups, filling almost to the top. Bake at 325° for 22-24 minutes or until cakes test done. Cool on wire racks. Store in an airtight container. **Yield:** 6 dozen.

Grandma's Chocolate Pudding

Donna Hughes, Rochester, New Hampshire

Grandmother always made this creamy, chocolaty pudding when we visited.

1 cup sugar
1/2 cup baking cocoa
1/4 cup all-purpose flour
2 cups water

3/4 cup evaporated skim milk
1 tablespoon vanilla
   extract

In a saucepan, combine sugar, cocoa and flour. Add water and milk; stir until smooth. Cook over medium heat, stirring constantly, until mixture comes to a boil. Cook until thick, about 1 minute. Remove from the heat; stir in vanilla. Cool to room temperature, stirring several times. Pour into a serving bowl or individual dishes. Serve warm or chilled. **Yield:** 6 servings.

NUTRITIONAL INFORMATION

Serving Size: 1/2 cup

Calories: 194
Total Fat: 1 gm
Calories from Fat: 5%
Saturated Fat: 1 gm
Cholesterol: 0
Sodium: 42 mg
Carbohydrate: 45 gm
Protein: 4 gm

Lemon Cheese Pie

Laura Odell, Eden, North Carolina

This pie is a great dessert for entertaining because it can be made ahead.

1 package (8 ounces) light
   cream cheese, softened
2 cups cold skim milk,
   divided
1 package (3.4 ounces)
   instant lemon pudding mix

1/2 teaspoon grated lemon
   peel
1 reduced-fat graham
   cracker crust (8 inches)

In a mixing bowl, beat cream cheese until smooth. Gradually add 1/2 cup milk. Sprinkle pudding mix over all. Gradually add lemon peel and remaining milk; beat until thickened, about 5 minutes. Pour into the crust. Freeze until ready to serve. **Yield:** 6 servings.

NUTRITIONAL INFORMATION

Serving Size: 1/6 recipe

Calories: 276
Total Fat: 8 gm
Calories from Fat: 25%
Saturated Fat: 3 gm
Cholesterol: 15 mg
Sodium: 523 mg
Carbohydrate: 42 gm
Protein: 8 gm

Strawberries with Lemon Cream

Marilyn Dick, Centralia, Missouri

If you're short on time, this is a tangy dessert you can whip up in a hurry! Dinner guests appreciate the fresh flavor of this treat. Our kids like it as a special snack.

1 pint fresh strawberries,
   sliced
1 tablespoon sugar
1 cup light whipped topping

2 cartons (8 ounces *each*)
   nonfat lemon yogurt
1 tablespoon grated lemon
   peel

Place strawberries in a medium bowl; sprinkle with sugar. In another bowl, fold whipped topping into yogurt; add lemon peel. To serve, layer strawberries and yogurt mixture in four parfait glasses. **Yield:** 4 servings.

NUTRITIONAL INFORMATION

Serving Size: 1/4 recipe

Calories: 190
Total Fat: 2 gm
Calories from Fat: 11%
Saturated Fat: 2 gm
Cholesterol: 3 mg
Sodium: 71 mg
Carbohydrate: 36 gm
Protein: 6 gm

Cherry Cobbler

Peggy Burdick, Burlington, Michigan

(Pictured on the front cover)

I've adapted this recipe to suit my family's tastes. It's delicious!

5 cups pitted canned
  tart red cherries
1/3 cup sugar
1/3 cup packed brown sugar
2-1/2 tablespoons cornstarch
1 teaspoon ground
  cinnamon
1/4 teaspoon ground nutmeg

2-1/2 tablespoons lemon juice
TOPPING:
1 cup all-purpose flour
1 tablespoon sugar
1 teaspoon baking powder
1/4 teaspoon salt
2 tablespoons margarine
1/3 to 1/2 cup skim milk

Drain cherries, reserving 1-1/4 cups juice; set cherries aside. In a saucepan, combine sugars, cornstarch, cinnamon and nutmeg; stir in lemon juice and reserved cherry juice. Bring to a boil, stirring occasionally; boil for 2 minutes. Add cherries; pour into an ungreased 9-in. square baking dish. For topping, combine flour, sugar, baking powder and salt; cut in margarine until crumbly. Stir in enough milk to moisten. Drop by rounded tablespoonfuls over cherries. Bake at 450° for 10-13 minutes or until golden brown. **Yield:** 9 servings.

Chocolate Angel Food Cake

Margaret Zickert, Deerfield, Wisconsin

You don't have to be blue if the doctor advises you—or a member of your family—to curtail fat. This good-for-you recipe earned a blue ribbon at a local fair's baking competition.

1 cup cake flour
1/2 cup baking cocoa
2 cups egg whites (14 eggs)

2 teaspoons cream of tartar
2 cups sugar
1 teaspoon vanilla extract

Sift flour and cocoa together three times; set aside. In a large mixing bowl, beat the egg whites until foamy. Sprinkle with cream of tartar and beat until soft peaks form. Gradually add sugar, about 2 tablespoons at a time, beating until stiff peaks form. Blend in vanilla. Sift about a fourth of the flour mixture over egg white mixture; fold in gently. Repeat, folding in remaining flour mixture by fourths. Pour into an ungreased 10-in. tube pan. Bake at 325° for 1 hour. Turn off the oven, but let cake sit in the oven for 5 minutes. Remove from the oven and immediately invert pan; cool. Loosen sides of cake from pan and remove. **Yield:** 12 servings.

Blackberry Dumplings

Liecha Collins, Oneonta, New York

(Pictured below)

As long as I can remember, my mother has been making these Blackberry Dumplings. They really do make you hurry through Sunday dinner! I'll often make them in winter just to have a taste of summer.

1 quart fresh *or* frozen
   (loose-pack) blackberries
1 cup plus 1 tablespoon
   sugar, *divided*
3/4 teaspoon salt, *divided*
1/2 teaspoon lemon extract

1-1/2 cups all-purpose flour
  2 teaspoons baking powder
1/4 teaspoon ground nutmeg
2/3 cup skim milk
Light whipped topping, optional

In a Dutch oven, combine the blackberries, 1 cup sugar, 1/4 teaspoon salt and lemon extract. Bring to a boil; reduce heat and simmer for 5 minutes. Meanwhile, in a mixing bowl, combine flour, baking powder, nutmeg and remaining sugar and salt. Add milk; stir just until mixed (dough will be very thick). Drop by tablespoonfuls into six mounds onto hot blackberry mixture; cover tightly and simmer for 15 minutes or until a toothpick inserted in a dumpling comes out clean. Spoon into serving dishes. Serve with whipped topping if desired. **Yield:** 8 servings.

NUTRITIONAL INFORMATION

Serving Size: 1/8 recipe
(calculated without
whipped topping)

Calories: 234
Total Fat: 1 gm
Calories from Fat: 2%
Saturated Fat: trace
Cholesterol: trace
Sodium: 333 mg
Carbohydrate: 55 gm
Protein: 4 gm

Spice Cookies with Pumpkin Dip

Kelly McNeal, Derby, Kansas

(Pictured above)

My husband and two children like to eat these cookies warm from the oven. Having a dip to go along with the cookies makes this recipe fun for parties. A co-worker gave me the recipe for the pumpkin dip, and everyone loves it.

NUTRITIONAL INFORMATION

Serving Size: 3 cookies and 1 tablespoon dip

Calories: 129
Total Fat: 5 gm
Calories from Fat: 31%
Saturated Fat: 1 gm
Cholesterol: 8 mg
Sodium: 174 mg
Carbohydrate: 21 gm
Protein: 2 gm

3/4 cup margarine, softened
1 cup sugar
1 egg
1/4 cup molasses
2 cups all-purpose flour
2 teaspoons baking soda
1 teaspoon ground cinnamon
1/2 teaspoon ground ginger
1/2 teaspoon ground cloves
1/2 teaspoon salt

PUMPKIN DIP:
1 package (8 ounces) light cream cheese, softened
1 can (18 ounces) pumpkin pie mix
2 cups confectioners' sugar
1/2 teaspoon ground cinnamon
1/4 teaspoon ground ginger

In a mixing bowl, cream margarine and sugar. Add egg and beat well. Add molasses; mix well. Combine flour, baking soda, cinnamon, ginger, cloves and salt; add to creamed mixture and mix well. Chill overnight. Shape into 1/2-in. balls; place 2 in. apart on ungreased baking sheets. Bake at 375° for 6 minutes or until edges begin to brown. Cool for 2 minutes before removing to a wire rack. For dip, beat cream cheese in a mixing bowl until smooth. Add pumpkin pie mix; beat well. Add sugar, cinnamon and ginger; beat until smooth. Serve with cookies. Store leftover dip in the refrigerator. **Yield:** 10 dozen (3 cups dip).

Creamy Peach Sorbet

Janice MacLeod, Ro ginia

Yogurt makes this from-scratch sher eamy, while nutmeg and vanilla add an interesting taste twis y to create refreshing desserts in minutes when you get a head st frozen fruit.

2 cups frozen unsweetened
  sliced peaches, partially
  thawed
2 tablespoons orange juice
  concentrate

1/8 teaspoon ground
  nutmeg
1 teaspoon vanilla
2 tablespoons sugar
1/2 cup plain nonfat yogurt

In a food processor or blender, chop the peaches. Add remaining ingredients; blend until creamy. Serve immediately or freeze until serving time. **Yield:** 4 servings.

Apple-Cherry Cobbler

Eleanore Hill, Fresno, California

Some of my fondest memories are of Saturday night dinners at my aunt and uncle's cozy farmhouse, because the family made an occasion of them. Those fun-filled times are fondly remembered whenever I prepare my aunt's favorite cobbler.

1 egg
1/2 cup sugar
1/2 cup skim milk
2 tablespoons vegetable oil
1 cup all-purpose flour
2-1/4 teaspoons baking powder
1 can (21 ounces) apple
  pie filling
1 can (21 ounces) cherry
  pie filling

1 tablespoon lemon juice
1 teaspoon vanilla extract
TOPPING:
1/3 cup packed brown sugar
3 tablespoons all-purpose
  flour
1 teaspoon ground
  cinnamon
1 tablespoon margarine

In a bowl, combine the first four ingredients. Combine flour and baking powder; add to egg mixture and blend well. Pour into a 13-in. x 9-in. x 2-in. baking pan coated with nonstick cooking spray. Combine pie fillings, lemon juice and vanilla; spoon over batter. For topping, combine brown sugar, flour and cinnamon; cut in margarine until crumbly. Sprinkle over filling. Bake at 350° for 40-45 minutes or until bubbly and cake tests done. If necessary, cover edges with foil to prevent overbrowning. **Yield:** 16 servings.

Grilled Peaches with Berry Sauce

Nancy Johnson, Connersville, Indiana

(Pictured below)

This unusual dessert is as pretty as it is delicious. Topped with brown sugar and cinnamon, the peaches come off the grill sweet and spicy. The raspberry sauce adds a refreshing touch.

NUTRITIONAL INFORMATION

Serving Size: 1/4 recipe

Calories: 80
Total Fat: 1 gm
Calories from Fat: 11%
Saturated Fat: trace
Cholesterol: 0
Sodium: 10 mg
Carbohydrate: 18 gm
Protein: 1 gm

1/2 cup sweetened frozen
   raspberries, partially
   thawed
1-1/2 teaspoons lemon juice
   2 medium fresh peaches,
   peeled and halved

5 teaspoons brown sugar
1/4 teaspoon ground
   cinnamon
1/2 teaspoon vanilla extract
   1 teaspoon margarine

In a blender or food processor, process raspberries and lemon juice until pureed. Strain and discard seeds. Cover and chill. Place the peach halves, cut side up, on a large piece of heavy-duty foil (about 18 in. x 12 in.). Combine brown sugar and cinnamon; sprinkle into peach centers. Sprinkle with vanilla; dot with margarine. Fold foil over peaches and seal tightly. Grill over medium-hot coals for 15 minutes or until heated through. Open foil carefully to allow steam to escape. To serve, spoon the raspberry sauce over peaches. **Yield:** 4 servings.

Strawberry-Rhubarb Pie

Helen Ward O'Key, Litchfield, Connecticut

I cook the old-fashioned way, using locally grown berries and garden rhubarb for this favorite. It's a tantalizing taste of spring.

3 cups sliced fresh *or* frozen rhubarb (1/2-inch pieces)	1 cup sliced fresh *or* frozen strawberries
1 cup water	1 envelope whipped topping mix
1 package (6 ounces) strawberry gelatin	1 reduced-fat graham cracker crust (8 inches)

In a saucepan, bring rhubarb and water to a boil; remove from the heat. Add gelatin and stir until dissolved; cool. Stir in strawberries; chill until it begins to thicken. Prepare whipped topping according to package directions using skim milk; fold half into rhubarb mixture. Pour into crust. Chill 2 hours or until firm. Top with remaining whipped topping. **Yield:** 8 servings.

NUTRITIONAL INFORMATION

Serving Size: 1/8 recipe
Calories: 233
Total Fat: 6 gm
Calories from Fat: 23%
Saturated Fat: 3 gm
Cholesterol: trace
Sodium: 165 mg
Carbohydrate: 42 gm
Protein: 4 gm

Christmas Rice Pudding

Barbara Garfield, Jamestown, New York

This is an old Swedish specialty that my grandma made on Christmas Eve.

1-3/4 cups uncooked long grain rice	4 cups skim milk
2 cups water	1-1/2 cups sugar
	2 tablespoons margarine

In a saucepan, combine the rice and water; simmer for 10 minutes. Add milk and bring to a boil. Reduce heat and simmer, uncovered, for 60-70 minutes or until rice is tender. Add sugar and margarine; mix well. Spoon into small bowls or dessert dishes. **Yield:** 8 servings.

NUTRITIONAL INFORMATION

Serving Size: 3/4 cup
Calories: 375
Total Fat: 3 gm
Calories from Fat: 8%
Saturated Fat: 1 gm
Cholesterol: 2 mg
Sodium: 89 mg
Carbohydrate: 79 gm
Protein: 8 gm

Apple Crunch

Hazel Fritchie, Palestine, Illinois

Apples and walnuts make this down-home dessert crunchy and delicious.

1 egg	1/2 cup chopped peeled apple
3/4 cup sugar	1/4 cup chopped walnuts
1/3 cup all-purpose flour	1 teaspoon vanilla extract
1 teaspoon baking powder	2-1/4 cups fat-free ice cream
1/8 teaspoon ground cinnamon	

In a mixing bowl, beat the egg. Combine sugar, flour, baking powder and cinnamon; add to egg and beat until smooth. Fold in apple, nuts and vanilla. Spoon into an 8-in. square baking pan coated with nonstick cooking spray. Bake at 350° for 25-30 minutes or until cake tests done. Cool. Serve with fat-free ice cream. **Yield:** 9 servings.

NUTRITIONAL INFORMATION

Serving Size: 1/9 recipe
Calories: 166
Total Fat: 3 gm
Calories from Fat: 14%
Saturated Fat: trace
Cholesterol: 24 mg
Sodium: 89 mg
Carbohydrate: 32 gm
Protein: 4 gm

Pumpkin Bread Pudding

Lois Fetting, Nelson, Wisconsin

This comforting dessert is old-fashioned but never out of style. I received this favorite pumpkin recipe from an elderly aunt. You can use cooked or canned pumpkin, so you can make it year-round.

4 cups cubed day-old whole wheat bread
1/2 cup chopped dates
1/3 cup chopped pecans, *divided*
2 cups skim milk
1 cup canned *or* cooked pumpkin

2 eggs, *separated*
2/3 cup packed brown sugar
1-1/2 teaspoons ground cinnamon
3/4 teaspoon ground nutmeg
1/4 teaspoon salt
1/8 teaspoon ground cloves

Combine bread cubes, dates and 1/4 cup pecans; place in a 2-qt. shallow baking dish coated with nonstick cooking spray. In a mixing bowl, combine the milk, pumpkin, egg yolks, brown sugar, cinnamon, nutmeg, salt and cloves; beat well. In a small mixing bowl, beat egg whites until stiff; fold into pumpkin mixture. Pour over bread cubes and toss gently. Sprinkle with remaining nuts. Bake, uncovered, at 350° for 1 hour or until a knife inserted near the center comes out clean. Serve warm or chilled. **Yield:** 8 servings.

NUTRITIONAL INFORMATION

Serving Size: 1/8 recipe

Calories: 219
Total Fat: 6 gm
Calories from Fat: 23%
Saturated Fat: 1 gm
Cholesterol: 54 mg
Sodium: 243 mg
Carbohydrate: 37 gm
Protein: 7 gm

Carrot Spice Cake

Karen Brodeen, Cook, Minnesota

I don't think a meal is complete until a sweet treat appears on the table. This cake is a dieter's delight because it's low in fat and cholesterol.

1-1/4 cups sugar
3/4 cup light corn syrup
3/4 cup skim milk
8 egg whites
2 cups all-purpose flour
2 teaspoons baking powder

2 teaspoons baking soda
2 teaspoons ground cinnamon
1/4 teaspoon salt
2 cups grated carrots

In a large mixing bowl, beat sugar, corn syrup, milk and egg whites. Combine dry ingredients; add to batter. Beat well. Pat carrots dry with paper towels; stir into the batter. Pour into a 10-in. fluted tube pan that has been coated with nonstick cooking spray and floured. Bake at 350° for 1 hour or until a toothpick inserted near the center comes out clean. Cool in pan for 10 minutes; invert onto a wire rack. Cool completely. **Yield:** 16 servings.

NUTRITIONAL INFORMATION

Serving Size: 1/16 recipe

Calories: 180
Total Fat: trace
Calories from Fat: 1%
Saturated Fat: trace
Cholesterol: trace
Sodium: 309 mg
Carbohydrate: 42 gm
Protein: 4 gm

Strawberry Angel Dessert

Mrs. J. Jelen, Mineota, Minnesota

(Pictured below)

Back when we lived on our farm, I made this recipe often during corn-shelling time. This light, cool dessert tastefully topped off a hot meal.

1 envelope unflavored
   gelatin
3/4 cup cold water
1/2 cup sugar
   1 package (10 ounces)
   frozen sliced strawberries,
   thawed

1 carton (8 ounces) frozen
   light whipped topping,
   thawed
5 cups angel food cake cubes
Fresh strawberries and mint,
   optional

NUTRITIONAL INFORMATION

Serving Size: 1/9 recipe
(calculated without garnish)

Calories: 210
Total Fat: 3 gm
Calories from Fat: 14%
Saturated Fat: 3 gm
Cholesterol: 0
Sodium: 144 mg
Carbohydrate: 42 gm
Protein: 3 gm

In a saucepan, combine gelatin and cold water; let stand 5 minutes to soften. Stir over low heat just until gelatin dissolves. Remove from the heat; add sugar. Stir until dissolved. Stir in undrained strawberries. Chill until partially thickened. Fold in whipped topping. Place cake cubes in a mixing bowl; pour strawberry mixture over cake and mix gently. Pour into an ungreased 8-in. square baking dish. Chill until firm. Garnish with strawberries and mint if desired. **Yield:** 9 servings.

273

Red, White and Blue Dessert

Sue Gronholz, Columbus, Wisconsin

(Pictured above)

Serving this rich, fresh-tasting dessert decorated like the flag is a great salute to the nation's independence! I used a new recipe I found and made some modifications based on tricks my grandma taught me.

NUTRITIONAL INFORMATION

Serving Size: 3/4 cup

Calories: 154
Total Fat: 2 gm
Calories from Fat: 14%
Saturated Fat: 2 gm
Cholesterol: 2 mg
Sodium: 128 mg
Carbohydrate: 29 gm
Protein: 5 gm

2 packages (8 ounces *each*) fat-free cream cheese, softened
1/2 cup sugar
1/2 teaspoon vanilla extract
1/2 teaspoon almond extract
4 cups light whipped topping
2 quarts strawberries, halved
2 quarts blueberries

In a large mixing bowl, beat cream cheese, sugar and extracts until fluffy. Fold in the whipped topping. Place a third of the mixture in a 4-qt. bowl. Reserve 20 strawberry halves and 1/2 cup blueberries for garnish. Layer half of the remaining strawberries and blueberries over cream mixture. Top with another third of the cream cheese mixture and the remaining berries. Spread remaining cream cheese mixture on top. Use reserved strawberries and blueberries to make a "flag" on top. **Yield:** 18 servings.

Spiced Peaches

Norma Erne, Albuquerque, New Mexico

This is a super summer dessert when peaches are plentiful. The sweet chilled fruit topped with sour cream and brown sugar is so refreshing.

1/2 cup sugar	6 fresh peaches, peeled and
1/2 cup water	halved
1/4 cup vinegar	1/2 cup nonfat sour cream
8 to 10 whole cloves	2 tablespoons brown sugar
1 cinnamon stick	

In a large saucepan, bring the first five ingredients to a boil. Reduce heat; simmer for 10 minutes. Add peaches; simmer until heated through, about 10 minutes. Pour into a shallow baking dish. Cover and chill 8 hours or overnight. Drain. Spoon peaches into serving dishes; top with a dollop of sour cream and sprinkle with brown sugar. **Yield:** 6 servings.

Cantaloupe and Raspberry Melba

Peggy Langen, Lanconia, New Hampshire

A chilled cranberry/almond sauce is a nice complement to the cantaloupe and raspberry mixture.

1/2 cup cranberry juice	3 cups cantaloupe cubes
1 tablespoon sugar	or balls
2 teaspoons cornstarch	1 cup raspberries
1/4 teaspoon almond extract	Fresh mint, optional

In a saucepan, blend cranberry juice, sugar and cornstarch. Cook and stir over medium heat until thickened. Stir in extract. Cool. When ready to serve, place cantaloupe and raspberries in individual bowls. Top with cranberry sauce; garnish with mint if desired. **Yield:** 4 servings.

Banana Cream Parfait

Judy King, Johnstown, Pennsylvania

This creamy dessert is a fantastic finale to any meal. I hope you enjoy it!

1 package (3.4 ounces)	1/2 cup graham cracker
instant banana pudding	crumbs
2 cups cold skim milk	2 medium ripe bananas,
	sliced

Prepare pudding according to package directions, using the skim milk. Sprinkle 1 tablespoon graham cracker crumbs each into four parfait or dessert glasses. Top with 1/4 cup pudding and half of the bananas. Repeat layers of crumbs, pudding and bananas. **Yield:** 4 servings.

Raspberry Baked Apples

Sue Hampton, Greendale, Wisconsin

Apples take on a summertime twist in this versatile dessert.

1/2 cup sugar
1 tablespoon quick-cooking tapioca
1/3 cup water

3 cups fresh raspberries
6 medium tart apples, quartered

In a bowl, combine sugar and tapioca. Stir in water and berries. Cut a lengthwise strip of peel from the center of each apple quarter; discard peel and stir apples into raspberry mixture. Pour into a shallow 3-qt. baking dish coated with nonstick cooking spray. Cover and bake at 350° for 1 hour or until apples are tender, spooning sauce over apples every 15 minutes. Serve warm. **Yield:** 10 servings.

Banana Tapioca Pudding

Michel Karkula, Chandler, Arizona

Served either warm or cold, this treat brims with old-fashioned taste.

2-3/4 cups skim milk
3 tablespoons quick-cooking tapioca
1/3 cup sugar

1 egg
1 teaspoon vanilla extract
2 medium ripe bananas, sliced

In a saucepan, combine milk, tapioca, sugar and egg; let stand for 5 minutes. Cook and stir over medium heat until mixture comes to a full boil; remove from the heat. Stir in vanilla and bananas. Cool for 20 minutes. Serve warm or cold. **Yield:** 6 servings.

Peppermint Kisses

Lynn Bernstetter, Lake Elmo, Minnesota

Family and friends request these cookies every Christmas. I'm always happy to make them.

2 egg whites
1/8 teaspoon salt
1/8 teaspoon cream of tartar
1/2 cup sugar

2 peppermint candy canes (one green, one red), crushed

In a mixing bowl, beat egg whites until foamy. Add salt and cream of tartar; beat until soft peaks form. Beat in sugar, 1 tablespoon at a time, until stiff and glossy. Spoon meringue into a pastry bag or resealable plastic bag. If using a plastic bag, cut a 1-in. hole in a corner. Squeeze 1-1/2-in. kisses of meringue onto ungreased foil-lined baking sheets. Sprinkle half with crushed red candy canes and half with green candy canes. Bake at 225° for 1-1/2 to 2 hours or until dry but not brown. Cool; remove from foil. Store in an airtight container. **Yield:** about 3 dozen.

Bird's Nest Pie

Jeannine Bates, Wauseon, Ohio

(Pictured below)

When we were kids, this was our favorite dessert at Grandma's house. I know we were fascinated by the name, but the real reason we liked it was because of its fantastic flavor.

5 medium apples, peeled
  and sliced
2 cups all-purpose flour
1 cup sugar
1/2 teaspoon baking soda
1/2 teaspoon cream of tartar
1 cup sour skim milk*

1 egg
TOPPING:
1/4 cup sugar
1/2 teaspoon ground
  cinnamon
1/4 teaspoon ground nutmeg

NUTRITIONAL INFORMATION

Serving Size: 1/12 recipe

Calories: 205
Total Fat: 1 gm
Calories from Fat: 4%
Saturated Fat: trace
Cholesterol: 18 mg
Sodium: 69 mg
Carbohydrate: 47 gm
Protein: 3 gm

Divide apples evenly between two 9-in. pie plates coated with non-stick cooking spray; set aside. In a mixing bowl, combine flour, sugar, baking soda, cream of tartar, sour milk and egg; mix well. Divide batter and pour over apples. Bake at 350° for 25-30 minutes or until pies are lightly browned and test done. Invert onto serving plates (so apples are on the top. Combine all topping ingredients; sprinkle over apples. Serve warm. (*To sour milk, place 1 tablespoon white vinegar in a measuring cup; add enough skim milk to equal 1 cup. Let stand for 5 minutes.) **Yield:** 12 servings.

Pineapple Sherbet

Barbara Libkie, Roswell, New Mexico

(Pictured below)

This was a favorite dessert at Thanksgiving and Christmas when our family gathered together—the holidays weren't complete without this homemade sherbet. I remember those days fondly whenever I make it.

1 quart buttermilk
1 can (20 ounces) crushed
   unsweetened pineapple,
   drained

1-1/3 cups sugar
1/2 cup chopped walnuts
1 teaspoon vanilla extract
Fresh pineapple slices, optional

In a bowl, combine the first five ingredients; mix well. Cover and freeze for 1 hour. Stir; return to freezer for at least 2 hours before serving. Garnish with pineapple slices if desired. **Yield:** 8 servings.

Puffed Wheat Balls

Lucile Proctor, Panguitch, Utah

Whenever my Grandma Hunt comes over, she makes her famous Puffed Wheat Balls by the dozen. Her grandchildren and great-grandkids love them.

12 cups puffed wheat cereal
2 cups packed brown sugar
1 cup light corn syrup

2 tablespoons margarine
1 cup evaporated skim milk
1/3 cup sugar

Place cereal in a large bowl; set aside. In a heavy saucepan, bring brown sugar and corn syrup to a boil. Add margarine. Combine evaporated milk and sugar; add to boiling mixture. Continue cooking until the mixture reaches 240° (soft-ball stage) on a candy thermometer. Pour over cereal and stir to coat. Shape into 2-in. balls. **Yield:** 3 dozen.

NUTRITIONAL INFORMATION

Serving Size: 2 balls

Calories: 178
Total Fat: 1 gm
Calories from Fat: 7%
Saturated Fat: trace
Cholesterol: 1 mg
Sodium: 56 mg
Carbohydrate: 41 gm
Protein: 2 gm

Strawberry Cloud

Patricia Kile, Greentown, Pennsylvania

I like to treat my family to this cool, no-bake concoction on hot days.

1 package (3 ounces) strawberry gelatin
1 package (3 ounces) cook-and-serve vanilla pudding mix

2-1/2 cups water
1 carton (8 ounces) frozen light whipped topping, thawed

In a saucepan over medium heat, cook and stir gelatin, pudding mix and water until mixture boils, about 15 minutes. Cool until partially set; fold in whipped topping. Spoon into eight individual dishes or parfait glasses. Chill until ready to serve. **Yield:** 8 servings.

NUTRITIONAL INFORMATION

Serving Size: 2/3 cup

Calories: 151
Total Fat: 4 gm
Calories from Fat: 23%
Saturated Fat: 4 gm
Cholesterol: 0
Sodium: 107 mg
Carbohydrate: 27 gm
Protein: 1 gm

Raisin Pudding

Margaret Vieth, Norwalk, Wisconsin

This old-fashioned dessert tastes like the comforting long-cooked puddings Grandma used to make, but it really is quick and easy to prepare. The flavor is wonderful. We have it often because my whole family enjoys it.

1 package (3 ounces) cook-and-serve vanilla pudding mix
1 cup skim milk
1/2 cup water

1 cup raisins
1/2 teaspoon vanilla extract
1-1/4 cups plain nonfat yogurt
Ground nutmeg, optional

In a saucepan, combine pudding mix, milk and water; cook over medium heat until thickened. Remove from the heat; stir in the raisins and vanilla. Cool for 15 minutes; stir in yogurt. Spoon into individual dessert dishes. Chill for 2-3 hours. Sprinkle with nutmeg if desired. **Yield:** 6 servings. **Editor's Note:** Sugar-free vanilla pudding can be substituted for the regular pudding.

NUTRITIONAL INFORMATION

Serving Size: 3/4 cup

Calories: 168
Total Fat: trace
Calories from Fat: 2%
Saturated Fat: trace
Cholesterol: 2 mg
Sodium: 170 mg
Carbohydrate: 38 gm
Protein: 5 gm

Light 'n' Luscious Trifle

Paula Marchesi, Rocky Point, New York

Fresh fruit and prepared angel food cake star in this version of a classic dessert. Make it for your next get-together and easily impress family and friends.

6 cups cubed honeydew melon
6 cups sliced fresh strawberries
1/2 cup strawberry all-fruit spread
2 packages (8 ounces *each*) fat-free cream cheese, softened
1-1/2 cups confectioners' sugar
1 cup (8 ounces) nonfat sour cream
2 cups light whipped topping
1 loaf (10-1/2 ounces) angel food cake, cubed
1/3 cup grated semisweet chocolate

In a large bowl, toss the honeydew and strawberries with fruit spread; set aside. In a mixing bowl, beat cream cheese and sugar until smooth. Add sour cream; mix well. Fold in whipped topping and cake cubes. Drain juice from fruit mixture. In a trifle dish or deep salad bowl, layer a third of the fruit, a third of the cake mixture and a third of the chocolate. Repeat layers twice. Serve immediately. **Yield:** 16 servings.

Old-Time Popcorn Balls

LaReine Stevens, Ypsilanti, Michigan

Our whole family loves popcorn. These are great anytime, especially for trick-or-treating or stocking stuffers. They always look appealing covered in clear plastic wrap and tied with a festive ribbon.

2 quarts air-popped popcorn
1/2 cup molasses
1/2 cup sugar
1/3 cup water
1 tablespoon vinegar
1 tablespoon margarine
1/4 teaspoon baking soda

Place popcorn in a large bowl and set aside. In a heavy saucepan, combine molasses, sugar, water, vinegar and margarine. Cook, without stirring, over medium heat until the mixture reaches 235° (soft-ball stage) on a candy thermometer. Add baking soda and stir well. Remove from the heat and immediately pour over popcorn, stirring gently with a wooden spoon until well coated. When cool enough to handle, quickly shape into 3-in. balls, dipping hands in cold water to prevent the syrup from sticking. **Yield:** 8 servings.

Cherry Fluff

Joyce Leach, Armstrong, Iowa

(Pictured above)

Chunky tart cherries, coconut, pecans and pineapple give substance to this lightly sweet make-ahead dessert. With its pastel color and fluffy look, it's perfect for a baby shower.

1 carton (8 ounces) frozen light whipped topping, thawed
1 can (20 ounces) crushed unsweetened pineapple, drained
1 can (21 ounces) cherry pie filling
1 can (14 ounces) fat-free sweetened condensed milk
1/2 cup flaked coconut
1/4 cup chopped pecans

Combine all ingredients in a large bowl; mix well. Chill overnight. **Yield:** 12 servings.

NUTRITIONAL INFORMATION

Serving Size: 2/3 cup

Calories: 250
Total Fat: 5 gm
Calories from Fat: 19%
Saturated Fat: 3 gm
Cholesterol: 0
Sodium: 49 mg
Carbohydrate: 47 gm
Protein: 3 gm

Very Raspberry Pie

Kathy Jones, West Winfield, New York

(Pictured above)

We live along a 130-year-old railroad track (our house once was a train station) edged a couple weeks a year with wild raspberries that I pick for my pie.

RASPBERRY TOPPING:
  6 cups fresh raspberries, *divided*
  1 cup sugar
  3 tablespoons cornstarch
  1/2 cup water
CREAM FILLING:
  1 cup light whipped topping
  1 package (8 ounces) fat-free cream cheese, softened
  1 cup confectioners' sugar
  1 reduced-fat graham cracker crust (8 inches)
Fresh mint, optional

Mash about 2 cups raspberries to measure 1 cup; place in a saucepan. Add sugar, cornstarch and water. Bring to a boil, stirring constantly; cook and stir 2 minutes longer. Strain to remove seeds if desired. Cool to room temperature, about 20 minutes. Meanwhile, for filling, beat whipped topping, cream cheese and confectioners' sugar in a mixing bowl. Spread into crust. Top with remaining raspberries. Pour cooled raspberry sauce over top. Refrigerate until set, about 3 hours. Store in the refrigerator. Garnish with mint if desired. **Yield:** 8 servings.

California Cranberry Torte

Pat Parsons, Bakersfield, California

I developed this torte myself, and it seems that everyone I serve it to enjoys it. This recipe requires relatively few ingredients, is quite easy to make, looks sensational and, most important, tastes great!

6 egg whites
1/4 teaspoon cream of tartar
1-1/2 cups sugar
1 teaspoon vanilla extract
1 can (16 ounces) jellied
  cranberry sauce

2 tablespoons raspberry
  gelatin, undissolved
1 carton (8 ounces) frozen
  light whipped topping,
  thawed

In a mixing bowl, beat egg whites until foamy. Add cream of tartar; beat until soft peaks form. Gradually add sugar, 2 tablespoons at a time, and continue beating until stiff and glossy. Add vanilla. Place plain brown paper or parchment on cookie sheets. Draw three 8-in. circles on the paper. Spoon the meringue into the circles, spreading with a knife. Bake at 250° for 1 hour. Meringues should sound hollow when tapped. Turn heat off and allow meringues to cool in the oven with the door open. Meanwhile, melt cranberry sauce in a saucepan over medium heat. Add gelatin and stir to dissolve. Cool. Fold 1 cup whipped topping into cranberry mixture. To assemble, place 1 tablespoon whipped topping in the center of serving platter to hold meringue in place. Top with a meringue shell; spread 1/3 of the cranberry mixture on top. Repeat with remaining meringues and cranberry mixture. Frost sides of torte with remaining whipped topping. If desired, a pastry tube can be used to decorate edges of torte. Chill 6 hours or overnight. **Yield:** 16 servings.

Pumpkin Whip

Linda Clapp, Stow, Ohio

Even though it's quick to prepare, this dessert has a creamy pumpkin taste and a golden harvest look.

1 package (3.4 ounces)
  instant butterscotch
  pudding mix
1-1/2 cups cold skim milk
1 cup canned *or* cooked
  pumpkin

1 teaspoon pumpkin pie
  spice
1-1/2 cups light whipped
  topping

In a mixing bowl, beat pudding and milk until well blended, about 1-2 minutes. Blend in pumpkin and pie spice. Fold in whipped topping. Spoon into six dessert dishes. Chill. **Yield:** 6 servings.

Light Chocolate Cake

Celeste Clarke, Wilmot, New Hampshire

Folks are surprised—and delighted—to hear this luscious chocolate cake fits into their low-fat diet. Applesauce, not oil, makes it moist and delicious.

2 cups sugar
1-3/4 cups all-purpose flour
3/4 cup baking cocoa
1-1/2 teaspoons baking soda
1-1/2 teaspoons baking powder
1 teaspoon salt
1 cup skim milk

Egg substitute equivalent
to 2 eggs
1/2 cup unsweetened
applesauce
2 teaspoons vanilla extract
1 cup boiling water

In a large mixing bowl, combine dry ingredients. Beat in milk, egg substitute, applesauce and vanilla. Add water; beat on medium speed for 2 minutes (batter will be very thin). Pour into a 13-in. x 9-in. x 2-in. baking pan coated with nonstick cooking spray. Bake at 350° for 30 minutes or until a toothpick inserted near the center comes out clean. Cool. **Yield:** 20 servings.

NUTRITIONAL
INFORMATION

Serving Size: 1/20 recipe

Calories: 139
Total Fat: 1 gm
Calories from Fat: 4%
Saturated Fat: trace
Cholesterol: trace
Sodium: 256 mg
Carbohydrate: 32 gm
Protein: 3 gm

Rhubarb Berry Delight

Joan Sieck, Rensselaer, New York

This flavorful dessert is great for a spring luncheon or a shower for a special bride-to-be. It's an instant success whenever I serve it. It takes time to prepare, but one taste and you'll agree it's worth the extra effort.

4 cups diced fresh *or*
frozen rhubarb
2 cups fresh *or* frozen
strawberries
1-1/2 cups sugar, *divided*
1 package (6 ounces)
raspberry gelatin

2 cups boiling water
1 cup skim milk
1 envelope unflavored
gelatin
1/4 cup cold water
1-1/2 teaspoons vanilla extract
2 cups (16 ounces) nonfat
sour cream

In a saucepan, cook rhubarb, strawberries and 1 cup sugar until fruit is tender. In a large bowl, dissolve raspberry gelatin in boiling water. Stir in fruit; set aside. In another pan, heat milk and remaining sugar on low until sugar is dissolved. Meanwhile, soften unflavored gelatin in cold water. Add to hot milk mixture and stir until gelatin dissolves. Remove from the heat; add vanilla. Cool to lukewarm; blend in sour cream. Set aside at room temperature. Pour a third of the fruit mixture into a 3-qt. bowl; chill until almost set. Spoon a third of the sour cream mixture over fruit; chill until almost set. Repeat layers twice, chilling between layers if necessary. Refrigerate until firm, at least 3 hours. **Yield:** 12 servings.

NUTRITIONAL
INFORMATION

Serving Size: 3/4 cup

Calories: 219
Total Fat: trace
Calories from Fat: 1%
Saturated Fat: trace
Cholesterol: 3 mg
Sodium: 79 mg
Carbohydrate: 50 gm
Protein: 5 gm

Poor Man's Cookies

Georgia Perrine, Bremerton, Washington

(Pictured below)

In the 1930's, producers of a popular radio program invited listeners to write in for this recipe. My mother changed the name from Jake and Lena Cookies to Poor Man's Cookies because they contained no eggs, milk or nuts. Despite the name, the cookies are rich in taste!

2 cups rolled oats	1/4 cup hot water
1 cup packed brown sugar	1/2 cup margarine, melted
1/2 cup sugar	and cooled
1 cup all-purpose flour	1 teaspoon vanilla extract
1/4 teaspoon salt	
1 teaspoon baking soda	

In a mixing bowl, combine oats, sugars, flour and salt. Combine baking soda and water; stir into oat mixture along with margarine and vanilla. Roll into walnut-size balls. Place on cookie sheets coated with nonstick cooking spray. Bake at 350° for 10 minutes or until golden brown. Remove from the oven; cool for 2 minutes before removing to a wire rack. **Yield:** 3-1/2 dozen.

NUTRITIONAL INFORMATION

Serving Size: 2 cookies

Calories: 135
Total Fat: 5 gm
Calories from Fat: 33%
Saturated Fat: 1 gm
Cholesterol: 0
Sodium: 125 mg
Carbohydrate: 21 gm
Protein: 2 gm

Cookie Capers

Unbaked cookie dough can be refrigerated for up to 2 weeks or frozen up to 6 weeks. It's convenient to have on hand when you want to bake up a batch in a hurry.

Try spraying beaters with nonstick cooking spray before mixing cookie batter to prevent clumping.

Use your electric knife to easily cut rolled and chilled cookie dough. You'll get perfectly even cookies every time.

Index